THE RED SWAN

The Red Swan

MYTHS AND TALES OF THE AMERICAN INDIANS

Edited by John Bierhorst

UNIVERSITY OF NEW MEXICO PRESS

ALBUQUERQUE

Library of Congress Cataloging-in-Publication Data
The Red Swan : myths and tales of American Indians / edited by John
   Bierhorst.
      p.   cm.
   Originally published: New York : Farrar, Straus, and Giroux, 1976.
   ISBN 0-8263-1355-8
      1. Indians—Religion and mythology.   2. Indians—Legends.
I. Bierhorst, John.
E98.R3R43   1992
299'.7—dc20   92-3299
                                                        CIP

Acknowledgment is made to the authors and publishers for permission to
reprint from the following (for titles of the selections reprinted, see Notes) :
Indian Tales by Jaime de Angulo, copyright 1950 by *The Hudson Review*,
copyright 1953 by Hill and Wang, Inc. / *The Tenetehara Indians of Brazil*
by Charles Wagley and Eduardo Galvão, copyright 1949 by Columbia
University Press / *Folk-Tales of Salishan and Sahaptin Tribes* (*Memoirs
of the American Folklore Society*, Vol. XI), edited by Franz Boas, copyright 1917 by The American Folklore Society / *The Ring in the Prairie*

Frontispiece: "Council Grove,"
drawn (and engraved?) by
[Jacques Hippolyte?]
Vanderburch   (*Private
collection*)

by John Bierhorst, © 1970 by John Bierhorst, The Dial Press / *Finding the Center* by Dennis Tedlock, © 1972 by The Dial Press / *By Cheyenne Campfires* by George Bird Grinnell, copyright 1926 by Yale University Press / *Four Masterworks of American Indian Literature*, edited by John Bierhorst, © 1974 by John Bierhorst, Farrar, Straus and Giroux, Inc. / *Xingu: The Indians, Their Myths* by Orlando Villas Boas and Claudio Villas Boas, translated by Susana Hertelendy Rudge, © 1970 by Orlando Villas Boas and Claudio Villas Boas, translation © 1973 by Farrar, Straus and Giroux, Inc.; Souvenir Press, London / *The Basic Writings of Sigmund Freud*, translated and edited by Dr. A. A. Brill, copyright 1938 by Random House, Inc., copyright renewed 1965 by Gioia B. Bernheim and Edmund R. Brill / *Civilization and Its Discontents* by Sigmund Freud, translated from the German and edited by James Strachey, © 1961 by James Strachey, W. W. Norton & Company, Inc.; The Hogarth Press, London.

Acknowledgment is made to the authors and publishers for permission to translate from the following books in German (for titles of the selections translated, see Notes): *Francisco de Avila* by Hermann Trimborn and A. Kelm, © 1967 Gebr. Mann Verlag, Berlin / *Religion und Mythologie der Uitoto* by K. T. Preuss, published 1921-3 by Vandenhoeck & Ruprecht, Göttingen / *Die Yamana (Die Feuerland Indianer*, Vol. 2) by Martin Gusinde, copyright 1937 by Martin Gusinde, Anthropos, Mödling bei Wein.

Contents

WINTER AND SPRING

THE BIRTH OF THE HERO

THE HERO AS PROVIDER

THE HERO AS DELIVERER

COMEDY OF HORRORS

JAGUAR AND FOX

GHOSTS

TALES OF THE WHITE MAN

MYTHS OF RETURNING LIFE

DEATH AND BEYOND

THE RED SWAN

INTRODUCTION

1

A myth is an unverifiable and typically fantastic story that is nonetheless felt to be true and that deals, moreover, with a theme of some importance to the believer. With this definition as a starting point, I will attempt to draw a few tentative conclusions about the nature of Indian myth, its scope, and, incidentally, its symbolism.

First let me say that although this book is concerned primarily with myth, it includes a sampling of mere tales as well. In other words, it includes stories based on real experiences that are at least partly *verifiable;* stories devoid of fantastic elements and therefore strictly *mundane;* and stories that may indeed be fantastic, and also safe from the harsh light of verification, but that are recognized as *fictitious* or *trivial*. It is interesting to note that the same story may be handled as a myth by one tribe and as a common tale by another. Certainly there is a broad meeting ground between the two categories, and even in the slightest of tales, told for entertainment only, there will be echoes of the great themes that belong to myth.

For convenience, the subject matter of Indian myth may be divided into four areas, as follows:

A / SETTING THE WORLD IN ORDER. The useful world is fashioned from the chaos of nature; that is, from nothingness, confusion, imbalance, or disarray. The idea is dramatized by myths in which the entire universe is made to issue, feature by feature, from the mind, the person, or the deeds of a being who represents humanity. But the same idea may be expressed more elegantly by focusing on a particular aspect of creation and subjecting it to one of the mythopoetic techniques of reversal, adjustment, partition, or assemblage. For example, a world where women behave like warriors is *reversed* so that men, not women, are warriors. A world that has no night is *adjusted* so that the day is half light, half dark. An undifferentiated world is made into heaven and earth by a woman *partitioned* into halves, the spiritual half thrown upward, the genital half thrown downward. Or, instead of partition into two, we may have partition into four; and this can be done either spatially, by imposing a cross on the earth's surface, or temporally, by postulating a series of four or five successive worlds, as in the typical origin myths of Mexico and the North American Southwest. Or, finally, the various parts of an inchoate world may be *assembled* by applying a rule of three, or a rule of five, or a rule of eleven, or a rule of fifty. In fact, almost any number can be used to express totality; and one can always find a tenuous analogy, if one must, to explain the choice: the human hand, for instance, has five digits. In the Schoolcraft version of the myth known as "The Red Swan," social order is brought to a wilderness by assembling three brides for three brothers. In another version of the same story, recorded by Leonard Bloomfield, eleven brides are collected for eleven brothers. Some of the most impressive displays of assemblage are to be found not in myth, however, but in ritual. When the Iroquois have been stricken by the death of a high chief, they effectively mend the disordered social fabric by reciting the names of each of their fifty chiefs in an elaborate chant known as "The Roll Call of the Founders," which creates a verbal diagram of the Iroquois world as a whole (imagined as a great longhouse stretching from the Mohawk Valley on the east to the shores of Lake Erie on the west). The recitation of the chant, as distinct from the chant itself, is called "putting the house in order."

B/ THE FAMILY DRAMA. This phrase was used by Malinowski in discussing the various conflicts and affinities rising out of the basic kinship unit called by Freud "the germ-cell of civilization." Few are the myths that do not in some way touch upon the special relationship between brother and sister, husband and wife, elder brother and younger brother, father and son, mother and son, or father and daughter. The typical problems are rivalry, aggression, and incest. The comforts are protection and sustenance. The entire cosmos is sometimes wishfully viewed as a nuclear family: the earth is the mother, the sky is the father, humanity is the child. But the dangers are not to be overlooked. Bears and ogres often turn out to be parents in disguise. Brothers turn out to be natural enemies. A father who admires his daughter too much may try to prevent her from marrying. It is surprising to learn how many Indian myths deal overtly with incest. But as Malinowski was at some pains to point out, the classic Freudian family cannot be taken as universal without serious qualifications. For example, in matriarchal societies the tutorial duties of the father are generally assumed by the mother's brother. And so, in many myths where we might expect to find a father-son conflict, we find instead a conflict between uncle and nephew. We must also note that in certain societies, according to Malinowski, the child-rearing pattern is conducive to an incestuous attraction not so much between mother and son as between brother and sister— though stricter Freudians would contend that the displacement is by no means culturally specific. Thus Ernest Jones can write: "As analytic work shows every day, this also . . . is a derivative of the fundamental Oedipus complex."

C / FAIR AND FOUL. Perhaps the most familiar figure in American mythology is the so-called trickster, a fluid personality portrayed in various stories as foolish, irresponsible, or patently evil. Yet at other times he may be responsible and wise. In the extended trickster cycle recorded and analyzed by Paul Radin, the hero progresses from utter worthlessness to a gradual understanding of social virtue. In general, the trickster tale affords the narrator an opportunity to flirt with immoral or antisocial temptations. Most of the tales, interestingly, are humorous. The tension between wise and foolish, responsible and irresponsible, or good and evil is actually resolved, however, in other kinds of narratives: myths in which a model bride is contrasted with a feckless one, a reluctant maiden receives her due punishment, a polite youth is rewarded, or a hero comes to grips with evil in the form of a monster. Or the tension may be resolved in such a way that neither fair nor foul seems favored. In the myth entitled "The Red Parrot," the father-like figure called Seigerani is presented as the giver of food and light; yet it is quite apparent, though he attempts to deny it, that Seigerani is synonymous with the shadowy Nadyerukudu, who takes away these gifts. In "The Hungry Old Woman" the hero, after perilous adventures, finds that he is reborn as a child—but with the white hair of old age. Does such a myth represent a triumph, in which the hero succeeds in combining the virtues of innocence and experience? Or is it an ironic commentary on the quest for rejuvenation? More likely the former, though the story admits of either interpretation. With an eye to such fusions of opposites, certain writers have spoken of Indian myth as "undifferentiated" or lacking in "dualism," as though it were blind to antithetical relationships. Clearly, however, it is not.

D/CROSSING THE THRESHOLD. Under this broad heading I propose to group five distinct, yet hardly disparate, types of passage from one state of being to another. The myths themselves will show that the five types are interrelated. *First:* The passage from unconsciousness to consciousness, often worked out as a transition from sleeping to waking or from gestation to delivery. Included here are the many stories in which humans emerge from an earth-womb. Those who trust the findings of psychoanalysis will also include certain flood myths and even those myths in which a creature dives through water, searching for earth; the waters are viewed as amniotic. *Second:* The ordeal of puberty, which finds its way into an enormous number of myths, usually with the implication of sexual arousal, often hinting at incest. Marriage is included. *Third:* Passage into and out of the animal world. The hero is either adopted by animals, marries an animal, or is literally transformed into an animal. Celestial bodies may take the place of animals. *Fourth:* Passage into and out of death. I here include descents to the underworld as well as death and resurrection. *Fifth:* The transition from nature to culture, symbolized by the acquisition of a superior game animal; a new abundance of game animals; corn as opposed to animal food; fruit; jewels; fire, or light; speech; knowledge in general; curiosity; food in general; or utensils, especially receptacles for grain or prepared food, such as pots, jugs, mortars, pitchers, baskets, or parfleches.

I hope my summary has not been too brief.

The point I wish to make now is that there is a kind of centripetal force operative in mythology, tending to draw all this material into a single narrative. The work may be accomplished in one of two ways, the more obvious method being simply to join a number of separate stories in series to form what may be called a "cycle." Various tribes of North and South America have yielded such cycles, and they are usually known as origin legends, or cosmogonies. Well-known examples are the Navajo Origin Legend and the Popol Vuh of the Quiché Maya. The Iroquoianist J. N. B. Hewitt was probably correct, however, in preferring the term *cosmology* for this type of composition. Although it regularly includes some manner of genesis, what it gives in general is more properly a *world view*. (The sixty-four myths and tales collected in this book, incidentally, are intended to do just that—provide the reader with an American Indian world view.) But this work of drawing together may also be achieved in myths of much smaller scale, in which all or most of the basic mythic materials are condensed in a species of novelette. I will cite just two examples: the myth of Geriguigatugo, chosen by Lévi-Strauss as the cornerstone of his monumental commentary on Indian mythology (because of "an intuitive feeling that it was both rich and rewarding"); and the story from Schoolcraft called "The Red Swan," of which more later.

As we observe this process of gathering in, we may ask if it is not possible to describe the material of myth with greater efficiency, and with more insight, than I have been able to achieve in the summary above. Before attempting to do so, however, I would like to make a few brief remarks on the subject of mythopoetic technique.

2

One of the problems with reading myth is that the reader, wittingly or unwittingly, approaches it expecting to find the same flowing narrative and fixed characters encountered in a modern novel or short story. The expectation may or may not be rewarded. Usually there is some kind of narrative thrust, which appears to link each incident with the incident that follows; and usually there is at least one character whose fortunes are pursued from beginning to end. But the texture will seem lumpy, and in many cases the mythopoet will appear to be slipping into non sequitur. If the myth is well made, however, and if the listener—or reader—takes the trouble to become acquainted with the mythic idiom, what had seemed lumpy and ill-digested will be perceived as vibrant and logical.

As a first step toward acquiring the ability to read myth, one may take note of just three of its peculiarities: (1) mythic narrative is self-reiterating; (2) mythic characters have a tendency to be "split," or "decomposed"; and (3) myth is "geometrical," expressing movement in terms of step-like increments and metaphor in terms of discrete symbols that remain uncombined.

When I say that myth is self-reiterating, I am thinking not only of the verbatim repetitiveness that characterizes far too many winter and campfire yarns but of a subtler kind of duplication in which an incident, an episode, or an entire story is transposed to a new level of meaning. A convenient illustration of this process is the widespread literary form I propose to call *double myth,* examples of which can be cited from Canada, the Great Plains, and ancient Peru.

A double myth is a myth divisible into two more or less equal parts, rehearsing the same plot twice, the second time with a quite different set of images and connotations. The Arapaho story entitled "Raw Gums and White Owl Woman" (p. 141) is in some ways typical; its basic plot is simply this: someone young puts an end to someone old. As told for the first time, it seems to have relatively little mythic interest: a voracious monster-baby, born with a set of teeth, goes around biting and eating old chiefs. But when the story is repeated, it wears a different dress: a good-natured youth, by mutual agreement, puts an end to the spirit of winter. Immediately the first telling assumes a depth of meaning it did not have before—unless of course the reader has fallen into the trap of supposing that the second telling is merely a continuation of the narrative. To get closer to the full meaning of this superb myth, one must juxtapose the second telling against the first.

Other double myths in the present collection are "Coniraya and Cahuillaca," "The Ring in the Prairie," "Why the Buzzard Is Bald," and "The Great Cavern of Darkness." The reader who examines these myths carefully, dividing them into their first and second parts, will have made a significant step toward the interpretation of native American literature.

The second peculiarity to which I would call attention is the device known as splitting. It will be observed that characters sometimes appear in the course of a narrative, or disappear, without motivation; there may be numerous characters popping in and out of the story with seemingly little connection to the narrative as a whole. In such cases one immediately suspects splitting. That is, a single character has been split, or decomposed, into two or more mythic personalities. Anyone who doubts that this process occurs, or that it is consciously manipulated by the mythmaker, may turn to the Seneca story entitled "Brother Black and Brother Red" (p. 91). It will be quite clear, I think, that the brother and his double are one and the same person and that the mythmaker is aware of the split.

Persons most frequently decomposed, aside from the self, are spouses, parents, and siblings—persons about whom one has ambivalent feelings. In the myth of Coniraya and Cahuillaca, the figure of the would-be wife has four manifestations: Cahuillaca herself, the two daughters of Pachacamac, and the mother called She-Who-Gives-Birth-to-the-Dove. The hungry old woman in the Anambé myth (p. 173) is also a wife-mother, i.e., one half of a split wife whose complement is her own daughter.

Other myths in which splitting occurs include "How Coyote Made the World," "A Gift of Honey," "Hiawatha," "The Red Swan," "The Master of the Red Macaws," and "Geriguigatugo."

Thirdly, myth may be described as discontinuous, or geometrical, by which I mean to imply not only that myth, like the graphic art with which it is contemporary, is patterned and formal but that it has something in common with the development of mathematics. If geometry is the precursor of calculus, myth is the precursor of modern literature. The latter in each case is synthesizing, the former is analytic. Myth, to take a specific point, seldom avails itself of the synthesizing figure of speech we generally call metaphor (including simile). Yet if we read through a story like "Raw Gums and White Owl Woman," briefly summarized above, we feel nonetheless that a metaphorical statement is being made. The principal images are these: an unpleasant baby with teeth, the chiefs whom he bites and eats; a genial youth, the winter spirit whom he outwits and replaces. Since this is a double myth—that is, a myth in which the basic elements are duplicated—then

$$\text{baby} = \text{youth}, \quad \text{chiefs} = \text{winter}, \quad \frac{\text{baby}}{\text{chiefs}} = \frac{\text{youth}}{\text{winter}}, \quad \textit{and}$$

$$\frac{\text{baby}}{\text{winter}} = \frac{\text{youth}}{\text{chiefs}}$$

where the full metaphorical effect is the sum of all these relationships. Without stopping to inquire whether this sort of poetry is too dry, or whether it is admirably chaste, we may ask first whether a statement of the same general drift, even allowing for the trivializing tone of the particular author quoted, is preferable as expressed in the modern idiom:

> To me it seems that youth is like spring, an over-praised season—delightful if it happen to be a favoured one, but in practice very rarely favoured and more remarkable, as a general rule, for biting east winds than genial breezes.

For the sake of clarity it should perhaps be pointed out that I do not mean to confuse modern literature in its entirety with that exhilarating twentieth-century spasm known as modernism. The latter, indeed, is at least partly an antiquarian movement, and in rejecting the synthesizing formulations of the general modern idiom as too profane, too overt—too common in our time—it has leaned heavily upon the resources of myth, admittedly so in the case of Joyce or Eliot, less specifically but with equal indebtedness in the works of such prose poets as Kafka and Robbe-Grillet.

Another, complementary aspect of the ancient, or mythic, idiom is the device I have called progressionism, whereby a change of being, direction, or location is expressed in terms of step-like increments. The hummingbird sequence in Schoolcraft's "Red Swan" (p. 277) can be used as an illustration. In this passage the hero, Odjibwa, descends to the underworld (as I will demonstrate more fully in a later paragraph), en route transforming himself first into a hummingbird, then into a speck of down or fluff. Both the bird and the fluff, incidentally, are pan-Indian symbols for the male seed. (Among the Guarani Indians a pregnant woman is said to have a hummingbird in her belly; the Aztec war god, Huitzilopochtli, is said to have been conceived of fluff or down.) To put it bluntly, the hero is implanting himself in the womb of the underworld so that he can be reborn. But what I wish to emphasize at the moment is merely the step-like manner in which he achieves this goal, making himself smaller and smaller in two discrete stages. A variant of the same sequence occurs in "Geriguigatugo" (p. 301), in which the author of the myth employs not only progressionism but both reiteration and splitting as well. The episode is told three times in succession: first, the hummingbird descends to the underworld *on behalf of* the hero; second, the dove descends; third, the mammori (a giant grasshopper) descends. Again the hummingbird is a semen symbol—and more besides. In the present context, as Lévi-Strauss has pointed out, the hummingbird represents something *high*. The grasshopper represents something *low*. The dove is in between. But Lévi-Strauss (for once) misses the sexual symbolism that justifies the configuration: the hummingbird, as indicated, symbolizes male generative power; the grasshopper symbolizes female generative power; the dove is a symbol of sexual innocence (or neutrality), a suitable midpoint between the coital male (on top) and his female partner (below): thus high-low-medium. We have a three-step progression, then, from high to medium to low, in which the hero, represented by three split manifestations, implants himself ever deeper in the underworld womb.

Other, excellent examples of progressionism can be found in "The Mice's Sun Dance" and "The Flight of Quetzal-coatl." The sequence just discussed has a close parallel in "The Ring in the Prairie," where the hero transforms himself first into an opossum, then into a mouse burrowing in rotten wood. The foul-smelling, or putrid, opossum and the mouse linked with rotten wood are both death symbols, which, taken together with their being smaller and yet smaller, indicate a descent to the underworld womb, just as in "The Red Swan" and "Geriguigatugo."

3

Returning now to the question of subject matter, I would like to emphasize the more or less inarguable fact that the typical myth concerns itself with at least one of the five types of transition listed above under part D of my summary—provided we also include, as a sixth type, the transition discussed under the heading "Setting the world in order" (part A). The six may be restated as follows: (1) transition from un-consciousness to consciousness, (2) sexual arousal, (3) passage through the animal (or the celestial) world, (4) passage through death, (5) transition from nature to culture, and (6) transition from chaos to order. I have already suggested that these transitions are interrelated. I could have gone a step further and said that they are mutually allegorical, even interchangeable.

The myths themselves show that this is true. Suppose, for example, we have a double myth in which, in the first instance, a solitary youth becomes a husband and father after making a symbolic passage through death; in the second instance, the same protagonist, again solitary, becomes once more a family man after making a passage through the celestial realm. (The myth is given in full on pp. 263–7; the underworld, or death, symbolism is discussed on p. 14.) From this much it should be clear that the trip to the celestial world (number 3 in the list above) serves the same purpose as the passage through death (number 4). We may therefore state, at least tentatively, that number 3 is equivalent to number 4.

Further exercises of the same sort, using other myths, could establish the interchangeability of all six types of transition. And in passing it may be of interest to note that this statement and the two paragraphs preceding it might serve as a brutally terse—and highly interpretive—synopsis of Lévi-Strauss's four-volume commentary on New World mythology: *The Raw and the Cooked, From Honey to Ashes, The Origin of Table Manners,* and *The Naked Man.* Yet we are left with a structure that has no name. If all these transitions are mutually allegorical, which of them, if any, is the primary referent? If myth has an inner axis, what precisely is it? Lévi-Strauss himself offers no answer, preferring simply to map out the interconnections. For him the essence of myth is its structure, not its content—at least in theory. In practice, however, he finds it convenient to refer back repeatedly to the so-called transition from nature to culture (number 5 in my list above), and I will do the same.

To explore for a few moments some of the other possibilities, let it be noted, first of all, that Jungian interpreters hark back typically to number 1, the progress from unconsciousness to consciousness, often represented in myths as birth or waking. Jung himself had a tendency to view the transition from nature to culture or, as we might say in the present context, the rise to civilization, as a gradual process of becoming conscious. (Animals are not "conscious" in the sense employed here.) Certainly there are many myths that bear him out, myths in which the world begins with gestation, in which a hero emerges from a womb, in which pre-humans are literally animals, or in which there is a gradual creation of the self. "The Beginning Life of the Hummingbird," "The Emergence," and "The Hungry Old Woman" are among the myths in the present collection that lend themselves to Jungian analysis. In some cases the Jungian material may be couched in symbol, as in the hummingbird episodes in "The Red Swan" and in "Geriguigatugo," discussed above in connection with progressionism.

An interpretation based on the ideas of Freud, on the other hand, would stress the value of number 2 (sexual arousal). To see how this might work, let us briefly construct a Freudian theory of mythic content, using the two myths that Freud himself composed. (It is remarkable that Freud could have believed in any myth, let alone one that he had invented, yet it is by no means clear that he declined to do so.) The earlier and better known of these is the story derived from Darwin's notion that primal man, as yet in a state of nature, had lived in bands, or "hordes," in which the sexual favors of the females were controlled by a single paternal male; when sons or younger brothers tried to challenge this arrangement, they were expelled. The myth seeks to explain, moreover, why tribal groups in various parts of the world hold a particular animal sacred—the totem animal—yet periodically kill and eat this animal to the accompaniment of elaborate ritual observances. With the foregoing explanation as prologue, I here reproduce Freud's myth in full:

> One day the expelled brothers joined forces, slew and ate the father, and thus put an end to the father horde. Together they dared and accomplished what would have remained impossible for them singly. Perhaps some advance in culture, like the use of a new weapon, had given them the feeling of superiority. Of course these cannibalistic savages ate their victim. This violent primal father had surely been the envied and feared model for each of the brothers. Now they accomplished their identification with him by devouring him and each acquired a part of his strength. The totem feast, which is perhaps mankind's first celebration, would be the repetition and commemoration of this memorable, criminal act with which so many things began, social organization, moral restrictions and religion.

This myth of the origin of society, from Freud's *Totem and Taboo,* is complemented by a second myth, also by Freud, seeking to explain the origin of fire. The second myth is from the much later *Civilization and Its Discontents:*

> It is as though primal man had the habit, when he came in contact with fire, of satisfying an infantile desire connected with it, by putting it out with a stream of his urine. The legends that we possess leave no doubt about the originally phallic view taken of tongues of flame as they shoot

upwards. Putting out fire by micturating—a theme to which modern giants, Gulliver in Lilliput and Rabelais' Gargantua, still hark back—was therefore a kind of sexual act with a male, an enjoyment of sexual potency in a homosexual competition. The first person to renounce this desire and spare the fire was able to carry it off with him and subdue it to his own use. By damping down the fire of his own sexual excitation, he had tamed the natural force of fire. This great cultural conquest was thus the reward for his renunciation of instinct. Further, it is as though woman had been appointed guardian of the fire which was held captive on the domestic hearth, because her anatomy made it impossible for her to yield to the temptation of this desire.

In the first myth we find the transition from nature to culture accompanied by sexual arousal (of the young males desiring their mothers and sisters); in the second we find the same transition made possible by sexual arousal deliberately damped. The myths present two sides of the same coin: culture flows from sexual energy, but only as it is converted to the uses of technology and sodality. Already the dilemma is plain. For the human species, culture is life; yet the damping, or rechanneling, of sexual instincts, which produces temptation, guilt, and perhaps also aggression, makes culture only barely tolerable. Sexual energy is therefore glorious and at the same time evil.

The first of Freud's myths has unmistakable parallels in Indian literature. The story called "The Boy and the Owls" (p. 270) could almost be treated as a retelling of it; a young man at the threshold of puberty establishes sexual intimacy with his mother and succeeds in killing—and eating—a forbidden animal (representing the generic father, specifically, in this case, the uncle); the spirit of the murdered uncle returns to haunt the boy in the form of owls (representing the boy's elder kinsmen, who may be regarded as split manifestations of the "dead" uncle). The forbidden-animal motif also turns up in "The Red Swan": a young man at the threshold of puberty kills—and skins—a forbidden bear and thereupon immediately makes contact with a potential bride (the red swan herself) who, as we learn, is a female controlled by a fatherly magician (a split manifestation of the hero's own father or elder brother). The result in each case is that the incestuous young man becomes a provider, or culture hero.

Again I will try to paraphrase the Freudian theory: without the energy bound up in incestuous cravings there can be no civilization, no culture; but this sexual energy must be redirected to the purposes of art, science, horticulture, husbandry, gathering, hunting, and socialization. There can be no incest per se. In myths of world collapse, especially in Mexican and Peruvian lore, the general destruction is attributed to the reemergence of incest. The partly historical, partly mythic narrative entitled "A Gift of Honey" (p. 101) may be taken as a typical example.

I turn now to category number 4, the passage through death. There was a time, beginning in the late nineteenth century and continuing well into the 1930's, especially in Germany, when this particular type of transition was regarded as the primary figure to which all myth referred. Myths, including Indian myths, are indeed replete with descents to the underworld, instances of death and revival, and numerous metaphorical variations upon the same theme, including the passage from winter to spring, the diurnal cycle of the sun, the loss and recovery of the moon, and even the Venus cycle. Presumably the idea takes its force from the observation of nature, which appears to dictate a circular law of life and death. Life, in fact, feeds on death; the grave is the seedbed; and so forth. The study of myth along these lines is known as nature mythology; closely related to it is the so-called ritual theory, by which a number of ingenious investigators, especially in Great Britain and especially in the wake of Frazer's *Golden Bough,* have attempted to show that myth itself is a direct outgrowth of revivalist ritual. Clearly this approach has great poetic merit, and if it has fallen from favor in recent decades, the reason perhaps is that it does not lend itself to scientific formulation. As we know, rejuvenation is merely a dream, a fantasy.

"The Red Swan," to which I have alluded previously, has one important episode that may be, indeed must be, treated in terms of nature mythology. This is the sequence beginning with the loss of the old magician's wampum scalp in a contest with enemies "as numerous as the hanging leaves"; the young hero, who goes among these enemies, retrieves the scalp, returns in the form of a hawk, whose cry is heard from a distance, and, placing the scalp on the old man's head, transforms him into a beautiful youth. Though the casual reader may doubt it, every element in this sequence is a symbol, either simple or complex, suggesting that the episode represents a (solar) descent to the underworld. To understand it we must refer to the related ethnography and to a vast web of interconnected myths stretching from Amazonia to the Great Lakes. In a Menominee variant of the very same myth, for example, the (white) wampum beads forming the old man's hair are shown to be laid out in rays. But I will not take up the enormous amount of space that would be needed to justify the entire symbolic fabric. Let it simply be proposed, if not proved, that the wampum hair represents the light of the sun, shorn by the "numerous" stars of night, and returned through the heroic labor of the planet Venus as morning star, appearing just before sunrise to extinguish the light of the offending "enemies," thus restoring the sun to its former beauty. On a second level the "numerous" enemies are the souls of the dead, whom the sun must encounter during its nocturnal west-east passage through the underworld. The hawk is a sun symbol, the cry of the hawk represents the voice of the sun as it breaks over the horizon. What the hero returns with, in effect, are the jewels of new life.

This brings us back to the transition from nature to culture (category number 5), which, as I have already stated, may be symbolized by the acquisition of a jewel. Perhaps the most obvious culture myth in the present collection is "The Red Swan" itself (as epitomized below—see pp. 25–6). Yet the same transition is implied with nearly equal force in many of the other myths, in which, for example, hunger is relieved by plenty ("The Boy and the Owls"), a serpent brings food ("Nephew Story"), an exploding serpent disseminates knowledge ("The Birth of Knowledge"), baskets are woven by a guilty heroine ("The Boy and the Deer"), or food and light are acquired by a guilty hero ("The Red Parrot").

What I have been attempting to do, then, is to demonstrate a little more fully how some of these elementary transitions are actually worked out in the myths and to suggest that at least several if not all of them may be used as axes upon which to turn a theory, whether Jungian, Freudian, or Frazerian. What I hope I have implied, moreover, is that inasmuch as these basic transitions are mutually congruent, if not quite synonymous, the various theories mentioned are all valid and must all be taken into account if one is to pursue, as I intend, a literary approach to myth—that is, an approach which recognizes the single myth as a work of art and proceeds to interpret it not merely for theory's sake but for itself.

In giving credence to Jungian emergence, the Freudian Oedipal theme, the sometimes tenuous constructs of nature mythology, and the Lévi-Straussian fantasy of transition from nature to culture (historically speaking, a non-event), I am well aware of having embraced a series of para-scientific notions that more skeptical observers have rejected as mere "myths." Yet this is precisely their value. The only artistic way to explain a myth is to tell another one; and this in fact is the native American method of exegesis—a subject to which I will return later.

4

Before proceeding, it may be well to emphasize a point that has perhaps already been conveyed, though without elaboration; namely, that the mythic transition is potentially both positive and negative, both fair and foul. Myths in which the positive thrust is unchecked, let it be added, are extremely rare.

With this in mind the varieties of transition, or threshold crossing, may be schematized as follows:

near side	threshold	far side
1 / unconsciousness ⟶	emergence ⟶	consciousness
2 / innocence ⟶	love ⟶	experience
3 / youth ⟵	death ⟵	age
4 / animality ⟶	transformation ⟶	humanity
5 / nature ⟶	progress ⟶	culture
6 / chaos ⟶	creation ⟶	order

Notice that transition 3, resulting in youth, or rebirth, moves in the "wrong" direction. It contradicts its five companions. Notice also that the "near side" entries are negative (that is, undesirable), except for number 3, which gives the "near side" in its entirety a somewhat positive, or desirable, coloration. By contrast the "far side" is all positive except, of course, for number 3, which taints the group as a whole. It is this contradiction, then, that myth attempts to resolve. Without it, there would probably be no myth. The question myth asks is this: How can we get to the far side while staying on the near side?.

The question may be answered by dramatizing one or more of the five "right" transitions, while at the same time either underscoring number 3 or, after the model supplied by number 3, reversing the direction of at least one of the other five. Or, number 3 itself may be reversed, then restored. Thus we have myths in which a protagonist flees from sexuality, often returning to his or her parent ("Coniraya and Cahuillaca," "How the Fog Came," "The Vampire Skeleton," "The Ring in the Prairie"); myths in which humans are permanently transformed into animals ("The Ring in the Prairie"); myths in which the cultural artifact, often a basket, rebels against its owner, is broken, or disappears ("How Night Appeared," "The Hungry Old Woman," "The Ring in the Prairie"); so-called eschatological myths in which cosmic order reverts to chaos ("The Red Parrot," "A Gift of Honey"); and myths in which a hero passes twice through death, once toward culture and once toward nature ("The Red Swan").

The Shawnee myth entitled "The Ring in the Prairie" is

evidently rich in these reversals. Without pausing to scruti-
nize every detail, it may be worthwhile to examine the story
in outline at least, remembering, to start with, that this is a
double myth.

In the first part the hero is united with his bride, yet the
final incident is a reversal, a flight from sexuality, with the
bride returning to her father. In the second part the couple is
reunited, yet again the final incident is a reversal, a transformation in which the hero and his bride, though still
united, revert to animality. If the first part leaves us with the
impression that the myth is tragic, the second part shows us
that we were not quite correct. The penultimate incident in
the second part, moreover, is this: as the stars reached out to
accept the gifts offered by the young hero, "a strange confusion immediately arose"; those "who selected tails or claws
were changed into animals and ran off"; the others "were
changed into birds, and flew away." What we are being
given, in mythic terms, is a transparent metaphor for the
progress from chaos to order, a setting-in-order of the world
by partition into two—by analogy, a separation of earth and
sky—precisely the same metaphor used by the poet Brow-
ning, slipping for one moment into the mythic idiom:

> *The lark's on the wing;*
> *The snail's on the thorn*

then catching himself in the notorious gloss ("God's in his
heaven— / All's right with the world") that the Shawnee
mythmaker, naturally, omits.

Thus the myth gives its stamp of approval—in effect a kind
of counterbalance—to the flight from vulnerability, summing
it all up in the final incident, which combines a reversal (re-

turn to the animal world) with a conventional advance (union of the sexes). In other words we can have it both ways. We can enjoy the full life of the "far side"—of culture, let us say, to pick one of the possible interpretations—while at the same time enjoying the safety of the "near side"—of nature, let us say—with its guaranteed protection against age, senility, and death. (Or can we? As I will demonstrate later, not all myth is so sanguine.)

5

Stories like "The Ring in the Prairie," in which the evils of culture yield to the restorative pull of nature, represent what is unquestionably myth's single greatest fantasy. If its lineaments seem less than familiar in the material reviewed thus far, they can to some extent be recognized more clearly in a yet more novelistic myth like "The Red Swan," in which the burden is carried not only in symbols but by the plot itself.

In this story, from the Chippewa, a boy whose deceased father had been a hermit—a pai-gwud-aw-diz-zid, one who dwells in a wilderness—grows to puberty without knowledge of women or worldly goods. He and his elder brothers, who now act as the boy's father, have remained in the forest, far removed from any village. As the plot gathers momentum, the boy, disobeying his brothers, shoots a bear (that the brothers had specifically forbidden him to kill), and immediately discovers the magnificent red swan who will lead him to prototypal villages, to the discovery of cooked food (hominy), who will in fact become his bride and help him turn the wilderness into a community. But in his first efforts to obtain the swan, the boy commits a fatal error. Attempting to shoot it, and having used up all his arrows without success, he runs home to get the three charmed arrows that had been kept in a hallowed medicine pack belonging to himself and his brothers. The first two miss the mark and are lost. With the third arrow he penetrates the swan; but she carries it off and it is not seen again. In order to obtain culture the young man, in effect, has traded his people's charm against mortality. Hence the well-known dilemma: with culture (or love) comes vulnerability to death. To compensate, when culture has at last been firmly established, the hero makes a special journey to the underworld realm of the dead and retrieves the lost medicine. Thus the hero is the *provider* in the first part of the myth; in the second part he becomes the *deliverer*.

In the cycle of Quetzalcoatl the remedy is the same, but realized in a more dramatic fashion. The deliverer himself, in his own flesh, makes the transit from old age to youth via death. The death and resurrection of Quetzalcoatl—an elegant example of literary progressionism in the American Indian style—is worked out in the mythic fragment commonly known as "The Flight of Quetzalcoatl" (really a flight from vulnerability), included as the final selection in this book. With Quetzalcoatl we have come a long way from "The Ring in the Prairie," and yet it should be clear that the underlying fantasy is unchanged.

Such myths as I have been discussing may be thought of as comedies, in the elevated sense of the term. But myth has its tragedies, too, in which the movement toward nature (or youth) is not strongly reiterated or is strongly iterated, then viewed with suspicion. Thus we have myths like "The Hungry Old Woman," in which the hero indulges in an elaborate, one might almost say epic, flight from sexuality, terminating in a Jungian reentry into the maternal womb, from which he is born again and delivered (by an American stork) to his mother's home; yet he is "old"; his hair is "white."

The same kind of thing happens in "The Man Who Loved the Frog Songs" (p. 149). In this little myth the movement toward nature is expressed in terms of the transition from winter (age) to spring (youth). But, alas, the completed transition is accompanied by vulnerability nonetheless. The man who rejoices in spring is no more protected than anyone else. Eliot's April is indeed the cruelest month. Its promise is pure fantasy.

6

Much more could be written, obviously, about the myths touched upon above, especially "The Flight of Quetzalcoatl" and "The Red Swan"; and I am tempted to give rather full interpretations of several other myths besides. Yet in the long run these exercises may be more satisfying to write than they are to read. What in fact I would rather do is leave the reader with the texts themselves, having provided what I should like to call a "grammar" and "vocabulary" of the mythic idiom as it is understood in the Americas.

Needless to say, such a reference work is not being furnished in these scant pages. One does not acquire Russian or Portuguese after plodding through merely a few dozen paragraphs devoted to its syntax, scattered with random offerings from its lexicon—even if it can be said, as I hope it can, that one's "ear" for the idiom has been improved.

The very idea that there exists a pan-Indian mythic idiom needs more general acceptance than it has heretofore enjoyed. The reluctance to acknowledge it is perhaps the principal reason that native American literature has been so little studied. Whereas the natural inclination of the Western scholar or critic is to approach the literature of a single culture, mastering its language and all its available ethnography, few outside the field of anthropology have cared to invest their talents in such an improbable undertaking. The results, one feels, would be meager. The truth is, we haven't as much information as we would like to have about even such a heavily documented culture as the Navajo. And if we turn to the Chippewa or the Bororo, the lack grows noticeably more acute. This combined with the fact that the labor of learning an Indian language can only be arduous. Thus, when all the work has been done, the student who has kept to Bororo studies must find that Bororo literature remains virtually a closed book. On the other hand, the myths of the Bororo share basic configurations with variants obtained from neighboring and even distant cultures. Indeed, the mythic variant in itself—provided we do not underestimate the pre-Columbian Indian as traveler and linguist—may be regarded as a natural form of aboriginal criticism, the basis for a comparative literature strictly within the confines of the Americas, grounded in native American techniques of explication.

When the Bororo mythmaker submits his variant of the hummingbird descent, partially discussed above (pp. 13–14), what he offers is both art and commentary. Using it, we are permitted to see more clearly what the Chippewa mythmaker is up to (p. 13), and with these two variants we recognize the configuration that would otherwise appear meaningless, if not puerile, in the equally competent Shawnee myth (see p. 14). Let it be emphasized, however, that not all variants deserve the same respect. The occasional watering down, as opposed to vigorous reinterpretation, of Mexican mythic materials, for example, by tribes farther north can be dreary and, in truth, puerile. In sum, then, the serious student of Indian literature must master two "idioms": a chosen language, in order that he or she may contribute to the continuing process of translation and textual criticism, and the general mythic idiom, which is pan-Indian.

But neither will the mythic idiom be easy to master. Its "grammar" has only begun to be formulated and its "vocabulary" remains uncompiled.

By "grammar" I mean the rules according to which certain symbols may be combined. By "vocabulary" I mean a catalogue of symbols coupled with their basic definitions, auxiliary meanings, and geographical range. The "grammar" would make it plain, for example, that configurations involving the number 5 are not necessarily synonymous by virtue of this feature alone; not only the configuration but also its context must be carefully weighed. It would formulate a more complete set of rules with regard to splitting, a fuller definition of the double myth, and more varieties of mythic transition. As a sampling of the "vocabulary" I offer these few partially worked-out entries from the nonexistent lexicon that a dedicated scholar with twenty or more years to devote (inspired by the labor of the distinguished folklorist Stith Thompson) might one day produce:

"Red duck." *see* Rubra avis.

"Red" macaw. *see* Rubra avis; Sun.

"Red" parrot. *see* Rubra avis.

"Red swan." *see* Rubra avis.

Roseate spoonbill. *see* Rubra avis.

Rubra avis. Woman, especially a bride; object of a young man's quest; man's "pet." Bride, as roseate spoonbill—

AMAZONIA: Kamaiurá (Villas Boas and Villas Boas 1972, p. 143). Bride, as "red" macaw—AMAZONIA: Kamaiurá (Villas Boas and Villas Boas 1972, p. 163). Bride, as macaw—CENTRAL ANDES: Canari (Cristobal de Molina in Markham 1873, p. 8); AMAZONIA: Tukuna (Nimuendaju 1952, p. 151). Bride, as "red swan"—UPPER MISSISSIPPI BASIN (former sporadic range of roseate spoonbill): Chippewa (Schoolcraft 1839, Vol. 2, p. 9), Menominee (Bloomfield 1928, p. 419), Osage (Dorsey 1904, p. 34), Oto (as "red duck") (Curtis 1907–30, Vol. 19, p. 166), Winnebago (as "white" swan with red-haired consort) (Radin 1972, p. 83). Object of young man's quest, as "red" macaw, probably *Ara chloroptera*—SOUTHERN BRAZIL: Bororo (Colbacchini 1925, p. 231). Man's "pet," as "red" parrot—AMAZONIA: Uitoto (Preuss 1921–3, Vol. 1, p. 207). A complex symbol incorporating Red (*see under* Red: Sun, Western sun, Menses) and Bird (*see under* Bird: Female phallus, Poison, Loss of paradise, Phoenix). *See also* Red and white; Sun.

And so the directives that I have attempted to provide are incomplete—a beginner's guide. Yet with this much and no more, the reader is urged to forge ahead, keeping in mind that the mythic idiom, though governed by rules, is flexible, capable of infinite variety; that reading or listening in itself is an act of creation; that the ultimate aim of dissection and exegesis is to dispense with dissection and exegesis, making way for a higher experience that proceeds—as expressed by one North American ethnographer-informant—"from vivid feeling within oneself, feeling as a moving current all the figures and the relationships" that belong to the whole mythology.

7

One of the purposes of the following collection, as already noted, is to present a comprehensive view of the world—the world of humanity—as perceived through the lens of American myth. For variety's sake I have drawn my examples from as many different cultures as possible, keeping in mind the conviction, or, as I believe it is fair to say, the observation, that ideas developed with peculiar brilliance by one culture are by no means alien to distant cultures where they may nevertheless be poorly developed or apparently lacking. My second, more immediate purpose is to display this brilliance as effectively as I can, and as a consequence certain sources and therefore, lamentably, certain cultures have been given short shrift. I include two selections from Gusinde's *Die Yamana*, but none from his equally compendious *Die Selk'nam*. I am an admirer of James Mooney's *Sacred Formulas of the Cherokees* (taken from old native manuscripts), yet can find little or nothing to equal it in Mooney's *Myths of the Cherokee*, valuable though that work unquestionably is. No Delaware myths are included and none from the Araucanian cultures of Chile.

Such omissions are due to missed opportunities on the part of Westerners, ruinous acculturation, or both. Modern times, on the other hand, do not always spell the end of good oral literature. Dennis Tedlock's "The Boy and the Deer," obtained from a Zuni informant in 1965, is clearly superior to other, similar Deer Boy tales collected forty years earlier.

In the notes provided for each selection, I make an attempt to identify the informant, the translator, and the collector and to give the date and place of collection, though in many cases this cannot be done. Of the sixty-four selections included, fifty-one are complete and unabridged, two are abridgments, and eleven are excerpts—as explained in the notes. The story titles are the original ones, except where otherwise noted. But it must be kept in mind that the "original" title is not necessarily the native title. Most often, in fact, it is the invention of the translator. I also make an informal effort to trace the publishing history of each myth or tale, most of which, I find, are not nearly so well known as they deserve to be. A few, by contrast, have been widely circulated. Probably the most famous of all Indian stories are Schoolcraft's, and of these I conclude that the best loved (though it is not one of the ones incorporated by Longfellow in his *Song of Hiawatha*) is the undoubtedly charming "Ring in the Prairie." I include this one and two others from Schoolcraft, as well as liberal selections from Magalhães, Grinnell, and Edward Curtis, three celebrated collectors whose works should be among the first consulted by anyone searching for Indian myths of more than average appeal.

The translations are anything but uniform. I have tolerated the rough, workmanlike versions of Dorsey and Kroeber, Schoolcraft's "polite" prose, the donnish prose-poetry of Leland, the severe paratactical style sometimes used by Boas and his school, and the quaint "missionary" style of Ixtlilxochitl and the anonymous compiler of "Histoyre du Mechique." But I have not tolerated them at their worst. Two of the Schoolcraft stories, for example, have been completely rewritten—yet with care taken to preserve the original tone and every precious nuance of meaning. One is tempted to edit out a phrase like "the fire of youth beaming from his eye." Can this be Indian? Yet I dare not get rid of it. I am convinced, moreover, that the story in which it appears ("The Ring in the Prairie") has solar allusions, and I suspect that the fire, perhaps even of "youth," has always been there in one form or another.

This kind of problem, fortunately, plagues only a small percentage of my material. It is with considerable confidence, as well as pleasure, that I present such superlative pieces as "The Rival Chiefs," "The Beginning Life of the Hummingbird," "How Night Appeared," and "The Flight of Quetzalcoatl," all of which have been taken directly from the native texts. Accuracy has been the primary concern throughout; and in a few cases it has even been possible to improve upon long-familiar versions of well-known stories—for example, the Bororo narrative entitled "Geriguigatugo" and the Uitoto creation myth beginning with the words "Was it not an illusion," both of which have been newly translated especially for this volume.

I am aware that the fitting of these selections into thematic groups is only partly successful. Many of the stories defy such rigid classification and there is much overlapping. I believe nonetheless that the arrangement will help the reader in making cross-cultural comparisons and will serve therefore as a starting point toward the interpretation of the more difficult myths.

J.B.

West Shokan, N.Y.
April 1975

The Dream Father

Indian mythology deals with the problem of ultimate origins by treating the Creation as a process of growing awareness or as a deliberate act of the imagination. The earth is supposed to have issued from the thoughts of a first Father, who gives his ideas substance by saying them out loud or by singing them.

THE BEGINNING LIFE OF THE HUMMINGBIRD

MBYÁ

Our First Father, the absolute, grew from within the original darkness.

The sacred soles of his feet and his small round standing-place, these he created as he grew from within the original darkness.

The reflection of his sacred thoughts, his all-hearing, the sacred palm of his hand with its staff of authority, the sacred palms of his branched hands tipped with flowers, these were created by Ñamanduí as he grew from within the original darkness.

Upon his sacred high head with its headdress of feathers were flowers like drops of dew. Among the flowers of the sacred headdress hovered the first bird, the Hummingbird.

As he grew, creating his sacred body, our First Father lived in the primal winds. Before he had thought of his future earth-dwelling, before he had thought of his future sky—his future world as it came to be in the beginning—Hummingbird came and refreshed his mouth. It was Hummingbird who nourished Ñamanduí with the fruits of paradise.

As he was growing, before he had created his future paradise, he himself, Our Ñamandu Father, the First Being, did not see darkness, though the sun did not yet exist. He was lit by the reflection of his own inner self. The thoughts within his sacred being, these were his sun.

The true Ñamandu Father, the First Being, lived in the primal winds. He brought the screech owl to rest and made darkness. He made the cradle of darkness.

As he grew, the true Ñamandu Father, the First Being, created his future paradise. He created the earth. But at first he lived in the primal winds. The primal wind in which our Father lived returns with the yearly return of the primal time-space, with the yearly recurrence of the time-space that was. As soon as the season that was has ended, the trumpet-vine tree bears flowers. The winds move on to the following time-space. New winds and a new space in time come into being. Comes the resurrection of space and time.

SOLITUDE WALKER

YUKI

The name of the Yuki Creator, Taikó-mol, means, literally, "Solitude Walker." The implement he uses is the lílkae, or "stone crook," four of which he arranges to form a cross, or, more precisely, a swastika.

There was only water, and over it a fog. On the water was foam. The foam moved round and round continually, and from it came a voice. After a time there issued from the foam a person in human form. He had wing feathers of the eagle on his head. This was Taikó-mol. He floated on the water and sang. He stood on the foam, which still revolved. There was no light. He walked on the water as if it were land. He made a rope and laid it from north to south, and he walked along it, revolving his hands one about the other; and behind him the earth was heaped up along the rope. But the water overwhelmed it. Again he did this, and again the water prevailed. Four times this was done.

Taikó-mol was constantly talking to himself: "I think we had better do it this way. I think we had better try it that way." So now he talked to himself, and he made a new plan. He made four lílkae, and planted one in the north and the others in the south, west, and east. Then he stretched them out until they were continuous lines crossing the world in the center. He spoke a word, and the earth appeared. Then he went along the edge and lined it with whale hide, so that the ocean could not wash away the earth. He shook the earth to see if it was solid, and he still makes this test, causing earthquakes.

The earth was flat and barren, without vegetation and rivers. And still there was no light. In the ocean were fish and other creatures, but on the earth was nothing. Yet Taikó-mol had the feathers of various birds. He laid buzzard feathers and eagle feathers on the ground, and they became mountains. With lightning he split the mountains, and streams issued forth. He made all the birds and beasts, which in those times were persons. Afterward he changed them into their present forms and created real human beings.

He built a house, and in it he laid sticks of mountain mahogany. Those with knobs on the ends were to be men, the smooth ones women, the small ones children. He said, "In the morning there will be much noise in this house. There will be laughing and talking." And in the morning the house was full of people, all laughing and talking. The earth was populated, and Taikó-mol went forth from the north all around the earth to give the tribes different languages. When all his work was done, he went up into the sky.

WAS IT NOT AN ILLUSION?

UITOTO

Was it not an illusion?

The Father touched an illusory image. He touched a mystery. Nothing was there. The Father, Who-Has-an-Illusion, seized it and, dreaming, began to think.

Had he no staff? Then with a dream-thread he held the illusion. Breathing, he held it, the void, the illusion, and felt for its earth. There was nothing to feel: "I shall gather the void." He felt, but there was nothing.

Now the Father thought the word. "Earth." He felt of the void, the illusion, and took it into his hands. The Father then gathered the void with dream-thread and pressed it together with gum. With the dream-gum iseike he held it fast.

He seized the illusion, the illusory earth, and he trampled and trampled it, seizing it, flattening it. Then as he seized it and held it, he stood himself on it, on this that he'd dreamed, on this that he'd flattened.

As he held the illusion, he salivated, salivated, and salivated, and the water flowed from his mouth. Upon this, the illusion, this, as he held it, he settled the sky roof. This, the illusion, he seized, entirely, and peeled off the blue sky, the white sky.

Now in the underworld, thinking and thinking, the maker of myths permitted this story to come into being. This is the story we brought with us when we emerged.

HOW COYOTE MADE THE WORLD

PIT RIVER

This humble myth is presented by anthropologist Jaime de Angulo as a dialogue between himself and his informant, whose words he translates in a bluntly colloquial style. Yet the underlying concepts are subtle. Note that the Creator is regarded as two separate persons, Silver Fox and Coyote, an idea de Angulo pretends to find surprising. The concept of a dual Creator, however, is both typical and widespread. One possibility is that the mythmaker perceives the spirit of the world to be split in half, half wise and half foolish, or, looked at from a slightly different angle, half good and half evil.

"Listen, Bill, tell me . . . do the Indians think, really think, that Coyote made the world? I mean, do they really think so? Do you really think so?"

"Why, of course I do . . . Why not? . . . Anyway . . . that's what the old people always said . . . only they don't all tell the same story. Here is one way I heard it: It seems like there was nothing everywhere but a kind of fog. Fog and water mixed, they say, no land anywhere, and this here Silver Fox . . ."

"You mean Coyote?"

"No, no, I mean Silver Fox. Coyote comes later. You'll see, but right now, somewhere in the fog, they say, Silver Fox was wandering and feeling lonely. *Tsikuellaaduwi maandza tsikualaasa.* He was feeling lonely, the Silver Fox. I wish I would meet someone, he said to himself, the Silver Fox did. He was walking along in the fog. He met Coyote. 'I thought I was going to meet someone,' he said. The Coyote looked at him, but he didn't say anything. 'Where are you traveling?' says Fox. 'But where are YOU traveling? Why do you travel like that?' 'Because I am worried.' 'I also am wandering,' said the Coyote; 'I also am worrying and traveling.' 'I thought I would meet someone, I thought I would meet someone. Let's you and I travel together. It's better for two people to be traveling together, that's what they always say . . .' "

"Wait a minute, Bill . . . Who said that?"

"The Fox said that. I don't know who he meant when he said *that's what they always say*. It's funny, isn't it? How could he talk about *other* people since there had never been anybody before? I don't know . . . I wonder about that sometimes, myself. I have asked some of the old people and they say: That's what I have been wondering myself, but that's the way we have always heard it told. And then you hear the Paiutes tell it different! And our own people down the river, they also tell it a little bit different from us. Doc, maybe the whole thing just never happened . . . And maybe it did happen but everybody tells it different. People often do that, you know . . ."

"Well, go on with the story. You said that Fox had met Coyote . . ."

"Oh, yah . . . Well, this Coyote he says, 'What are we going to do now?' 'What do you think?' says Fox. 'I don't know,' says Coyote. 'Well then,' says Fox, 'I'll tell you: LET'S MAKE THE WORLD.' 'And how are we going to do that?' 'WE WILL SING,' says the Fox.

"So, there they were singing up there in the sky. They were singing and stomping and dancing around each other in a circle. Then the Fox he thought in his mind, CLUMP OF SOD, come! ! That's the way he made it come: *by thinking*. Pretty soon he had it in his hands. And he was singing all the while he had it in his hands. They were both singing and stomping. All of a sudden the Fox threw that clump of sod, that *tsapettia*, he threw it down into the clouds. 'Don't look down!' he said to the Coyote. 'Keep on singing! Shut your eyes, and keep them shut until I tell you.' So they kept on singing and stomping around each other in a circle for quite a while. Then the Fox said to the Coyote, 'Now, look down there. What do you see?' 'I see something . . . I see something . . . but I don't know what it is.' 'All right. Shut your eyes again!' Now they started singing and stomping again, and the Fox thought and wished: Stretch! Stretch! 'Now look down again. What do you see?' 'Oh! It's getting bigger!' 'Shut your eyes again and don't look down!' And they went on singing and stomping up there in the sky. 'Now look down again!' 'Oooh! Now it's big enough!' said the Coyote.

"That's the way they made the world, Doc. Then they both jumped down on it and they stretched it some more. Then they made mountains and valleys; they made trees and rocks and everything. It took them a long time to do all that!"

"Didn't they make people, too?"

"No. Not people. Not Indians. The Indians came much later, after the world was spoiled by a crazy woman, Loon. But that's a long story . . . I'll tell you someday."

From the Body of Our Mother

Ritual of the Indians of
Hispaniola in honor of the earth
goddess. Adapted and engraved
by Bernard Picart, 1721
(*Private collection*)

The earth has often been imagined as a woman. A number of Indian tribes, especially in North America, revere her as the source of life. Yet the idea of the earth is still attributed, in many cases, to a pre-existing father figure.

THE FLAMING ROCK

OMAHA

At the beginning all things were in the mind of Wakonda. All creatures, including man, were spirits. They moved about in space between the earth and the stars. They were seeking a place where they could come into a bodily existence. They ascended to the sun, but the sun was not fitted for their abode. They moved on to the moon and found that it also was not good for their home. Then they descended to the earth. They saw it was covered with water. They floated through the air to the north, the east, the south, and the west, and found no dry land. They were sorely grieved. Suddenly from the midst of the water uprose a great rock. It burst into flames and the waters floated into the air in clouds. Dry land appeared; the grasses and the trees grew. The hosts of spirits descended and became flesh and blood. They fed on the seeds of the grasses and the fruits of the trees, and the land vibrated with their expressions of joy and gratitude to Wakonda, the maker of all things.

EARTH GODDESS

AZTEC

Quetzalcoatl and Tezcatlipoca represent the bright and dark aspects of the Creator. The earth herself is the nourisher of life; but she is also the burial ground of the dead. One purpose of this myth is to validate the Aztec custom of sacrificing live human hearts.

The gods Quetzalcoatl and Tezcatlipoca brought the earth goddess Tlalteuctli down from on high. All the joints of her body were filled with eyes and mouths biting like wild beasts. Before they got down, there was water already below, upon which the goddess then moved back and forth. They did not know who had created it.

They said to each other, "We must make the earth." So saying, they changed themselves into two great serpents, one of whom seized the goddess from the right hand down to the left foot, the other from the left hand down to the right foot. As they tightened their grip, she broke at the middle. The half with the shoulders became the earth. The remaining half they brought to the sky—which greatly displeased the other gods.

Afterward, to compensate the earth goddess for the damage those two had inflicted upon her, all the gods came down to console her, ordaining that all the produce required for human life would issue from her. From her hair they made trees, flowers, and grasses; from her skin, very fine grasses and tiny flowers; from her eyes, wells and fountains, and small caves; from her mouth, rivers and large caves; from her nose, valleys and mountains; from her shoulders, mountains.

Sometimes at night this goddess wails, thirsting for human hearts. She will not be silent until she receives them. Nor will she bear fruit unless she is watered with human blood.

THE EMERGENCE

JICARILLA APACHE

Gestation myths are typical of the Pueblo, Navajo, and Apache tribes of the southwestern United States. The earth is thought of as a primal womb; the underground mountain

*suggests pregnancy; the twelve-step ladders correspond to the
birth canal.*

In the beginning nothing was here where the world now
stands; there was no ground, no earth—nothing but Darkness, Water, and Cyclone. There were no people living. Only
the Hactcin existed. It was a lonely place. There were no
fishes, no living things.

All the Hactcin were here from the beginning. They had
the material out of which everything was created. They made
the world first, the earth, the underworld, and then they
made the sky. They made Earth in the form of a living woman
and called her Mother. They made Sky in the form of a man
and called him Father. He faces downward, and the woman
faces up. He is our father and the woman is our mother.

In the beginning there were all kinds of Hactcin living in
the underworld, in the place from which the emergence
started. The mountains had a Hactcin, the different kinds of
fruit each had one, everything had a Hactcin.

It was then that the Jicarilla Apache dwelt under the earth.
Where they were there was no light, nothing but darkness.
Everything was perfectly spiritual and holy, just like a
Hactcin . . .

Then those four, White Hactcin, Black Hactcin, Holy Boy,
and Red Boy, brought sand. It was sand of four colors. They
brought pollen from all kinds of trees . . . They leveled off
a place so they could work with the sand. They smoothed
down the place with eagle feathers.

They had earth of four colors there too: black, blue, yellow, and glittering.

First they laid the sand down evenly. Then they made four
little mounds of earth with the dirt. In each one they put

some seeds and fruits . . . The mounds of earth were in a row extending from east to west. The first one was the one of black earth, next the one of blue earth, then the one of yellow earth, and last the one of glittering earth.

Before the mountain started to grow, the Holy Ones took a black clay bowl and filled it with water. They did this because water was needed to make the mountain grow. How could it grow that tall without water? When they did this there was still no single tall mountain there. But they put the clay bowl of water there and then added all the things . . . and the mountain began to grow . . .

Then the two Hactcin and Holy Boy and Red Boy started to sing. They sang and sang and after a while all the fruit began to grow in these piles of earth . . .

Every time the mountain grew there was a noise . . . All the four mounds of earth, as they grew, merged and became one mountain . . .

All those who were present helped. They all worked to make the mountain grow. It was getting large. The people wanted to travel on it. The mountain had much fruit on it now. There were cottonwood and aspen trees on it and streams of water flowed from it too. It was very rich in everything. Yucca fruit and all other fruits were growing on it by this time, all kinds of berries and cherries . . .

Now all the people came together . . . and sang, and the mountain began to grow again. It grew just a little higher. It grew four times and then it wouldn't rise any more.

The four Holy Ones went up the mountain . . . They saw that the top of the mountain was still a little way from the sky and from the hole through which they could see to the other earth. So they all held a council to decide what they would do next.

They sent up Fly and Spider. The spider put his web all around, and the fly and the spider went up on it. That is why, in February or March, when the first warm weather starts and the first flies appear, they come on the sunbeams, which stand for the spider's web. You will see the sun's ray come through the window and the fly will come in on it, right into the house.

Those two went up where the sun was. They took four rays of the sun, each of a different color, and pulled on them as if they were ropes. They pulled them down to the mountaintop. The ropes came down, black, blue, yellow, and glittering, one on each corner of the opening. From these rays of the sun the four Holy Ones made a ladder. Out of the same material they made twelve steps and placed them across . . .

Ancestral Man was the first of the people to ascend. Ancestral Woman followed and was the first woman to emerge. Both walked up with age sticks in their hands. They were dressed as White-Shell Woman and Child-of-the-Water dress for the girl's puberty ceremony now. The other people followed. The men were to the east, the women to the west, and the children to the north and south.

After the people the animals came.

The people emerged from a hole in a mountain. At that time this was the only mountain on the earth, besides Flint Mountain to the east. The other mountains grew up later . . . Some say that the emergence mountain lies north of Durango, Colorado. Others say it is near Alamosa, Colorado. It was called Big Mountain.

Sky is our father, Earth is our mother. They are husband and wife, and they watch over us and take care of us. The earth gives us our food; all the fruits and plants come from the earth. Sky gives us the rain, and when we need water we pray to him. The earth is our mother. We came from her. When we came up on this earth, it was just like a child being born from its mother. The place of emergence is the womb of the earth.

THE MOTHER OF ALL THE PEOPLE

OKANAGON

Old-One, or Chief, made the earth out of a woman, and said she would be the mother of all the people. Thus the earth was once a human being, and she is alive yet; but she has been transformed, and we cannot see her in the same way we can see a person. Nevertheless, she has legs, arms, head, heart, flesh, bones, and blood.

The soil is her flesh; the trees and vegetation are her hair; the rocks, her bones; and the wind is her breath.

She lies spread out, and we live on her. She shivers and contracts when cold, and expands and perspires when hot. When she moves, we have an earthquake. Old-One, after transforming her, took some of her flesh and rolled it into balls, as people do with mud or clay. These he transformed into the beings of the ancient world.

THE ORIGIN OF NUNIVAK ISLAND

NUNIVAK ESKIMO

Two brothers lived together in a far land. One was still very young and weak, so that when the elder went on hunting trips he packed the younger on his back. One spring, when the younger was quite grown up, they made a kayak and went hunting, but though they went far, they saw no game. At last, almost exhausted, they stopped by some anchor ice, intending to go home the following day. That night a stiff blow came up. "Let us go home!" often cried the younger.

"No, we shall set out for home tomorrow," always answered the elder. The frightened younger brother cried so loudly that the elder threatened, "You had better stop that crying. If you do not, a spirit will hear you."

But the crying continued. When the moon broke through the clouds for a brief moment, the elder saw, on looking up, something coming down to the water. Frightened, he exclaimed, "I told you not to cry! I told you that a spirit would hear you! Now look and see what is coming down to us!"

The younger stopped wailing, and they watched. The spirit came closer. singing as it approached, "I hear people preparing for the night. I want them for my own. I shall have them for my own."

The spirit woman, with fancy trimming on her parka and holding something inside it, stepped on their kayak. Said she, "I heard that you are in trouble. I have come to help you."

"I told my brother over and over that I would take him home tomorrow, but he wants to go now."

The spirit woman took something from her parka and threw it on both sides of the kayak, and it became land. The younger brother turned into a woman, whom the elder married. Then all animals, both of land and sea, became so numerous that the man, who was a great hunter, was able to provide everything in great plenty.

Once, while hunting, his bow string broke, so he returned home to have his wife make him a new one. As she was shredding sinew, he lay beside her watching, and began to tease her. As she edged away, he moved toward her, continually teasing, until at last she thrust her sinew threader toward him. This she did many times, whenever he moved closer. Finally he became very still. Frightened by his quietness, she looked at him very carefully and saw that his body was full of tiny holes. Then she carried the corpse outside and buried it.

That night the spirit woman entered and inquired for the man. "My husband broke a bow string and came home for a new one. He went out again and has not returned since," the wife lied.

The spirit, not quite satisfied with the answer, searched about the house, finally asking, "Where did he go? Did he really go?"

"Yes, he went away, taking his new bow string with him."

One winter night, as the woman built her fire, the smoke hung in the room instead of going through the smoke hole, so she went outside to build a windbreak. While she was busy, the spirit woman returned and sat down to watch. As she reclined, she felt something protruding into her back, something which felt like a human knee bone. She dug, and found the body of the man, punched full of holes.

She asked the woman, "Why did you lie to me? You said your husband had gone away, but you killed him."

"He was teasing me, but I only motioned at him with my sinew threader, and that had to happen."

"Why did you do that? You were intended to live together as man and wife."

The woman sprang to her feet to run away. As she did so, the spirit woman reached out to grab her, but just grazed the sole of her foot. As the woman disappeared, she sang:

> *Up shall I go;*
> *Up shall I go;*
> *To the middle of the sky shall I go.*
> *Where all the spirits go, there shall I go.*
> *Up shall I go.*

The spirit woman felt so distressed because the man had been killed and the woman had gone to the sky that she broke her knife in two, inserting the halves into her upper jaws to make long fangs. Then she turned into a wolf, and all of her wolf offspring later became humans.

SEDNA AND THE FULMAR

CENTRAL ESKIMO

From the flesh of her body Sedna dispenses seals and fish. But she is also the ruler of the underworld realm of the dead, called Adlivun.

Once upon a time there lived on a solitary shore an Inung with his daughter, Sedna. His wife had been dead for some time and the two led a quiet life. Sedna grew up to be a handsome girl and the youths came from all around to sue for her hand, but none of them could touch her proud heart. Finally, at the breaking up of the ice in the spring, a fulmar flew from over the ice and wooed Sedna with enticing song. "Come to me," it said; "come into the land of the birds, where there is never hunger, where my tent is made of the most beautiful skins. You shall rest on soft bearskins. My fellows, the fulmars, shall bring you all your heart may desire; their feathers shall clothe you; your lamp shall always be filled with oil, your pot with meat." Sedna could not long resist such wooing and they went together over the vast sea. When at last they reached the country of the fulmar, after a long and hard journey, Sedna discovered that her spouse had shamefully deceived her. Her new home was not built of beautiful pelts but was covered with wretched fishskins, full of holes, that gave free entrance to wind and snow. Instead of soft reindeer skins her bed was made of hard walrus hides and she had to live on miserable fish, which the birds brought her. Too soon she discovered that she had thrown away her opportunities when in her foolish pride she had rejected the Inuit youth. In her woe she sang: "Aja. O Father, if you knew how wretched I am, you would come to me and we would hurry away in your boat over the waters. The birds look unkindly upon me, the stranger; cold winds roar about my bed; they give me but miserable food. O come and take me back home. Aja."

When a year had passed and the sea was again stirred by

warmer winds, the father left his country to visit Sedna. His daughter greeted him joyfully and besought him to take her back home. The father, hearing of the outrages wrought upon his daughter, determined upon revenge. He killed the fulmar, took Sedna into his boat, and they quickly left the country which had brought so much sorrow to Sedna. When the other fulmars came home and found their companion dead and his wife gone, they all flew away in search of the fugitives. They were very sad over the death of their poor murdered comrade and continue to mourn and cry until this day.

Having flown a short distance, they discerned the boat and stirred up a heavy storm. The sea rose in immense waves that threatened the pair with destruction. In this mortal peril the father determined to offer Sedna to the birds and flung her overboard. She clung to the edge of the boat with a death grip. The cruel father then took a knife and cut off the first joints of her fingers. Falling into the sea, they were transformed into whales, the nails turning into whalebone. Sedna holding on to the boat more tightly, the second finger joints fell under the sharp knife and swam away as seals; when the father cut off the stumps of the fingers they became ground seals. Meantime the storm subsided, for the fulmars thought Sedna was drowned. The father then allowed her to come into the boat again. But from that time she cherished a deadly hatred against him and swore bitter revenge. After they got ashore, she called her dogs and let them gnaw off the feet and hands of her father while he was asleep. Upon this he cursed himself, his daughter, and the dogs which had maimed him; whereupon the earth opened and swallowed the hut, the father, the daughter, and the dogs. They have since lived in the land of Adlivun, of which Sedna is the mistress.

The Lure of the Serpent

"Storing Their Crops in the
Public Granary." Southeastern
United States. Painted *circa*
1565 by Jacques Le Moyne,
engraved *circa* 1590 by Theodore
De Bry   (*Picture Collection,
New York Public Library*)

Deep in the mythic past, there was a time when all things were free. There were no social responsibilities and food was magically abundant. When it appeared that there might be such a thing as hunting or planting, then the easily obtained food suddenly vanished; the natural world became hard to control. This important transition—from nature to culture, or, as we might say, from childhood to adulthood—is symbolized in myths the world over by the figure of the serpent. The serpent imparts the knowledge of culture and is thereafter associated with all that culture implies, including wisdom, life, vulnerability to death, and loss of innocence.

THE BIRTH OF KNOWLEDGE

DIEGUEÑO

Earth was a woman and water a man. Earth was beneath water. She bore two sons, and she named them Chakopá and Chakomát. Chakopá was elder and Chakomát was younger. They stood up and pushed with their hands, raising the water until it formed the sky. Then they were standing on the earth. The younger was blind.

First they made the sun, then the moon, then the stars. The younger brother rolled clay into a flat disc and threw it into the western sky. It slipped down twice. He tried it in the southern sky, but it slipped down twice. He tried it in the north, and again it slipped down twice. He tried it in the east, and it remained without slipping so rapidly. The elder brother said it felt too hot, and it was raised higher. Three times it was moved higher, until it felt right. In the same way the moon was finally fixed in place, but it was too cold, and three times it was moved higher until it was right. For the stars many small pieces of clay were scattered in the sky. Then was begun the creation of people out of clay. They lay there sleeping, and then began to come to life. This happened at the mountain Wíkami.

The people planned a ceremony, and built a large enclosure of brush. Then they sent a messenger to bring the great serpent Umaí-huhlyá-wit from the ocean. He came and coiled himself in the enclosure; but he could not get his entire length inside. On the third morning, when he had coiled as much of his body as the enclosure would contain, the people set fire to it and burned him. His body exploded and scattered. Inside his body was all knowledge, comprising songs, magic secrets, ceremonies, languages, and customs. Thus these were scattered over the land and different people acquired different languages and customs.

HOW NIGHT APPEARED

ANAMBÉ

In the beginning there was no night. It was always day. Night was asleep at the bottom of the water. There were no animals. All things could speak.

The daughter of the Great Serpent, they say, was married to a young man. This young man had three trustworthy servants. One day he called the three servants and said to them, "Go! Be off! My wife refuses to sleep with me." The servants departed.

Then he called his wife to sleep with him. His wife answered, "It isn't night yet."

"There is no night, only day."

"My father has night. If you wish to sleep with me, send to the river for it."

He called back the three servants and his wife sent them to her father's house to ask for a tucuma nut.

When they arrived at the Great Serpent's house, he gave them the tucuma nut, perfectly closed. "Here it is," he said. "Take it. Be careful not to open it! If you open it, you will be lost."

The servants departed. They heard a sound inside the tucuma nut: tan tan tan, tan tan tan. It was the sound of crickets and toads that sing in the night.

After the servants had traveled some distance, one of them said to his companions, "What is that sound? Come, let's see."

But the helmsman said, "No. Never. We would all be lost. Paddle on! Keep moving."

They moved on. They kept hearing a sound. They had no idea what the sound might be. At last, when they had gone a very long way, they all got together in the middle of the canoe to open the tucuma nut to see what was inside.

One of them made a fire; they melted the pitch that covered the hole in the tucuma nut. They opened it and at once there was thick night.

Then the helmsman said, "We are lost! At home the young woman already knows we have opened the tucuma nut." They went on.

At home, the young woman was saying to her husband, "They've let out the night! We must watch for the dawn."

Then all the things that were lying about in the woods were changed into animals and birds. All the things that lay in the river were changed into ducks and fish. The basket became a jaguar.

The fisherman and his canoe were changed into a duck; his head became the head of the duck; his paddle became the legs of the duck; his canoe became the duck's body.

When the daughter of the Great Serpent saw the morning star, she said to her husband, "Dawn has come. I will divide the day from the night."

Then she rolled up a thread and said, "You be the cujubí. Sing when dawn comes." And so she made the cujubí: she whitened its head with white clay, she reddened its legs with urucú. She said to it, "You will always sing when dawn comes."

Again she rolled up a thread, and said, "Be the inambu." She took ashes and rubbed it, saying, "You shall be the inambu, that sings in the evening, at night, at midnight, past midnight, and in the early part of the morning."

From then on the birds have sung at their appointed times

and also when dawn comes to brighten the day. When the three servants arrived, the young man said to them, "You were not trustworthy. You let out the night. You caused all the things to be lost. For this you will be changed into monkeys —forever. You will live in trees."

THE THEFT OF NIGHT

TENETEHARA

This little story epitomizes the ideas expressed more fully in the preceding myth.

A long time ago, the sun was continually in the sky. There was no night and the Tenetehara slept in full daylight. Deep in the forest an old woman kept Night closed up in several vessels. Mokwaní, a young man who could run extraordinarily fast, decided to go to steal Night from the old woman. He went to her house, and calling her grandmother, he asked if she would give him Night. She showed him the vessels and asked him to choose one. He picked a small pot. He broke it open and out came darkness, with owls and bats. Mokwaní ran as fast as he could, back to the village, followed by the darkness, but by the time he arrived the darkness had disappeared and it was daylight again.

He told the people what he had seen and done. They suggested that he return to the house of the old woman who was the owner of Night. This time, when she asked him to choose, he picked a larger pot. He broke it and more darkness came out. He began running back toward the village, but Night overtook him and he was transformed into a night bird whose sad song people can still hear during the night from deep in the forest.

NEPHEW STORY

COOS

The translator of this myth found it necessary to add certain words and phrases in order to complete the meaning for readers of English. These additions are printed in italic.

Five brothers lived *together*. Their father and mother were alive. Their sister was in the habit of bathing all the time. She used to go bathing early in the morning, and would go bathing in the evening. She would always *do* that way.

Once she went bathing. The young woman was swimming *where* there was a somewhat deep place. She swam naked. One day a small snake was swimming. The snake was as large as a hair *and* was very pretty. It swam towards her. She stretched out her hand, and the little snake came into her hand. She went ashore with it. The woman picked up a little moss and put *the snake* there. Then the woman dressed, and went home with it.

She took it into the house. She took it there where her bed was. "What am I going to do with it?" Thus she was thinking. Then she gathered moss. Indeed, she worked hard. There she put the pet. "What may it do?" Thus the woman was thinking.

The parents *of* the woman did not know it. Every evening she would go bathing. Then she examined the pet. It was big already. The woman was glad when she saw that it was large. Not long *afterwards* it grew up. The woman was again picking moss. The woman was always bathing; and whenever she came home, she would examine it.

She examined it once, and it seemed as if a lump was on its head. She examined it, and verily she saw *what was* about to develop into horns. She saw that *they were* large already. Thus she said, "You shall take care of me, my pet." Thus she said. She was glad when she saw it. Her elder brothers, her mother, and also her father came to know it. "What do you intend to do with it?" And the young girl answered thus, "Verily, I will raise it."

The horns were sticking out already. The horns stretched out to *the roof of* the house. Thus she said to her elder brother, "Tear off these boards." Indeed, her elder brother tore them off. The two tips passed out of the house when the horns grew. It looked very pretty when they grew up. *The snake* coiled many times as it lay. The head was sticking out *from* the middle. It looked everywhere.

One morning it disappeared. "Where may it have gone?" Thus the young girl was thinking. Suddenly they heard something. They heard something back in the woods. So they looked there, and ahead of them they saw coming the grown-up snake. Thus the young girl spoke: "Indeed, it is my pet that is coming." The pet was dragging *something*. The pet had horns. It was dragging deer. The young girl was very glad when the *pet* brought home deer. There the pet came back again, and lay down *where it used to* lie.

Five times it went into the woods. It also brought as many elk; *namely*, five *times*. And also five deer it dragged *home*. They were very glad. They became rich when their food was being bought. The two horned *tips* passed out from *the roof of* the house. It seemed as if the young girl was afraid of the pet. So *they* let it rest. Their house was full of food. People were buying their food.

Whenever her pet would disappear, the young girl would think thus: "Where may it have gone?" Suddenly she saw a wind on the water. "What may be the thing I see on the water? I never saw such a wind." Suddenly she saw *the pet* swimming in the water. Behind *it* a whale was coming. It brought the whale ashore when it returned. They cut *the whale* into pieces. Again the pet came back, where it usually lay.

Five times it was dragging *something from* the ocean. It kept on bringing home as many whales. The owners became rich while the *food* was being bought. Thus it said to its master: "I am going home to the ocean. I shall not come back. This will be the end. I shall leave you now. You shall not think of me. Whenever the time comes, I will again give you a whale. You shall watch for it." Thus it spoke to its master. "I will always be *the cause of it,* whenever the water gets rough." Thus it spoke. "Whenever a person travels in a canoe *and* the water gets rough, I shall cause the water to go under the canoe."

Indeed, it was thus. The nephew—*that is, the pet*—went

home to the ocean. It may be there today. It went out to the mouth of the river, and let itself down there into the water.

Now this is the end.

THE BOY AND THE DEER

ZUNI

This rather long myth is typical of the novelistic style of many Zuni narratives. Though it is possible to read it as a latter-day allegory of the coming of culture, symbolized by hunting and basketry—with its concomitant burden of guilt and punishment (the boy's father, a serpent in other, related myths, is here replaced by the sun)—one is more likely to be struck by the attention lavished on mood, characterization, manners, and locale.

Departing from the usual method of translating narrative as straight prose, Dennis Tedlock, who collected the story, has attempted to convey some of the subtler aspects of the original performance. The slash (/) indicates a pause, often imperceptible, of a half second or more, depending on the whim of the narrator. A new paragraph implies a pause of at least two seconds. Vowels followed by dashes are to be held for about two seconds. Use a hushed voice for italicized words, a loud voice for words printed in capitals. Passages with words underlined or overlined are to be chanted: chant overlined words about three half tones higher than normal, underlined words about three half tones lower. Special direc-tions appear in parentheses, e.g., "(sharply)." Audience responses are labeled "(audience)."

SON'AHCHI. / (*audience*) Ee————so. / SONTI LO——— ————NG AGO. / (*audience*) Ee————so. / THERE WERE VILLAGERS AT HE'SHOKTA / and / up on the Prairie-Dog Hills / the deer / had their home.

The daughter of a priest / was sitting in a room on the fourth story down weaving basket-plaques. / She was always sitting and working in there, and the Sun came up / every day when the Sun came up / the girl would sit working / at the place where he came in. / It seems the Sun made her pregnant. / When he made her pregnant / though she sat in there with-out knowing any man her belly grew large. / She worked o————n for a time / weaving basket-plaques, and / her belly grew large, very very large. / When her time was near / she had a pain in her belly. / Gathering all her clothes / she went out and / went down to Water's End.

On she went until / she came to the bank / went on down to the river, and washed her clothes.

Then / having washed a few things, she had a pain in her belly.

She came out of the river. Having come out she sat down / by a juniper tree and strained her muscles: / *the little baby came out.* / She dug a hole, put juniper leaves in it / then laid the baby there. / She went back into the water / gathered all her clothes / and carefully washed the blood off herself. / She bundled / her clothes / put them on her back / *and returned to her home at He'shokta.*

And the DEER / who lived on the Prairie-Dog Hills / were going down to DRINK, going down to drink at dusk. / *The*

Sun had almost set when they went down to drink and the little baby was crying. / "Where is the little baby crying?" they said. / It was two fawns on their way down / with their mother / who heard him. / The crying was coming from the direction of a tree. / They were going into the water
and there / they came upon the crying. / Where a juniper tree stood, the child / *was crying.*

The deer / the two fawns and their mother went to him.

"Well, why shouldn't we / save him? / Why don't you two hold my nipples / so / so he can nurse?" that's what the mother said to her fawns.

The two fawns helped the baby / suck their mother's nipple and get some milk. / *Now the little boy*
was nursed, the little boy was nursed by the deer / o————
————n until he was full. / Their mother lay down cuddling him the way deer sleep / with her two fawns / together / lying beside her / and they SLEPT WITH THEIR FUR AROUND HIM. / They would nurse him, and so they lived on, lived on. / As he grew / he was without clothing, NAKED. / His elder brother and sister had fur: / they had fur, but he was NAKED and this was not good.

The deer / *the little boy's mother* / spoke to her two fawns: "Tonight / when you sleep, you two will lie on both sides / and he will lie in the middle. / While you're sleeping / *I'll go to Kachina Village, for he is without clothing, naked, and / this is not good.*"

That's what she said to her children, and / there / at the village of He'shokta
were young men / who went out hunting, and the young men who went out hunting looked for deer. / When they went hunting they made their kills around the Prairie-Dog Hills. / And their mother went to Kachina Village, she went

o————n until she reached Kachina Village. / It was filled with dancing kachinas.

"My fathers, my children, how have you been passing the days?" "Happily, our child, so you've come, sit down," they said. / "Wait, stop your dancing, our child has come and must have something to say," then the kachinas stopped. / The deer sat down *the old lady deer sat down.* / *A kachina priest spoke to her:* / "Now speak. / You must've come because you have something to say." "YES, in TRUTH / I have come because I have something to SAY. / *There in the village of He'shokta is a priest's daughter* / who abandoned her child. / We found him / we have been raising him. / But he is poor, without clothing, naked, and this / is not good. / So I've come to ask for clothes for him," that's what she said. / "Indeed." "Yes, that's why I've come, to ask for clothes for him." / "Well, there is always a way," they said. / Kyaklo / laid out his shirt. / Long Horn put in his kilt and his moccasins.

And Huututu put in his buckskin leggings / he laid out his bandoleer.

And Pawtiwa laid out his macaw headdress.

Also they put in the BELLS he would wear on his legs.

Also they laid out

strands of turquoise beads / moccasins. / So they laid it all out, hanks of yarn for his wrists and ankles / they gathered all his clothing. / *When they had gathered it his mother put it on her back:* "Well, I must GO / but when he has grown larger I will return to ask for clothing again." / That's what she said. "Very well indeed." / *Now the deer went her way. / When she got back to her children they were all sleeping. / When she got there they were sleeping and she / lay down beside them. / The little boy, waking up / began to nurse, his deer mother nursed him / and he went back to sleep.* So they spent the night and then / (*with pleasure*) the little boy was clothed by his mother. / His mother clothed him.

When he was clothed he was no longer cold. / He went around playing with his elder brother and sister, they would run after each other, playing. / They lived on this way until he was grown. / And THEN / they went back up to their old home on the Prairie-Dog Hills. Having gone up / they remained there and would come down only to drink, in the evening. / There they lived o————n for a long time / until / from the village / *his uncle / went out hunting. Going out hunting / he came along / down around / Worm Spring, and from there he went on towards*

the Prairie-Dog Hills and came up near the edge of a valley there. / When he came to the woods on the Prairie-Dog Hills he looked down and / THERE IN THE VALLEY was the herd of deer. In the herd of deer / there was a little boy going around among them / dressed in white. / He had bells on his legs and he wore a macaw headdress. / *He wore a macaw headdress, he was handsome* surely it was a boy / *a male / a person among them. / While he was looking* the deer mothers spotted him. / *When they spotted the young man they ran off. / There the little boy outdistanced the others.*

"Haa———, who could that be?" / That's what his uncle said. *"Who / could you be? Perhaps you are a daylight person."* / That's what his UNCLE thought and he didn't do ANYTHING to the deer. / *He returned to his house in the evening.*

It was evening / dinner was ready *and when they sat down to eat / the young man spoke: /* "Today, while I was out hunting / when I reached the top / *of the Prairie-Dog Hills, where the woods are, when I reached the top* THERE in the

VALLEY was a HERD OF DEER. / There was a herd of deer
and with them was a LITTLE BOY: / whose child could it
be? / When the deer spotted me they ran off and he outdistanced them. / *He wore bells on his legs, he wore a macaw
headdress, he was dressed in white."* / That's what the young
man was saying / telling his father. / It was one of the
boy's OWN ELDERS / his OWN UNCLE had found him. (*audience*) Ee————so. / His uncle had found him.

Then / he said, "If / the herd is to be chased, then tell
your Bow Priest." / That's what the young man said. "Whose
child could this be? / PERHAPS WE'LL CATCH HIM." / That's
what he was saying. / *A girl* / *a daughter of the priest said,*
"Well, I'll go ask the Bow Priest." / She got up and went to
the Bow Priest's house. / *Arriving at the Bow Priest's house
/ she entered:* / "My fathers, my mothers, how have you
been passing the days?" "Happily, our child / so you've
come, sit down," they said. "Yes. / Well, I'm / asking you to
come. / Father asked that you come, that's what my father
said," that's what she told the Bow Priest. / "Very well, I'll
come," he said. / *The girl went out and went home* and after
a while the Bow Priest came over. / He came to their house
/ while they were still eating.

"My children, how are you / this evening?" "Happy / sit
down and eat," he was told. / He sat down and ate with them.
/ *When they were finished eating,* "Thank you," he said.
"Eat plenty," he was told. / *He moved to another seat*
and after a while / the Bow Priest questioned them: /
"NOW, for what reason have you / summoned ME? / Perhaps
it is because of a WORD of some importance that you have
/ summoned me. You must make this known to me / so that
I may think about it as I pass the days," that's what he said. /
"YES, in truth / today, this very day / my child here / went

out to hunt. / *Up on the Prairie-Dog Hills, there* / HE SAW
A HERD OF DEER. / But a LITTLE BOY WAS AMONG THEM. /
Perhaps he is a daylight person. / Who could it be? / He
was dressed in white and he wore a macaw headdress. / When
the deer ran off he OUTDISTANCED them: / he must be very
fast. / That's why my child here said, 'Perhaps / they should
be CHASED, the deer should be chased.' / He wants to see him
caught, that's what he's thinking. / Because he said this / I
summoned you," he said. "Indeed." / "Indeed, well

perhaps he's a daylight person, what else can he be? / It
is said he was dressed in white, what else can he be?" / That's
what they were saying. / "WHEN would you want to do this?"
that's what he said. / The young man who had gone out hunting said, "Well, in four days / so we can prepare our
weapons" / That's what he said. / "So you should tell your
people that in FOUR DAYS there will be a deer chase." / That's
what / he said. "Very well."

(*sharply*) Because of the little boy the word was given
out for the deer chase. / The Bow Priest went out and
shouted it. / When he shouted, the VILLAGERS / heard him.
/ (*slowly*) "In four days there will be a deer chase. / A
little boy is among the deer, who could it be? With luck / you
might CATCH him. / We don't know who it will be. / You
will find a child, then," that's what he SAID as he shouted.

Then they went to sleep and lived on with anticipation. /
Now when it was the THIRD night, the eve of the chase

the deer / spoke to her son / when the deer had gathered:
/ "*My son.*" "*What is it?*" he said. / "Tomorrow we'll be
chased, the one who found us is your uncle. / When he found
us he saw you, and that's why

we'll be chased. / They'll come out after you: / your
uncles.

(*excited*) The uncle who saw you will ride a spotted horse, and HE'LL BE THE ONE who / WON'T LET YOU GO, and / your elder brothers, your mothers / no / he won't think of killing them, it'll be you alone / he'll think of, he'll chase. / You won't be the one to get tired, but we'll get tired. / It'll be you alone / WHEN THEY HAVE KILLED US ALL / and you will go on alone. / Your first uncle / will ride a spotted horse and a second uncle will ride a white horse. / THESE TWO WILL FOLLOW YOU. / You must pretend you are tired but keep on going / and they will catch you. / But WE / MYSELF, your elder SISTER, your elder BROTHER / ALL OF US / will go with you. / Wherever they take you we will go along with you." / That's what his deer mother told him *that's what she said.* / THEN HIS DEER MOTHER TOLD HIM EVERYTHING: "AND NOW / I will tell you everything. / From here

from this place / where we're living now, we went down to drink. When we went down to drink / it was one of your ELDERS, one of your OWN ELDERS / your mother who sits in a room on the fourth story down making basket-plaques: / IT WAS SHE / whom the Sun had made pregnant. / When her time was near / she went down to Water's End to the bank / to wash clothes / and when you were about to come out / she had pains, got out of the water / went to a TREE and there she just DROPPED you. / THAT is your MOTHER. / She's in a room on the fourth story down making basket-plaques, that's what you'll tell them.

THAT'S WHAT SHE DID TO YOU, SHE JUST DROPPED YOU. / When we went down to drink / we found you, and because you have grown up / on my milk / and because of the thoughts of your Sun Father, you have grown fast. / Well, you / have looked at us / at your elder sister and your elder brother / and they have fur. 'Why don't I have fur like them?'

you have asked. / But that is proper, for you are a daylight person. / That's why I went to Kachina Village to get clothes for you / the ones you were wearing. / You began wearing those when you were small / before you were GROWN. / Yesterday I went to get the clothes you're wearing now / the ones you will wear when they chase us. When you've been caught / you must tell these things to your elders.

When they bring you in / when they've caught you and bring you in / you / you will go inside. When you go inside / your grandfather / a priest / will be sitting by the fire. 'My grandfather, how have you been passing the days?' / 'Happily. As old as I am, I could be a grandfather to anyone, for we have many children,' he will say. / 'Yes, but truly you are my real grandfather,' you will say. / When you come to where your grandmother is sitting, 'Grandmother of mine, how have you been passing the days?' you will say. / 'Happily, our child, surely I could be a grandmother to anyone, for we have the whole village as our children,' she will say. / Then, with the uncles who brought you in and / with your three aunts, you will shake hands. / 'WHERE IS MY MOTHER?' you will say. / 'Who is your mother?' they will say. 'She's in a room on the fourth story down making basket-plaques, tell her to come in,' you will say.

Your youngest aunt will go in to get her. / When she enters: / (sharply) 'There's a little boy who wants you, he says you are his mother.' / (tight) 'How could that be? I don't know any man, how could I have an offspring?' / 'Yes, but he wants you,' she will say / and she will force her to come out. / THEN THE ONE WE TOLD YOU ABOUT WILL COME OUT: / you will shake hands with her, call her mother. 'Surely we could be mothers to anyone, for we have the whole village as our CHILDREN,' she will say to you. / 'YES, BUT

TRULY YOU ARE MY REAL MOTHER. / There, in a room on the fourth story down / you sit and work. / My Sun Father, where you sit in the light / my Sun Father / made you pregnant. / When you were about to deliver / it was to Water's End / that you went down to wash. You washed at the bank / and when I was about to come out / when it hurt you / you went to a tree and just dropped me there. / You gathered your clothes, put them on your back, and returned / to your house. / But my MOTHERS / HERE / found me. When they found me / because it was on their milk / that I grew, and because of the thoughts of my Sun Father / I grew fast. / I had no clothing / so my mother went to Kachina Village to ask for clothing.' / THAT'S WHAT YOU MUST SAY."

That's what he was told that's what his mother told him. "And / tonight / (*aside*) we'll go up on the Ruin Hills." / That's what the deer mother told her son. "We'll go to the Ruin Hills / we won't live here any more. / (*sharply*) We'll go over there where the land is rough / for TOMORROW they will CHASE us. / Your uncles won't think of US, surely they will think of YOU / ALONE. They have GOOD HORSES," that's what / his mother told him. It was on the night before / that the boy / was told by his deer mother. / *The boy became / so unhappy.* / They slept through the night / *and before dawn the deer / went to the Ruin Hills.*

They went there and remained, and the VILLAGERS AWOKE. / It was the day of the chase, as had been announced, and the people were coming out. / They were coming out, some carrying bows, some on foot and some on horseback, they kept on this way / o————n they went on / past Stone Chief, along the trees, until they got to the Prairie-Dog Hills and there were no deer. / Their tracks led straight and they followed them. / *Having found the trail they went on until / when they reached the Ruin Hills, there in the valley / beyond the thickets there / was the herd, and the / young man and two of his elder sisters were chasing each other /* by the edge of the valley, playing together. *Playing together / they were spotted.* / The deer saw the people. / *They fled.* / Many were the people who came out after them / *now they chased the deer.* / Now and again they dropped them, killed them. / Sure enough the boy outdistanced the others, while his mother and his elder sister and brother / still followed their child. As they followed him / he was far in the lead, but they followed on, they were on the run / and sure enough his uncles weren't thinking about killing deer, it was the boy they were after. / And ALL THE PEOPLE WHO HAD COME KILLED THE DEER killed the deer <u>killed the deer</u>. / Wherever they made their kills they gutted them, put them on their backs, and went home. / Two of the uncles

then / went ahead of the group, and a third uncle / (*voice breaking*) *dropped his elder sister / his elder brother / his mother.* / *He gutted them there* / while the other two uncles went on. As they went ON / the boy pretended to be tired. The first uncle pleaded: "Tísshomahhá! / STOP," he said, "Let's stop this contest now." / That's what he was saying as / the little boy kept on running. / As he kept on his bells went telele. / O————n, he went on this way / on until *the little boy stopped and his uncle, dismounting / caught him.*

Having caught him / (*gently*) "Now come with me, get up," he said. / His uncle / *helped his nephew get up, then his uncle got on the horse.* / They went back. They went on / *until they came to where his mother and his elder sister and brother were lying / and the third uncle was there. The third uncle was there. /* "So you've come." "Yes." / *The little boy spoke:* "This is my mother, this is my / elder sister, this is my elder brother. / They will accompany me to my house. / *They will accompany me,*" *that's what the boy said. /* "*Very well.*" / *His uncles put the deer on their horses' backs. /* On they went, while the people were coming in *coming in, and still the uncles didn't arrive, until at nightfall /* *the little boy was brought in, sitting up on the horse. /* *It was night and the people, a crowd of people, came out to see the boy as he was brought in on the horse through the plaza /* *and his mother and his elder sister and brother /* *came along also /* *as he was brought in. /* *His grandfather came out. When he came out the little boy and his uncle dismounted. /* *His grand-father took the lead with the little boy following, and they went up. /* *When they reached the roof his grandfather /* *made a corn-meal road /* *and they entered. /* *His grandfather entered /* *with the little boy following /* *while his /* *uncles brought in the deer. When everyone was inside*

the little boy's grandfather spoke: "*Sit down,*" *and the little boy spoke to his grandfather as he came .to where he was sitting: /* "Grandfather of mine, how have you been pass-ing the days?" *that's what he said. /* "Happily *our child / surely I could be a grandfather to anyone, for we have the whole village as our children.*" "*Yes, but you are my real grandfather,*" *he said. /* When he came to where his grand-mother was sitting *he said the same thing. /* "*Yes, but surely I could be a grandmother to anyone, for we have many chil-dren.*" "*Yes, but you are my real grandmother,*" *he said. /* He looked the way / his uncle had described him, he wore a macaw headdress and his clothes were white. / He had new moccasins, new buckskin leggings. / He wore a bandoleer and a macaw headdress. / He was a stranger. / He shook hands

with his uncles and shook hands with his aunts. / "WHERE
IS MY MOTHER?" he said.

"She's in a room on the fourth story down weaving basket-
plaques," *he said.* / *"Tell her to come out."* / *Their younger
sister went in.* / "Hurry and come now: / some little boy
has come and says you are his mother." / (*tight*) "How could
that be? / *I've never known any man, how could I have an
offspring?" she said.* / "Yes, but come on, he wants you, he
wants you to come out." / *Finally she was forced to come
out.* / The moment she entered the little boy / *went up to
his mother.* / "Mother of mine, how have you been passing
the days?" / "Happily, but surely I could be anyone's /
mother, for we have many children," that's what his mother
said. / *That's what she said.*

"YES INDEED / but you are certainly my REAL MOTHER. /
YOU GAVE BIRTH TO ME," he said.

Then, just as his deer mother had told him to do / *he told
his mother everything:*

"You really are my mother. / In a room on the fourth
story down / you sit and work. / As you sit and work / the
light comes through your window. / My Sun Father / made
you pregnant. / When he made you pregnant you / sat in
there and your belly began to grow large. / Your belly grew
large / you / you were about to deliver, you had pains in
your belly, you were about to give birth to me, you had
pains in your belly / you gathered your clothes / and you
went down to the bank to wash. / When you got there you /
washed your clothes in the river. / When I was about to
COME OUT and caused you pain / you got out of the water
/ you went to a juniper tree. / There I made you strain
your muscles / and there you just dropped me. / When you
dropped me / you made a little hole and placed me there. /

You gathered your clothes / bundled them together / washed all the blood off carefully, and came back here. / When you had gone / my elders here / came down to DRINK / and found me. / They found me.

I cried / and they heard me. / Because of the milk / of my deer mother here / my elder sister and brother here / because of / their milk / I grew. / I had no clothing, I was poor. / My mother here went to Kachina Village to ask for my clothing.

That's where / she got my clothing. / That's why I'm clothed. Truly, that's why I was among them / that's why one of you / who went out hunting discovered me. / You talked about it and that's why these things happened today." (*audience*) Ee————so. / That's what the little boy said.

"THAT'S WHAT YOU DID AND YOU ARE MY REAL MOTHER," that's what he told his mother. At that moment his mother / embraced him *embraced him*. / His uncle got angry *his uncle got angry*. / He beat / his kinswoman / *he beat his kinswoman*. / That's how it happened. / The boy's deer elders were on the floor. / *His grandfather then* / spread some covers / *on the floor, laid them there, and put strands of turquoise beads on them*. / *After a while they skinned them*. / With this done and dinner ready they ate with their son.

They slept through the night, and the next day / the little boy spoke: "Grandfather." "What is it?" / "Where is your quiver?" he said. "Well, it must be hanging in the other room," he said.

He went out, having been given the quiver, and wandered around. / He wandered around, he wasn't thinking of killing deer, he just wandered around. / *In the evening he came home empty-handed*. / *They lived on and slept through the night*. / *After the second night he was wandering around again.* / *The third one came* / and on the fourth night, just after sunset, his mother / spoke to him: "I need / the center blades of the yucca plant," she said. / "Which kind of yucca?" / "Well, the large yucca, the center blades" *that's what his mother said. "Indeed.* / Tomorrow I'll try to find it for you," he said. / (*aside*) She was finishing her basket-plaque and this was for the outer part. (*audience*) Ee————so. / That's what she said. / The next morning, when he had eaten / *he put the quiver on and went out.* / He went up on Big Mountain and looked around until he found a large yucca / with very long blades.

"Well, this must be the kind you talked about," he said. It was the center blades she wanted. / *He put down his bow and his quiver,* got hold of the center blades, and began to pull. / (*with strain*) He pulled

it came loose suddenly / *and he pulled it straight into his heart.* / *There he died.*

He died *and they waited for him but he didn't come.*

When the Sun went down / *and he still hadn't come, his uncles began to worry.* / *They looked for him.* / *They found his tracks, made torches, and followed him* / until they found him with the center blades of the yucca in his heart.

Their / *nephew* / *was found and they brought him home.* / *The next day*

he was buried. / Now he entered upon the roads / of his elders. / THIS WAS LIVED LONG AGO. LEE————SEMKONIKYA.

A Gift of Honey

"Manner in Which the Inca
Marries Those of His Own
Blood." Engraved by Claude
Du Bosc after the drawing by
Bernard Picart, 1731   (*Private
collection*)

The social order makes a curious demand: we must live in close contact with parents, siblings, and other relatives, yet there must be no hint of sexual intimacy. The brother who falls in love with his sister, the marriageable maiden who refuses to leave home, and the uncle who covets his niece are among the most common figures in Indian mythology. Yet the relationship is often obscured or denied, even as it is being presented.

BROTHER BLACK AND BROTHER RED

SENECA

There was a lodge in the forest where very few people ever came, and there dwelt a young man and his sister. The youth was unlike other persons, for one half of his head had hair of a reddish cast, while the other side was black.

He used to leave his sister in the lodge and go away on long hunting trips. On one occasion the young woman, his sister, saw, so she thought, her brother coming down the path to the lodge. "I thought you just went away to hunt," said the sister. "Oh, I thought I would come back," said he.

Then he sat down on the bed with the sister and embraced

her and acted as a lover. The sister reproached him and said that she was very angry. But again he endeavored to fondle her in a familiar way, but again was repulsed. This time he went away.

The next day the brother returned and found his sister very angry. She would scarcely speak to him, though hitherto she had talked a great deal.

"My sister," said he. "I am at loss to know why you treat me thus. It is not your custom."

"Oh, you ought to know that you have abused me," said the girl.

"I never abused you. What are you talking about?" he said.

"Oh, you know that you embraced me in an improper way yesterday," said the sister.

"I was not here yesterday," asserted the youth. "I believe that my friend who resembles me in every respect has been here."

"You have given a poor excuse," replied his sister. "I hope your actions will not continue."

Soon the brother went away again, stating that he would be absent three days. In a short time the sister saw, as she thought, a figure looking like her brother skulking in the underbrush. His shirt and leggings were the same as her brother's and his hair was the same. So then she knew that her brother had returned for mischief. Soon he entered the lodge and embraced her, and this time in anger she tore his cheeks with her nails and sent him away.

In three days the brother returned with a deer, but his sister would not speak to him. Said he, "My sister, I perceive that you are angry at me. Has my friend been here?"

It was some time before the sister replied, and then she

wept, saying, "My brother, you have abused me and I scratched your face. I perceive that it is still torn by my fingernails."

"Oh, my face," laughed the brother. "My face was torn by thorns as I hunted deer. If you scratched my friend, that is the reason I am scratched. Whatever happens to either one of us happens to the other." But the sister would not believe this.

Again the brother went on a hunting trip, and again the familiar figure returned. This time the sister tore his hunting shirt from the throat down to the waistline. Moreover, she threw a ladle of hot bear grease on the shirt. This caused his quick departure.

Returning in due time, the brother brought in his game and threw it down. Again the sister was angry and finally accused him. Pointing to his grease-smeared, torn shirt, she said that this was evidence enough.

"Oh, my sister," explained the brother, "I tore my shirt on a broken limb as I climbed a tree after a raccoon. In making soup from bear meat I spilled it on my shirt." Still the sister refused to believe him.

"Oh, my sister," said the brother, in distressed tones, "I am greatly saddened to think you will not believe me. My friend looks exactly as I do, and whatever happens to him happens to me. I shall now be compelled to find my friend and bring him to you, and when I do I shall be compelled to kill him before you for his evil designs upon you. If you would believe me, nothing evil would befall us, but I now think I myself shall die."

The sister said nothing, for she would not believe her brother.

The brother now began to pile up dried meat and to repair

the lodge. He then went out into the forest without his bow and arrows, and in a short time returned with another man exactly resembling him, and whose clothing was spotted and torn in a similar way. Leading him to the lodge fire, he began to scold him in an angry manner. "You have betrayed me and abused my sister," he said. "Now is the time for you to die." Taking out an arrow from a quiver, he cast it into the heart of his double and killed him. The sister saw her assailant fall to the floor, and then looked up as she heard her brother give a war cry and fall as dead, with blood streaming from a wound in his chest over his heart.

THE PRICE OF A WIFE

NUNIVAK ESKIMO

Though courted by all the youths of the village, the young woman prefers to remain with her father. Nothing short of an act of supernatural violence can persuade her to change her mind.

In a village by the sea lived a hunter, Kaiúga, and his daughter, Mírok. Mírok refused to consider seriously the youths of the village, and whenever one proposed marriage she would accept his gifts and carry food to him in the men's house. If he was liked by her, she would bring back the empty dish, but never again would she take food to him. Thus the father found himself burdened with an unapproachable daughter and all the youths of the village as sons-in-law. In his distress, he ran his fingers through his hair so much that it stood on end permanently.

One day an umiak containing a man and a woman, who were messengers, pulled up to the village. The woman went direct to Mírok and said, "Unugchoaóchin told me to fetch you to him."

"I have beads on my bed and my possessions are here beside me. Can he replace what I now own?"

"Yes, will you come now?"

"Can Unugchoaóchin spread sealskins from the umiak to his house for me to walk on?"

"It can be done."

"Will Unugchoaóchin have caribou skins spread from his door to the men's house for me to walk on when I carry food to him? Will the meat be caribou breast?"

"If you will come with me, all shall be done."

"Will Unugchoaóchin have caribou skins spread from my door to the urine pot, and will he have two reindeer hides to stand on and reindeer fur for drying?"

"If you will come with me, it shall be done. He told me to fetch you."

"Will Unugchoaóchin have three grease pots, one with blubber, one with grease, and one inlaid with ivory?"

The woman messenger hesitated. Angrily Mírok exclaimed, "Even if Unugchoaóchin is a good man and if he were here, I should throw urine in his face!"

The messenger went back to the umiak, and they pushed off, anchoring some distance from shore. Then the other messenger opened a box containing an inner box, inside of which was a small whale of carved ivory. This, attached to a long string, he dropped overboard, and sang:

> *Down there below me;*
> *Down there below me;*
> *Under the waves;*
> *Come up, daughter Mírok.*

At once the messengers heard the voice of Mírok on the shore, shouting as if in pain, "Oh, oh! My arm has gone!" At the same instant a whale thrust his head above the sea, bearing the arm of Mírok. This the man with the whale-power took aboard. Again and again he sang, and each time the whale brought up some part of Mírok. As soon as all the parts were there, the man assembled them and clothed her. When he had reached the village of Unugchoaóchin, he bade her remain aboard while he spread sealskins from boat to house for her to walk on.

Mírok felt greatly humiliated for having asked for so much. She saw many riches in the house: nose- and ear-beads, clothing, and all necessaries. There were three grease pots, one with blubber, one with grease, and one inlaid with ivory. She found fresh caribou breast to eat, and caribou skins to walk on to the men's house and to the urine pot, all as she had desired.

Unugchoaóchin, a great hunter, married her, thus winning her over all the youths of her village and the surrounding country.

THE RED PARROT

UITOTO

A man would not ordinarily louse his own niece—or put his fingers in her hair for any reason whatever. True to the fashion of many of the great myths of North and South America, this little story from western Amazonia begins with a touch of incest.

Dyaere lived there with his brother's parrot—his brother Seigerani, into whose daughter's hair the sun threw lice. But Dyaere prepared a remedy. He cured her, and the lice the sun had thrown were removed from her hair.

Then, because he had cured her, Dyaere demanded payment. He asked for the pet. "Brother, give me your pet!" "What would you do with my pet? You're too poor to feed it." "I want it!" "Don't ask! If you ask, I'll refuse." "You refuse me then?"

"Take the other parrot, the one over here!" "I don't want that one. I'll take this one up here, the one with all the feathers." "What for, you fool? Why must you have it? Such a price to pay! You can't do this to me, it's too much. You're taking my pet!"

The one he wanted was the red parrot, the beautiful red parrot with the flame-colored tail that his brother refused to give him—the flame-colored tail that could be seen from afar lighting up the lodge, so that the lodge itself shone with a red glow. This is what Dyaere wanted.

"Brother, let me take it! How can you deny me what I ask?" "You have no shame, or you'd take the other one instead. How can you ask for my pet, as poor as you are and so lazy? So lazy! What will you feed it? You've planted no cacao, your wife has no peanuts and you no corn. These are the things I feed it. But what about you if you take my pet? Truly you have no shame, asking for my pet. All right, take it! But take care of it and don't let it come back to me. Take good care of it, feed it, so it won't come back to me," Seigerani said, and in great anger he handed over the pet he had persistently refused to give him. Then, so that he might feed his pet, he gave him cacao, also peanuts and corn.

Dyaere took the food Seigerani had given him and went off with the pet. When he got back to his wife, he told her what had happened. Then he set the parrot on a forked stick and put all the cacao down for it to eat.

It quickly finished the cacao, and the next morning he put the peanuts down for the pet to eat. These too were quickly finished, for the parrot was a glutton. The following morning he gave it the corn, and it too was soon finished. Then everything Dyaere had brought was gone. The parrot had eaten it all.

And so it flew back to Seigerani, and Dyaere came to fetch it. "Brother, didn't my pet come here?" "What did I tell you?" "Never mind, I'm asking you if you have my pet." "When you went off with it, I told you not to let it fly back here. I haven't seen it; but before you took it, I told you not to let it come home to me. No, it didn't come here," he said.

The parrot sat at the door of the calabash people and picked their fruit and hacked it apart until nothing was left. "Dyaere's pet has picked all the fruit from our calabash tree. Not a one is left," said Nadyerekudu. "My tree is ruined. Why wasn't he watching his pet?"

As he spoke, he hit the parrot with a stick and ruined its tail feathers. They fell off in tatters. Then he seized the parrot and brought it inside the lodge. Its tail was gone—destroyed. Then he kept it there under a pot.

Dyaere kept looking for the pet. He asked Seigerani, "Brother, didn't my pet come here?" No answer. Angrily he protested to Seigerani: "Seigerani, I said 'Didn't my pet come here?' "

"Where are you going?" "Seigerani, why don't you answer my question?" "Oh, what did you ask?" "Where is my pet?" "You're looking for it at my place? Before I gave it to you, I warned you it might come back to me," he answered. "Then where is it?"

And with that, the one who had hit it and concealed it under the pot let it go, and balancing with its beak it hobbled toward Dyaere. The pet was no longer flame-colored. The pet had been ruined.

Dyaere was angry. He let it fly back to Nadyerekudu's people. He was angry. "Why did you people ruin my pet? Now where will you hide?" he said, full of rage. With that it began to rain, and the sky did not stop. Down it came.

Then the people spread the word, saying, "Dyaere spoke forth the rain. He pulled it down." And it kept on raining, and the earth grew soft and miry. "What has Dyaere done to us? Where can we hide? Why was his pet injured?" they asked. And "Where can we stay?" Because of Dyaere's anger, the sky was falling. It was coming down as rain. "What has happened? The earth is all soft."

Then the woman Kuidonyo and the man Varaseko fell from the sky and ran back and forth outside the door. "Whose children are you? They'll drown! Where are you from?" the people cried. "I, Varaseko, am from the sky."

"Who are their parents? Whose children are these?" "I, Kuidonyo, am from the sky," said the woman, and as she spoke she ran back and forth outside the door.

Then Dyaere took tobacco juice and made himself drunk. He placed his labret in his lower lip. Then he sat on the beam above the door and destroyed the earth.

The water rose and covered the softened earth. And then with the power of his labret he threw the people in. Dyaere made all the people drown, pulled them into the rushing water, made all the pots roll into the rushing water. Nothing was left. The people all drowned together.

Just then two men were fishing, Egoramui and Kuireifoma. Then a grating trough fell in front of them. They noticed it: "How pretty this is! We'll take it with us." And they put it in their carrying bag to take back to the village, it was so pretty. Then they started to carry it home.

But it worked loose and fell to the ground. So they packed it up again, and this time it pulled the whole load down. What were they to do? And while they were struggling, Dyaere allowed them to drown in the rushing water, together and in the same place.

The people could not run away. And all the tribes that had been created in the beginning were drowned by Dyaere—without mercy—because the red parrot's tail had been ruined. The tribes that had come first were destroyed by Dyaere. We had not yet arrived. We came afterward.

A GIFT OF HONEY

AZTEC

The Aztecs looked back on their opulent predecessors, the Toltecs, with a fascination not unlike that of Christian Europe contemplating the rise and fall of Rome. The brief "history" of the Toltec empire given below has been taken from the writings of the native chronicler Ixtlilxochitl, whose information was derived, at least in part, from ancient pictographic books now lost. Observe how the narrator handles an unmentionable situation: the girl's outraged father and her seducer appear in the story as though they were separate persons. Yet we are told that the girl is a member of the seducerking's "own lineage"; and we know from another, not wholly dissimilar, version of the same "history" that the unfortunate maiden is none other than the king's daughter.

In the year 1 Flint a party of feuding Toltecs was exiled from Old Tlapallan on the western sea. When they had fled their home, their priest, Huematzin, warned them that they would again be punished in a year 1 Flint. But in the years between, they would enjoy an age of prosperity, traveling eastward to fertile new lands where they would find vassals who would continue to serve them for as long as the omens were favorable, even down to the tenth generation. But upon the completion of 512 years, there would be born to the throne a mysterious lord whose authority would be upheld by some and contested by others. At birth he would be recognized by certain marks on his body, in particular a natural crown of curly hair. At the beginning of his reign he would be wise and just, later becoming foolish and unlucky. Because of him the people would suffer lightning, hail, frosts, famine, rainstorms, and other scourges sent down from the skies. Members of his own lineage would rebel against him. Unnatural portents would signal the end. The rabbit would grow horns; the hummingbird, spurs. Rocks would sprout fruit. Matrons making pilgrimages to temples would seduce the priests. The end would come in a year 1 Flint.

So the Toltecs set out in the direction of the rising sun. As they traveled eastward, they sowed new fields and founded new towns. They founded Tollantzinco. There they built a great house of beams, with room enough for all the people. They moved on and founded the city of Tollan, capital of the new realm. The year was 1 House, omen of wealth and empire.

The Toltecs were superb artisans, skillful architects, woodworkers, and silversmiths. They mined gold and cut jewels. They were poets, orators. They painted books. They cultivated corn, cotton, peppers, beans, and other crops. The women excelled at spinning and weaving. They wove elegant robes of many colors.

To their first king they gave the name Jewel-Who-Sheds-Light. By him they were eased and enlightened, freed from toil and persecution. With the people's consent he reigned for fifty-two years, as did each of the kings who followed him, down to the sixth king, whose name was Mitl. It was Mitl who built the temple in honor of the water goddess, the Temple of the Frog, all embellished with gold and jewels. The Frog itself was of jadestone. Mitl ruled for fifty-nine years, followed by his widow, who ruled for four. Upon her death, her son Tecpancaltzin ascended the throne.

In the tenth year of Tecpancaltzin's rule, a beautiful young woman arrived at the palace together with her mother and father, bearing a gift for the king. This gift, it is said, was the dark honey of the maguey, also the sugar made from this honey. It was they who had discovered it; and because it was a thing of novelty, they had come to present it to the king. As they were nobles, members of the king's own lineage, moreover, they were received with great courtesy. The king was delighted with the gift and found himself much taken with the young woman, whose name was Xochitl. He commanded her parents to send him more of this gift, to be brought by Xochitl herself, alone and unaccompanied, except that she might have with her a woman servant. Suspecting nothing, the parents consented.

Several days later Xochitl came back with her woman servant, carrying honey, honey-sugar, and maguey preserve. She was announced as the daughter of Papantzin, discoverer of the honey. Delighted, the king commanded that she be brought in alone with her gift, and that the old servant, who was the girl's nurse, be settled in a room apart, where she was to be given robes and gold and suitably entertained until time for her to return home with her mistress. The king's orders were carried out.

When the king set his eyes on the gift, he was well pleased. Then he spoke to Xochitl of his longing for her and begged her to satisfy his desire, promising to bestow many favors on her family. Over and over he pleaded, as she protested, until at last, realizing she had no choice, she gave in to his will. When his lewd desire had been satisfied, he had her removed to a well-guarded retreat outside the city, sending word to her parents that he had entrusted her to certain matrons who would prepare her for her coming marriage to a prince of the realm. This as a reward for the gift they had sent him.

Xochitl's parents had no power to challenge the king. They

pretended they were glad, though in fact they were bitter.

As the king often visited his lady Xochitl, she soon became pregnant. She gave birth to a son, whom the king named Child-of-the-Maguey. This child bore the marks that had been predicted by the priest Huematzin.

Xochitl's parents persisted in trying to learn where their daughter was hidden. But the city of Tollan was large, many lords had their houses there, and not until three years had passed did they discover her whereabouts. They learned she was guarded in a fortress on top of the hill called Palpan, surrounded by loyal retainers who kept her from view. In particular, the king had ordered that none of his own kinsmen be allowed to enter. So Xochitl's father was at some pains to think how he might pass the guards unrecognized.

At last he disguised himself as a peddler, and the guards, believing him harmless, permitted him to enter, after he had bribed them with certain presents. He went in and proceeded to look around. Presently he found himself in a garden, where he saw his daughter holding a child in her arms. He approached her, filled with joy, and said, "Is this why the king has put you here, to play with children?" He did not know that the child was his own grandson. His daughter then told him the truth, though not without shame, while Papantzin, out of pride, kept his anger concealed.

Some days later Papantzin went to the king and complained openly of the insult he had received. But Tecpancaltzin comforted him, telling him not to be troubled, for this was the act of a king and therefore no cause for offense. Moreover, the child would be heir to the throne, as the king was unmarried and had no intention of taking a wife. Many favors were bestowed on Papantzin, and he and his family were given permission to visit Palpan as often as they liked, on the condition that they keep Xochitl's presence there a secret, as did those few who were entrusted to guard her. For if the tribute lords who served the king were to hear of it, they would condemn it as evil. Somewhat consoled, Papantzin returned to his home, and from that day on, he and his wife went often to visit their daughter at Palpan.

After fifty-two years as king, Tecpancaltzin retired from the throne and arranged for the succession of his son, Child-of-the-Maguey, called also Topiltzin. Topiltzin was virtuous and very wise. There were other lords, however, who had a legitimate claim to be king. But because they were tenured in distant provinces, Tecpancaltzin felt safe in ignoring them. He chose two members of his personal following to serve as co-regents with Topiltzin. So Tollan, as previously, was ruled by a three-member regency, with Topiltzin as king and principal ruler, just as his father had been before him.

By the time he had ruled for forty years, Topiltzin had changed, and the people of Tollan began to follow his evil example, committing grave and abominable sins. Prominent women made pilgrimages to temples and sacred cities, where they coupled with the priests. The king, his court, and his vassals persisted in hideous deeds, until one day the king, while strolling through his groves and gardens, noticed a rabbit with horns like a deer, also a hummingbird with large spurs, sipping nectar.

The following year the Toltecs suffered heavy rains and windstorms. Many buildings were destroyed. For a hundred days it rained, and after the flood there was drought, followed by frosts, lightning, and hailstorms. All the trees and even the magueys were killed. Then came worms and grasshoppers, destroying the crops. And then there were wars with the three rival lords, who had been deprived of their rightful inheritance by Topiltzin's father. At that time the stored corn was consumed by weevils.

One day a beautiful baby, white-skinned and fair-haired, was found on a hilltop outside the city. The people brought it in to show it to the king; but when he saw it, he feared it as an evil omen and had them take it back. After a while the baby's head began to rot, and from the stench many people died. The Toltecs would have killed it, but those who made the attempt died before they could reach it. As the odor spread, it caused a plague throughout the land. Nine out of every ten Toltecs died.

Some days later, when the plague had passed, Topiltzin, seeing that his rivals' armies were closing in, sent them gold, robes, and jewels. He also sent them a ball court as big as a medium-sized room, made of four kinds of jewels—jadestone, redshell, whiteshell, and turquoise—and with it a ball of redstone, proposing that, inasmuch as the four jewels were of equal beauty, so he and they would rule the empire as equals, giving precedence wherever necessary to him who might score a goal; and in such an event the other three would acquiesce, and all the people and their descendants would live in harmony and lasting peace. These and many other messages Topiltzin sent his rivals, fearing that otherwise they might soon seize the empire for themselves.

The gift was received, but the fighting did not stop. At last Topiltzin was forced to leave the city. Many Toltecs had been killed. Surveying the dead and depopulated land, the rival armies merely sacked the temples and carried off the palace treasures, returning to their own countries, leaving no one behind them. For now the land was drought-ridden, infested, and unproductive. The year was 1 Flint, and in that year the days of Tollan came to an end.

Tales of War

Hidatsa warrior. Painted in 1833
by Karl Bodmer, engraved *circa*
1840 by Rawdon, Wright &
Hatch   (*Picture Collection,
New York Public Library*)

Punishment for guilt may come in the form of natural disasters; or, as in the extraordinarily explicit "Legend of Korobona," it may be administered by the hand of an aggressive neighbor. Often the hostilities between nations become integrated into the pattern of tribal life, as the tale entitled "Home Boy" suggests. Or they may be transmuted into quite different forms of behavior, as in the bizarre "Rival Chiefs," the story of two Kwakiutl lords who professed to be friends.

THE LEGEND OF KOROBONA

WARRAU

From her home in the hills, Korobona could look out over the forest below and see a beautiful lake in the distance. She and her younger sister would sometimes talk of going down to this lake to bathe, but their brothers had told them never to do so, warning that the place was fatal.

Korobona could not resist. "Come with me," she said to her sister one day. "Nothing can harm us." At first the sister refused. But Korobona continued to plead with her. At last she consented to go and the two young women set off through the forest.

When they had reached their destination, they removed their clothes and began to bathe. The waters were clear and beautiful. Fearlessly, Korobona swam out toward the middle of the lake, her sister close behind. As she swam, she noticed a piece of wood sticking up. Laughing, she reached out and grasped it. At that moment a man-like form arose before her. It seized her and ordered the younger sister to go back to the shore. Then it took Korobona beneath the water.

When it had released her, the sisters returned home. They did not tell their brothers where they had been. But after a time, when Korobona had given birth to a child, the brothers knew the truth and were wild with anger. The eldest brother determined to kill the child. But Korobona pleaded so insistently that at length he relented and the child was spared. This child was a girl.

After a while Korobona again felt herself drawn to the lake. She had heard that the spirit of the place was a serpent, sometimes appearing in human form, sometimes as a being half man, half serpent. She wondered if this could be true. Though her sister tried to dissuade her, Korobona once again set out through the forest.

This time she waited at the edge of the lake. At first she saw nothing. But the serpent had already spied her and was gliding toward her, under the water. Peering down from the bank, she saw what looked like a seed floating on the surface. In fact it was the serpent's head. As she bent over to look down, the man-snake rose up and seized her, just as he had done once before.

Korobona was now afraid to return home. She waited alone in the forest. When her time came, she gave birth to a boy, beautifully formed, yet somehow not unlike a serpent. At first she wept, then she fled. But she could not keep herself from returning to where the child lay hidden among the trees. Often she went there to care for her baby.

One day a hunter passing through the forest heard the child's cry and reported it to Korobona's brothers. The four brothers went at once to the place where the cry had been heard, and while two of them dragged their sister home, the other two pierced the child with an arrow. Then they told Korobona: "The child is dead." But seeing their sister's grief, they permitted her to go back and make her baby a grave.

Unbeknown to her brothers, Korobona revived the child. She concealed him in a thick tree and returned often with food. The boy grew rapidly and soon was large beyond his years. He was also wise.

Once, while out hunting, the brothers noticed footprints that they recognized as belonging to Korobona. Then they knew her secret. The next time she set off for the forest, they ran after her, waving arrows and stone war clubs. Korobona rushed to her son and tried to shield him. But her brothers aimed their arrows carefully and shot him dead despite their sister's efforts. Afterward, they cut the body to pieces. When they had finished, their sister cursed them, predicting that the evil they feared would come in due time nonetheless, and that the blame would now be theirs, not hers.

Korobona remained behind to keep away the carrion-eating beasts. She collected her son's remains and covered them over with leaves and red flowers. As the mother watched, the heap began to stir. At first a head and shoulders appeared, then the full form of a man, armed with bow and arrows and a war club. His short black hair was decorated with white down. His skin was somewhat lighter than that of the Warraus. On his cheeks and forehead he wore red paint.

This was the first Carib warrior, born to terrorize the Warraus.

When the four brothers saw the Carib coming, they called their own warriors together; but they were powerless against his superior strength. He drove them from their homes, seized their possessions, and took their daughters to be his wives.

This is why the Warraus, who in days long past had come down to earth from the sky, now live in the lowlands, among the swamps.

HOME BOY

HIDATSA

In the days of Tattooed Face and Good Fur Robe, there lived in one of the villages near Heart River the son of Black Coyote. He was a handsome, well-formed young man, with long brown hair, and his beauty and elegant dress won the admiration of all the women; for his soft thick buffalo robe was decorated with eagle feathers, and at the shoulders dangled pure white weasel skins. From his lance, too, fluttered many eagle feathers. While he was in appearance the ideal warrior youth, he had never been on the war path. He would stroll through the village singing, or perhaps climb to the top of his father's lodge to gaze upon the young women as they passed. His actions were so peculiar as to bring upon him the ridicule of the men, for it seemed to them that he should desire to win honors in strife, and on account of his reluctance to join the warriors he was derisively called Home Boy.

On the south side of Heart River, where it emerges from the hills and flows across the valley, rises a high butte. Men would often go there to fast, but never stayed more than a day or two, for something in that place seemed to frighten them. One day Black Coyote called his son to him and said:

"You have no deeds; you are nothing. It is time you distinguished yourself in some manner, for you are a strong young man. Go up on that hill and fast for a time; perhaps the spirits will help you."

So Home Boy went to the hill and stood upon its summit, crying to the spirits. During the night he heard sounds as though the enemy were coming. He could almost feel the ground tremble under their horses' hoofs, and terrified he fled back to the village. In the morning the people went to the hill to verify his story, but they saw no broken ground or trampled grass.

His father said, "You are a coward! What do you suppose people will think of you if you always remain in the village, doing nothing? Tonight you must go to the hill again and stay there no matter what happens."

So Home Boy went again to the hill and cried. Again he heard the enemy coming, and turning, seemed to see a party of mounted warriors charging upon him. The one in advance discharged an arrow, which pierced him, and as he fell the others swept by and struck him with their coupsticks. Then the spirits promised Home Boy that he should kill many enemies and count many coups. He returned to the village in the morning.

Shortly afterward the village was attacked by the Sioux, but Home Boy took no part in the battle; at night, however, after the enemy had withdrawn, he went out and dragged the bodies of their slain into a row. Taking the eagle feathers from his lance, he laid one on the dead body of each warrior, and said, "Here is something for you to take on your long journey." Then he lay down in the middle of the row. In a vision as he slept there, the spirits of the dead came and told him to arise and to be not afraid, for they were to make great medicine for him. One of the warriors then took his bow and shot his arrows through Home Boy. This made him invulnerable.

But when war parties formed, Home Boy still remained behind, and the finger of scorn was ever pointed at him. One day he and his friend were sitting on the housetop watching the people assemble for the Dahpiké. Suddenly Home Boy leaped up and said with determination, "Today I will dance in the lodge of the sun!" His friend looked at him in wonder, for only warriors of note participated in that ceremony. But he went with Home Boy to the sun lodge, and watched his sober face as he marched in carrying his lance.

The people were at first astonished at his temerity, then they began to laugh and to nudge each other, saying, "Look, Home Boy is going to dance; he must be growing foolish!" He boldly stepped up to the bowl of white clay with which the warriors painted themselves, and with which they smeared stripes across their arms to represent the coups they had struck. Home Boy painted himself, and placed a wisp of grass in his hair, a symbol worn only by scout leaders, to represent the hills from which they had viewed the enemy's country.

His mother and sisters drew their blankets over their faces and went out. His father said, "I have tried to rear my son from childhood according to our traditions and customs, and to make him a brave warrior, but now before all my people he has disgraced me." And drawing his blanket over his head, he too went out.

The warriors sat in four rows according to the rank their deeds gave them. Home Boy, with a wolf skin thrown over his shoulders and lance in hand, stepped into the front line, as though he had a perfect right to be there. As the warriors danced out of the lodge, making a circle and reentering, Home Boy danced with them. He stepped on the black stone at the foot of the sun pole, thus swearing that he spoke only the truth; and though he had performed no deeds in war, he told of his visions, while the people all laughed at him.

A short time after the dance a war party was about to start, and as they marched around the village singing, Home Boy joined them and sang with them. The chief said, "Young man, you always sing with these war parties, but you never go out to fight. You are making us ashamed."

His friend, who was one of the party, drew him aside and said, "You must go with us, or you can never hold up your head in this village again."

Home Boy replied, "My friend, I am going. I shall not join you now, but I shall be with this party when it reaches the enemy. Four days from now you will hear from me. Procure some buffalo meat for me, the muscles of the foreleg, the shoulder blade, the tongue, and an intestine stuffed with chopped meat. When you camp the fourth night, watch which way the wind blows and listen carefully and you will hear me howl like a wolf. Then bring out the four pieces of meat and throw them to the big white wolf you will see outside, but do not come too near it. Say, 'Here is some food for you, wolf.' Early in the morning join the scouting party and you will meet a lone wolf coming toward you. Say to those with you, 'There is Home Boy. He has seen the enemy, and I have seen them second.' They will laugh at you, but do not heed them. Remember what I say, and do these things."

The second day after the war party had left, Home Boy told his mother to make him some moccasins, for he wished to go on the war path. His mother begged him not to go. "You have never been away from the village since you were born," she said, "and you will surely be lost." But his determination was firm, and he went out of the lodge, leaving his mother to begin work on the moccasins. When Black Coyote came in, his wife told him of their son's intention, and the father replied, "Let him go. I have done everything I could to rear him well, but he has brought shame on our household. Perhaps he will die somewhere. It is well."

The morning of the fourth day the son went to his mother and said, "Are my moccasins ready?" She gave them to him, and Home Boy said, "Mother, come with me until I ford the river; then you may return home." She went with him, and when they reached the stream, he leaped into the water and disappeared, and a moment later a white wolf emerged, dripping, at the other side. She waited long for a glimpse of Home Boy, but in vain; and she was puzzled, but remembering all the queer actions of her son, she came to the conclusion that he had done something wonderful. The wolf looked back once, and then trotted away.

Home Boy's friend sat that night in the brush shelter, feasting with the others on the buffalo they had killed, and he laid aside certain portions of the meat, saying, "This is for Home Boy."

The others laughed, and said ironically, "Yes, that is for Home Boy!"

Soon they heard the wolf-howl outside, and the friend jumped up, saying, "Home Boy has come!" and, picking up the meat, ran out.

The chief, who had brought his beautiful young wife with him, in the belief that she and Home Boy were lovers, now turned to her and said sneeringly, "There is your sweetheart howling outside." And they all laughed.

When the young man came back into the lodge, the people asked, "Did you see your friend?"

"Yes," he replied, "Home Boy was out there"; but they laughed at him derisively.

The next morning, when the scouting party went out, Home Boy's friend accompanied them. The sun was halfway to the zenith when they saw a wolf running toward them along a ridge, now and again looking backward across his shoulder. The young man with the scouts said, "There is Home Boy. Whatever he sees, I claim second honor." The others smiled, and cheerfully assented. They saw the wolf run into a little coulee, and suddenly on the rim appeared Home Boy, dressed in a beautiful war shirt and fringed leggings. His face was painted and his hair tied with strips of wolf skin.

The scouts were filled with astonishment and wonder. In answer to their questions, he said, "Nearby is a large war party camped in a circle. They are so close you had better return to the main body." When the scouts were some distance from the camp, they began to run zigzag as a signal that they had seen the enemy. The warriors came out and piled up buffalo chips, and, forming in a half circle behind the heap, stood singing and awaiting the return of the scouts. Home Boy ran at their head, his long brown hair flowing in the wind, and the tail of his wolf skin streaming behind him.

When he reached the buffalo chips, he kicked the pile over, signifying that he would count coup on the enemy in the battle. The warriors were amazed, and murmured in awe-stricken tones, "Home Boy is here!"

He told them that a great number of the enemy were encamped but a short distance away, and that they had better prepare at once for a battle. His report caused great excitement, and the chief spread a buffalo robe on the ground and invited Home Boy to speak with him privately. "There are timber and water here," the youth told him, "and it is a good place to fight. My plan is to take warriors who are swift runners and strong. I will leave a number of these men at three points between here and the enemy. With the fourth party we will make the attack and surprise our foe; then we will retreat to the third body, and they will cover our retreat to the second, and so on to this camp, where we will make a stand together." The chief called a number of the older men and told them of the plan; they approved it.

To Home Boy was given the command, and he started out with the best warriors, leaving the inexperienced men and the old fighters in camp. At selected points he left reserve forces, and at the last stop he told the chief that from there to the enemy's camp the distance was great. "I shall take only my friend with me," said Home Boy, "for the way is long and some of you might tire and be unable to retreat." So the two set out alone and reached the enemy's camp after dark. "Whatever I do," said Home Boy, "follow right behind me and you shall have second honor."

They lay in the brush all night. Early in the morning one of the women of the village came out to work on a hide while the air was cool. Home Boy stole upon her through the grass and, rising beside her, pierced her with his lance, and his friend counted second coup. The death cry of the woman roused the village, and Home Boy said, "Start back as fast as you can, and after I have scalped the woman I shall follow you." Waving the bloody scalp and picking up the bone hide-scraper which the woman had dropped, he started after his friend, while the warriors of the village followed in hot pursuit. Soon his friend began to tire, and Home Boy said, "Swing your head from side to side, and blow like a wolf." When he did so the young man began to feel refreshed. But his feet grew heavy again, and Home Boy said, "Put your hands in front of you, and lope like a wolf." That again brought renewed strength, and when for the third time he became exhausted, Home Boy said, "Pretend you have a tail, and put it between your legs as a wolf does when he is pursued." This gave the young man strength enough to reach the third party of warriors, where a sharp fight took place. Home Boy fought bravely, and went forward to meet a single advancing warrior, whom he killed with his lance, and his friend close behind counted second coup.

Then they retreated to the spot where the second party waited, and another engagement occurred; again Home Boy killed an enemy, and his friend counted second coup. And so it was until they reached the main camp on the river, where, in the sight of all, Home Boy killed one of the bravest warriors of the enemy. Here the fighting was very severe, and the enemy were soon driven back.

After the battle was over, Home Boy gave the scalp of the woman he had killed to the chief and the hide-scraper to his wife. The chief was ashamed when he remembered what he had said of Home Boy the evening before, and invited him to sit beside him, while his wife brought food to Home Boy and held a horn of water to his lips.

When the war party started homeward, the hero told his friend that he himself would go alone. He watched the others out of sight, then started off and reached the village on the night of the next day, coming in while all were asleep. He hung his lance and robe where he usually kept them, over the headrest of his bed, and lay down to sleep. When the father awoke in the morning and saw his son lying there, he said to himself, "I suppose he was lost in the hills, and came home after wandering about." But his mother, as always, was glad to see him, and prepared food for him, and when he had eaten he lay down to sleep again. Soon the returning war party was heard across the river. The people gathered at the bank, and some paddled across in bull boats to welcome them. They told of their triumphs, but above all praised the bravery and leadership of Home Boy. His parents heard, but, thinking the people were still ridiculing their son, covered their heads and went back into their lodge. As was the custom, the clansmen of the father came to the lodge and sang the praises of Home Boy, but instead of bringing out gifts as was usual when a young man had returned from his first war party with deeds of valor to his credit, Black Coyote sat inside in deep humiliation.

Soon an old woman entered and pulled a blanket from the bed of Home Boy's mother; another took a robe from the pile on which Black Coyote sat. When he saw these signs, he called in Home Boy's friend and said, "Is it true, my child, what these people are saying?"

"Yes," he answered, "it is all true."

Black Coyote's eyes were filled with tears, and he pulled the blankets from his son and said, "My son, tell me truly, did you do these things?"

"Father, look at my lance," said Home Boy. When Black

Coyote beheld the lance covered with blood, he was convinced, and knew it was all true.

A few days later, when quiet was restored, the chief told his wife to clean the lodge well and to make it smell sweet with incense. Then he sent her to invite the young man, as he wished to speak to him. When Home Boy entered, the chief said:

"Young Wolf, you have brought great honor to me. You scalped the enemy in the village and brought the scalp to me. All your brave deeds are good. I said that you were foolish when you danced in the sun lodge, but I did not know your medicine then. My wife is handsome and good. She looks with favor upon you; whenever you come near she is pleased. Take her for your own."

Home Boy replied, "Old Man Wolf, your speech is good. I fought that day to prove to you that what you had said was wrong. I killed the enemy in the village that your name might be in the mouths of all. As for this young woman, I admire her only with my eyes. I will come and eat with you and talk with you, but she must throw away any affection she may have for me. I will be a warrior under your leadership and help you in many battles. You shall be known as a great chief among us."

Home Boy fought and lived for many years. He continued to bear the name of Home Boy, and it became a good name, for he won his eagle feathers many times over.

THE RIVAL CHIEFS

KWAKIUTL

In her well-known book Patterns of Culture, *Ruth Benedict used a synopsis of this purportedly true story to illustrate her thesis that the Kwakiutl belong to an inherently "Dionysian" culture: zesty, violent, and obsessively extravagant. The tale is here given in full.*

1

There were Kwakiutl living at Crooked Beach. Fast-Runner, chief of the Sun tribe, and Throw-Away, chief of the Hair-Turned-Up-in-Front tribe, were friends. Well, it is said they really loved each other. They were long-time friends. They watched each other's thoughts.

Now, one day the Kwakiutl were feeling low. Well, then Throw-Away asked for the thoughts of his friend, saying he was going to give a feast with many salmon berries for the Kwakiutl clans. Fast-Runner answered him at once: "O friend! Your words are good. Our tribe will be happy, for they are feeling very low."

So Throw-Away ordered his attendants to sweep out his house. The house was swept; the attendants put on their cedar-bark belts and went out to invite the Kwakiutl on behalf of their chief. Well, when the guests arrived, Throw-Away sent his attendants back out to call Fast-Runner again. So they called him one more time. At last Fast-Runner came into the house and Throw-Away invited him to sit in the rear.

When he had settled himself, the feasters began to sing feasting songs, four songs for feasting.

When the feasters were finished singing, then four small canoes were brought into the house. Well, now, the insides of these canoes were not washed out before they were used, before many salmon berries were poured into them. Then the four little canoes were filled half full of salmon berries; and a box of grease was put into each canoe. When they were ready, then one of the canoes was lifted up and put down in front of Fast-Runner and his clan, the Sun tribe. One was put down before Wrong-Around-World and his clan, the Mamtakila. One was put down in front of Met-by-Chiefs and his Chiefs clan. And the last one was put before Copper-Maker, who was chief of the Breakers-of-All-Tribes.

Well, as soon as everything had been put on the floor, Fast-Runner lay down on his back and covered his face with his black bear blanket. Well, Throw-Away asked his attendants to tell the feasters to go ahead and use their spoons and eat, for all the feasters carried spoons in the folds of their blankets. But they all kept looking at Fast-Runner; they knew his heart was bad. Then all the feasters lay down on their backs. After a while, Fast-Runner had his attendant stand up and speak to his fellow feasters: "O fellow tribesmen! See our chief here on the floor, here in the house of his friend, Throw-Away. He says he will not eat these dirty things of this dirty chief. Could he not have washed out his canoes, his feasting dishes, before he filled them with salmon berries?" For they had been used as soaking tubs for smoked halibut heads. "So, Throw-Away, it is your wish that the soot in your feasting dishes be eaten with spoons!"

Well, immediately Throw-Away stood up. He ignored his attendants and spoke directly: "O friend! Don't you talk proudly! You talk as if you had much. Keep it up! Do what you will!" Then Fast-Runner rose to his feet: "O friend, Throw-Away! I will not eat this filth you give me for food, O dirty man! And now I will meet your dirty deed. Yes, you are right: I have much." Then he sent his attendants to go get his copper, Sea Monster.

When the four attendants returned with the copper, they gave it to Fast-Runner. He took it and walked to the middle of the house and pushed it under the fire. Well, then, he put out the fire with it. Immediately, Throw-Away took out his own copper, Looked-at-Askance, and pushed it under the feasting fire. Well, with his copper he built up the fire again, so it wouldn't die out. It was just as if he had fueled the fire.

Then Fast-Runner sent his attendants to go get his other copper, Crane. As soon as they returned, they gave it to Fast-Runner and he pushed it into his friend's fire. So again he put out the fire.

It was just as if he had covered his friend's fire with the many blankets a copper is worth, so the fire burned nothing. That's what it means to "put out the fire" at a feast. But as for Throw-Away, it was as if he were lighting the fire with his copper, as if he were fueling it with grease. That's why he pushed his copper into the fire, so the feast fire wouldn't die out in his house.

Well, as soon as Fast-Runner had pushed his copper under the fire, Throw-Away asked his Hair-Turned-Up-in-Front clan for another copper. But there was no copper. Then Throw-Away was beaten: the feasting fire was extinguished in his house. The feasters left; they never ate the salmon berries that had been given in the feast.

2

Well, the next day Fast-Runner wished to know the thoughts of his friend. So he ordered his attendants to go and invite those who had been to Throw-Away's house the day before. Soon the guests came into the house, all but Throw-Away. Then Fast-Runner sent his attendants to call him again. Well, not long after that, Throw-Away came in. Then Fast-Runner drew him apart from his clan and had him sit beside the fire, with two attendants on either side. As soon as he had been settled, they began the songs of the feast giver: four songs were sung.

When the feasters had finished singing, four boxes of crab apples were laid on the floor just inside the door of the feasting house. Also four boxes of grease were brought, two double-headed serpent dishes, and two grizzly-bear dishes. Also one wolf dish. These were the feasting dishes of Fast-Runner. Then cherries were poured, then crab apples, until the feasting dishes were just half full. Then the grease was poured into them. Well, then, they were full of it.

Now the first dish was set before Throw-Away. Then, when all the feasting dishes had been set out, Fast-Runner's attendants urged the feasters to go ahead and eat with their spoons. Immediately Throw-Away stood up and spoke, saying, "O friend! Who will taste these feast-foods? Not I! You are really a dirty man, friend! For you have not washed the insides of your feasting dishes." Then he sent his four attendants back to his house on an errand. Very quickly they returned, bringing the copper, Day Face. Immediately Throw-

Away took the copper and shoved it under the fire. So he put out the fire in Fast-Runner's house.

Then Fast-Runner stood up and said, "O friend! Now my fire is put out. Now go and sit down while I think what to do." This he said with some excitement, for now he was dancing his fool-dance. Then he ordered his attendants to go see what they could find in the house of his father-in-law, Moving-Load. Well, the four attendants had not yet left when Moving-Load himself stood up in the house, for he had also come as a feaster. He said, "O son-in-law! Send them to go bring four flat-bowed canoes for your fire here in the house."

At once Fast-Runner sent out his four attendants and also his young men to break the four new flat-bowed canoes into pieces. Well, it wasn't long before they returned, carrying the broken canoes on their shoulders. Then they were piled on the fire.

Now truly with this, the fire in the house was burning high. And Fast-Runner hoped that Throw-Away would run from the heat. Surely he would be roasted if he did not run. But Throw-Away just lay down on his back beside the fire. He never moved, though the skin of his knees became blistered. He covered his face with his black bear blanket, and only the blanket was scorched. When the fire died down, he sat up and ate crab apples from his dish. It was as if he was not harmed by what had been done to him, though in fact he was burned. So as soon as the feasters had eaten the crab apples, they were praised by Fast-Runner's attendants. Then the feasters went out of the house.

3

Well, a long time passed and nothing like this happened again. Then one night Throw-Away invited his clan and told them he was going to give a winter-dance. The clan was grateful for his words. He was trying to see what he could do to beat Fast-Runner; so that's why he spoke as he did, and he said so. Well, it wasn't long before Fast-Runner found out what Throw-Away had said. Then one night he, too, invited his clans and told them he would give a winter-dance. For he wanted to be always equal to his rival. When his words were finished, they all went out of the house.

Not long after that, Throw-Away's little son and daughter disappeared for their pre-initiation retreat. But the next night Fast-Runner's full-grown son and his two full-grown daughters disappeared. And the night after that, yet another full-grown son of Fast-Runner's disappeared for his retreat.

Well, then, the time came for the Kwakiutl to dance the winter-dance. Then Throw-Away hired the wood carver to carve a precious sea-monster mask for his daughter to wear when she reappeared as an initiate at the winter-dance. And the boy, when he reappeared, would be a grizzly bear. But Fast Runner was listening to Throw-Away's words.

Now at last it was almost time to meet the initiates. The Kwakiutl clans sat down in the singing house. And Fast-Runner sat down with them, for all the men went to the singing house. When they were finished, they left for home. Night came and the tribes sought to bring back their initiates. It was dawn when they finished. Immediately the two disappeared children of Throw-Away were brought out onto the beach; then the war-dancer girl had her head cut off. Well, then, the grizzly bear struck with his claws at a large flat-bowed canoe, and the canoe was given to Fast-Runner.

When the singing for the war-dancer was finished, they left the beach and went inside the winter-dance house. As night came, the captured initiates were brought to their senses by singing: the war-dancer, wearing the precious sea-monster mask, arose and stood up in the rear of the house. Well, that was all that was done. Then Throw-Away was finished giving his winter-dance.

4

Now it was Fast-Runner's turn. At night he sent his attendants to secretly invite his clans. As soon as they all came in, the door to Fast-Runner's house was barred. Then Fast-Runner's attendant told the clan what they must do: in the evening of the following day they were to go and sit in the winter-dance house; then their chief would again do harm to his friend, Throw-Away, by showing his disappeared ones. "So we must all be ready to help him when he meets his rival!" The clan all said they were ready. When their words were finished, they went out of the house. And as soon as they had left the house, they went to bed.

They awoke late the next day. Immediately the winter-dancers went and washed themselves and their women and children.When they were finished, Fast-Runner invited them to come to his house for breakfast. After they had eaten, Fast-Runner's attendants whispered to the winter-dancers that they were to go inland to a secret singing place. Immediately all the men got up and went into the woods.

There they sat down on the ground, and the song masters began the two songs of the war-dancers, also the two grizzly-bear songs. When the song masters had finished, Fast-Runner spoke, saying, "O friends! now you will all dress up this night, that you may be happy on account of my deeds!" And all the winter-dancers answered him, saying, "This we shall do." At once the four attendants came up and asked to wash the bodies of those who had dances. Then as soon as the four attendants had finished, the men singers came home from the woods.

Now all the winter-dancers and their women and children got ready. Then they tried to bring back the disappeared ones. They had just finished when dawn came. Then the four attendants went and brought four great flat-bowed canoes and moored them, together with four long poles. Then they covered them over with boards and all the winter-dancers went out on the boards and into the canoes—not all, however. It seems that the grizzly bears, the fool-dancers, and all those having dances did not go with them to bring home the initiates; they just sat in the winter-dance house. But the homecoming did not take long, and soon they were seen rounding the point at the northern end of Crooked Beach.

Well, they came up to the beach at the winter-dance house and then one of the grizzly-bear novices lay down inside the bow of one of the big canoes, and the other grizzly bear did the same in the bow of another canoe. Then the two war-dancers were sung for. As soon as they had been sung for, then a stout male slave was sent to stand with a pole up front in the largest of the flat-bowed canoes. The moment he took his position, a warrior named Frowned-Upon seized him there in the canoe. Then his friend, Warrior-All-Round-the-World, took his knife and cut in a circle close to the edge of the slave's hair. As the knife met the cut, he pulled off the scalp.

Well, they pushed the slave out of the canoe. As soon as he
hit the water, the cannibals, grizzly bears, and fool-dancers
came out from the winter-dance house; then they chased the
slave as he ran along Crooked Beach. As the grizzlies and fool-
dancers chased him, they tried to spear him; they threw
stones at him. Then the grizzlies struck at him with their
claws. He had not reached the south side of Crooked Beach
before he fell down dead. Well, then, dead he was.

Immediately, the fool-dancers cut the dead slave into
pieces and the cannibals came down the beach to eat him.
Also the grizzly bears and the fool-dancers asked to eat of it.
It didn't take long to eat him all up, for there were a hundred
and twenty men eating the dead slave. Well, now, they say
the grizzly-bear novices took up the scalp and played with it,
tossing it back and forth; then they received food.

And so that is how Fast-Runner killed his slave on account
of his rival, Throw-Away. Then Throw-Away was beaten.
Well, as soon as the two grizzly bears were finished playing
with the scalp, Fast-Runner took it and gave it to Throw-
Away. He said, "Well, friend, now this will be yours." With
that, all those who had surrounded the former disappeared
ones went out of the canoe.

When evening came, Fast-Runner's attendants went out
and issued the call. Soon the Kwakiutl clans came into the
house, and at once the two grizzly bears were tamed. When
this had been done, the two war-dancers sang their sacred
songs. Then, when they'd finished, the song masters began to
sing; and the two war-dancers came dancing out of the house,
then back into the house and around the fire. When the finishing song had been sung, the speaker of the house went up
to where the two war-dancers were standing and asked one of
them to name her desire. Immediately she answered, "We

wish to be put in the fire." The speaker of the house repeated these words to his clan. Then the four attendants of Fast-Runner spoke, saying, "O shamans, let us for once obey this desire of our friends! Come, take two short roof boards and tie the war-dancers to them!"

Then Frowned-Upon and his friend, Warrior-All-Round-the-World, invited the two war-dancers to come and be tied to the roof boards. Immediately, the boards were brought and put down in the rear of the house; then the two war-dancers were taken and laid on their backs and tied to the boards with cedar-bark rope. When this had been done, thick blocks of firewood were brought and stacked up in a pile all around the fire, enclosing it. A tall man sticking his head up could hardly look over it. Then it was ready.

Now they were calling for the war-dancers to be thrown on the fire. Well, then, two roof boards were brought in just like the ones on which the war-dancers were lying. Hemlock branches were taken and fashioned into head-rings just like those worn by the real war-dancers. Then they tied them around the heads of two female slaves. The slaves were laid on their backs on the roof boards and tied with cedar-bark rope in the same manner as the war-dancers. Then the two warriors said to the two women slaves, "O children! do not scream when you are put on top of this fire. If you scream, you will not come back to life after four days. The moment you scream, we will strike the nape of your neck so that you die, and by this you will be dead and stay dead." Then both the poor women slaves spoke and said, "Go on, do it quickly. Our hearts are strong. We will not scream, so that it will not be long before we come back to life again." Now they were ready.

Then Fast-Runner invited the fool-dancers to bring forth

the tied war-dancers so that they could be put on the fire. As
the fool-dancers came, then all the winter-dancers stood up
in the house. There was much confusion and running about.
The fool-dancers picked up the war-dancers and went around
with them in the rear of the house, then up toward the door,
then back again toward the rear. Then they went into the
back inner room on the right-hand side. There they put down
the real war-dancers, hid them, picked up the two slaves, and
went out at the left-hand side. Then they carried them
around, and while one slave was carried toward the door and
put down, the other was carried toward the rear and put down
at the same time, so that there was one on each side of the
piled-up fire. Then the two slaves were stood upright and put
on top of the pile. Well, then, it is said they never screamed
when they were shoved down. Then they were dead.

As soon as they were burned to ashes, then two small boxes
were brought and put down on the floor at the rear of the
house—no, one of them was put down at the door. Well, they
picked out the slaves' bones with tongs and put one slave into
each box. Then they put the lids on the boxes and set them
down on the floor at the rear of the house. Well, on the fourth
day, after being four days concealed in the house, the war-
dancers sang their sacred songs; they pretended to come
alive. Well, then, it is said Throw-Away was truly beaten after
that.

Well, Throw-Away said he would go make war on the
Nootka. He said he would go by way of Nimkish Lake. Well,
it is said they poled their canoes on the river, and as soon as
they reached the road to Nootka Inlet they split each of the
canoes into three pieces and carried them over the mountain
on their shoulders. When they got to the river at Nootka
Inlet, they sewed the canoes together and drifted down-

stream; at the mouth of the river they paddled through a narrow passage. Then they were startled and shot by arrows; Throw-Away and his crew were killed. Only one came back to tell the story of how Kwakiutl men had been killed. Then Throw-Away was beaten after that. Well, then, this is the end.

Winter and Spring

"An Old Man in His Winter
Clothes." Secotan. Drawn by
John White, 1585–6. Engraved
by Theodore De Bry *circa* 1590
(*Picture Collection, New York
Public Library*)

The changing of the seasons provides myth with one of its most characteristic metaphors. Spring is the time of deliverance and renewal—yet spring is not gentle. Its cruelty becomes increasingly apparent in these four myths from Ontario, Oklahoma, Wisconsin, and Tierra del Fuego.

SAPLING AND FLINT

MOHAWK

The cruelty of winter is represented by Tawiskaron (ta-WIS-ka-ron), whose name means "flint."

As Sapling was traveling, he came to the shore of a lake; and there before him he saw Tawiskaron, making a bridge out of stone. Already the bridge extended far into the lake. Tawiskaron went on working as Sapling came to meet him.

"Tawiskaron, what are you doing?" he said.

"I'm making a road." And he pointed out beyond the bridge: "There on the far shore live cruel, enormous beasts.

When my road is done, it will be their path. They will come here regularly to eat human flesh."

Then Sapling said, "You must not go on with this work. Your mind is bad."

"I will not stop my work," he replied. "It is good. These beasts will come here regularly to feed on human flesh." And he went on building his bridge.

Sapling returned to shore. In the brush alongside the lake he saw a bird sitting on a branch. It was the bluebird. He said to her, "Kill a cricket. Pull off one of its hind legs and carry it in your mouth. Then go to where Tawiskaron is working. Sit down beside him and let out with a cry."

The bird answered, "Yo!" Then it went to look for a cricket. After a while it found one, seized it, and killed it. Then it pulled off the hind leg, took it in its mouth, and flew to where Tawiskaron was building his bridge. It alighted close to where he was working and uttered the cry: "Kwa! Kwa! Kwa! Kwa! Kwa!"

Tawiskaron raised his head, looked around, and caught sight of the bird. He thought he saw that it held the thigh of a man in its mouth, all covered with blood. Then Tawiskaron jumped up. He didn't stop. He fled. And as fast as he fled, the bridge he had made disappeared behind him.

RAW GUMS AND WHITE OWL WOMAN

ARAPAHO

This ritual-like myth from Oklahoma is reminiscent of the mainly Old World lore compiled by Frazer in The Golden Bough, *in which it was shown that the fear of senescence and the loathing of accumulated sin might be washed away by the murder of a king who had run his term. The Arapaho have no kings. But note that the murder victims belong to "the good classes of people." The burden of guilt, or evil, is transferred to winter in the person of White Owl Woman. Revival is suggested by the tree burial of the murdered chiefs and by the melting of snow.*

There was a camp circle near the river. The ground was covered with snow and there prevailed sharp winds.

In a family, there was a young baby just born. Both parents were very fond of the new baby. As is the custom, this baby was nicely wrapped up with buffalo chips, remnants of buffalo hide, and other pieces of skin of animals.

The young baby was growing fast and was plump, and at times very noisy, especially in the forepart of the night. Of course the parents would do all they could to calm him, but he would cry freely until perfectly exhausted and then go to sleep. Early in the morning, when the old folks got up, they saw their baby nearly out of his cradle, but still sound asleep. "Well, well, I am so surprised to see our baby so lively. Surely he is doing well and you can see that he has tried to get out," said the wife, smiling as she began to unwrap him. The child was gentle of disposition during the day and slept

most of the time. When the night came on, the mother again
wrapped the baby as usual and placed him to sleep. Finally
the parents retired, lying on each side of their child.

Sometime during the night, this child got out of his cradle
and wandered off. Towards dawn he would come back to his
cradle without disturbing his parents. In the morning, when
the parents got up, they again saw their child nearly out of
the cradle, but still sound asleep. "Oh! my dear child is so
active and thriving. Just look at his broad breast and arms,"
said the wife, as she at this time started the fire. "Yes, he is
quite a boy now," said the husband. The young baby was still
asleep. Late in the day he awoke and began to cry, but closed
his lips tightly. After the mother had unwrapped him, he
moved his hands and feet continually and gazed out of the
top of the tepee into the deep atmosphere. Early at night the
mother again wrapped the child comfortably and placed it to
sleep. After the folks had spent some time chatting and telling
stories, they both retired.

After they had gone to sleep, the baby got out of his cradle
and wandered off. Again, in the morning, they found it partly
in the cradle, still sound asleep.

Before leaving their breakfast they heard across the camp
circle much weeping and wondered. Another chief had died
early in the morning.

Since this baby was born, frequent deaths occurred at
night among the good classes of people. The people began to
wonder at it, and prayed for the discontinuance of lamentations. During the day this young baby was exceedingly joy-
ful, but closed his lips most of the time. The parents began to
suspect the child at this time, because he would be sleeping
yet, when people were stirring about. They decided to watch

him during the night, but somehow they could not keep awake.

The next night the mother wrapped the baby and placed it to sleep. Both the father and the mother lay on each side of their child, so as to find out its strange way. For a long time they kept awake, watching their child. Towards midnight they went to sleep; and the young child, hearing his parents snoring away, worked himself gradually out of his cradle and wandered off. In the morning when the parents got up, this young baby was snoring with elevated head and mouth closed.

While they were eating their breakfast, and occasionally glancing at the child, the mother saw him open his mouth, and she saw in his teeth fresh morsels of human flesh. "Say, man, turn and look at those teeth with morsels of human flesh. There is the identical person who kills those chiefs. The baby, though human in form, must be a mystery," said the mother to her husband. After the mother unwrapped the child, it began to stretch itself and work its limbs all day long. Of course he would go to sleep at intervals.

At this time the parents both slept during the day, in order to find out the strange disposition of the child. Night came and the mother wrapped the baby rather tightly and placed it in the center of the bed to sleep. When all the people had gone to sleep and all the lights in the camp were out, the parents pretended to go to sleep, lying on each side of their child. Late in the night this young baby, Raw Gums, woke up and fretted and cried loudly, but these parents both snored. Raw Gums, believing they were both sound asleep, went his way, slowly leaving his cradle. At times he would look to see if they were really sound asleep. Raw Gums then took his pieced buffalo robe and went out toward a chief's tepee. This chief was the only surviving ruler of the tribe, and there was much lamentation among the people on account of the recent losses.

Shortly after Raw Gums had gone, the parents peeped through the breastpin holes of their tepee and watched their child. "Just look at him, will you? He is such a mysterious being, and we have got to do something to prevent him from doing his wrong deeds," said the wife, with deep breath. "Well, yes, we shall plan to get rid of him soon, before he kills any more," said the husband. Raw Gums walked briskly to the chief's tepee and entered it. At this time of night there was a deep calm in the camp; even the dogs were sound asleep.

The parents watched the child closely until he came out, carrying the chief in his arms toward the river. "Say, look at him, with that big man in his arms!" said the wife. "Yes, I think he is a dreadful being; watch him closely, to see what he will do with the man," said the husband.

Raw Gums ate this chief's flesh and left only the bones. How Raw Gums killed the chiefs was a mystery. The parents saw him climbing the cottonwood snag, which had square edges at the top, and drop the remnant of the chief into the body of the snag. This snag was hollow from top to bottom. After they had seen what their child was doing at that time of night, they both went to sleep. About twilight Raw Gums went back to the tepee and entered. Walking slowly toward the bed, and breathing easily, he managed to get back to his own cradle without disturbing the parents; but they both heard him entering the tepee, and lay awake.

After the parents had noticed the child's deed with the chief, they were so afraid that they slept in bed watching the child for fear of being injured. Just as soon as the sun had risen, they got up from bed and the wife made the fire.

"While the child is still sleeping, please boil enough beef this morning and clean out the tepee and spread some mats for seats," said the husband to his wife. So his wife hurried in preparing the food, and soon got it ready. Raw Gums was still sleeping, all wrapped up, when the invitation was announced to the men to assemble in this tepee. When the men had seated themselves, they were in somewhat gloomy spirits, because another chief had recently died. This invitation was an unusual thing, because in the camp they were still mourning.

"Well, young men, I have this day called you together in order to decide on the best plan to get rid of this child. Our chiefs have been taken away by this cruel child. How he kills them is a mystery. But we have good proof, for we saw pieces of human flesh remaining in his teeth. Until lately, while he has slept, his mouth has always been closed, but yesterday, while we were eating our breakfast, my wife called me to look at his teeth, and to my surprise I saw that some time he had eaten human flesh. Then my wife and I slept all day and watched him last night until he got out of his cradle and went to that chief's tepee. After he had done some act inside, he came out, carrying the remnant of the man to the river. Reaching a cottonwood snag, he climbed it with the body and dropped the body in the hole in the snag. When we both saw him doing this, we began to be afraid of him. Now, since you men are supposed to correct the evils and suppress disorder and violence in the tribe and camp circle, I want you to consider and devise a plan to get rid of this cannibal child," said the husband.

After the man had informed the men who had killed the chiefs, they were very much amazed and said nothing for some time. Finally they left it all entirely with the father, and told him to punish his child in the best way. So after the men had eaten the feast provided and had gone back to their respective tepees in despair, the father told his wife to provide him with fat from the tripe and unwrap the child. Without much conversation with his wife, in order to prevent the child from knowing, he then carefully wrapped this baby with the fat, and with all his might threw it out of doors, and at the same time he called the dogs to plunge for it.

When Raw Gums lighted on the ground, he became a young man, wearing his remnant buffalo robe, and began to dance around the circle, singing thus: "A skeleton! A skeleton!"

When the bereaved families heard about Raw Gums's conduct and the disposition of the chiefs' bodies, they went to the cottonwood and cut it down. At the foot of this hollow snag they found the skeletons of their chiefs. The people, seeing that Raw Gums was an extraordinary man, and on account of the recent mourning among the people, broke camp and left the locality.

When the people had deserted the place, an old woman, White Owl Woman, came to the place. "Well, I am so glad to see you; did you see me coming?" said old White Owl Woman. "Yes, I am enjoying myself on this old camp ground," said Raw Gums. "Let us challenge each other to an exhibition of power. We will erect a bluestem and burn it at the bottom. If this blade of grass falls toward you, then you will have to seek for good food," said old White Owl Woman. "All right, I am up to all kinds of fun," said Raw Gums. So old White Owl Woman made the fire and staked the bluestem and started it to burn at the bottom. The bluestem burned and fell toward Raw Gums. He then at once got up and went to the deserted camping places and brought in a good dried beef, with some tenderloin fat, and gave it to old White Owl Woman, who ate it. After she had eaten the beef, she staked another bluestem by the fire and started to burn it, and it fell toward her. She then got up and went to the deserted places, and in a short time brought in tenderloin and dried beef with thick fat, and gave it to Raw Gums, who at once ate it. Again she staked a bluestem by the fire and it burned at the bottom, falling toward the young man. Raw Gums then got up and went away to a deserted place and soon brought in a nice fat roll of pemmican, mixed with berries, and gave it to old White Owl Woman, who at once ate it. "You are a good one, grandchild," said old White Owl Woman, who at the same time broke off another bluestem, staked it, and burned it at the bottom. This stem fell toward old White Owl Woman. "Well, I cannot help it, the bluestem burned and fell over to me. So I have to go out and provide the food," said she. So she went about the deserted places and soon brought in a delicious roll of pemmican, mixed with berries, and delivered it to Raw Gums. Raw Gums received it and ate it with much relish.

"Now, dear grandchild, I shall ask some more questions, and if you can answer them I shall consider that you are a powerful man with intelligence. In the first place, can you tell me what is the most essential article?" said old White Owl Woman. "Well, there is only one article which I consider to be essential for all purposes, and that is a moccasin," said Raw Gums. "That is very good, dear grandchild," said old White Owl Woman. Raw Gums was impatient. "Say, dear grandchild, what is it that never gets tired motioning people to come over?" said old White Owl Woman, hastily. "Let me see—oh! It is the earflaps of the teepee that wave people to come," said Raw Gums, clearing his throat. "Now, can you tell me what it is that never gets tired of standing in an upright position, and is very attentive on all occasions?" said old White Owl Woman. "Well, old woman, I cannot think of anything but tepee pins, they never get tired of listening and always are waiting to hear more," said Raw Gums. "Well, dear grandchild, what is it that has two paths?" "Ha, ha! It is the nose: there is no other thing that bears two holes," said Raw Gums. "Which travels fast?" said old White Owl Woman, lazily. "It is the brain [thought] that travels swiftly and at great distance," said Raw Gums. "What animal is harmless to all?" said old White Owl Woman. "Well, the most harmless creature is a rabbit, and its color signifies purity and benevolence," said Raw Gums, with louder voice. "Which of the two hands is the most useful?" asked old White Owl Woman. "Let me see—oh, yes, it is the left hand, because it is harmless, pure, and holy," said Raw Gums.

"Well, grandchild, you have answered my questions readily, and so this day is a glory to you. You may now strike my head at the top," said old White Owl Woman, stooping down. Raw Gums then struck her head with a stone sledge and burst her skull, and so scattered the brains, which were the snow, melting away gradually. That is why there is a season of vegetation.

THE MAN WHO LOVED
THE FROG SONGS

MENOMINEE

There was once a man who received a revelation from the head of all the frogs and toads. Now, in the early spring, when the frogs and toads thaw out, they sing and shout more noisily than at any other time. So this man made it a practice to listen for the first frogs of spring. He loved their songs and tried to learn something from them. He would stand near puddles, marshes, and lakes to hear them. And once, when night came, he lay down on the ground to hear them better.

In the morning, when he woke up, the frogs spoke to him, saying, "We are not happy, but in a very deep sadness. You seem to like our crying, but our reason for weeping is this: in early spring, when we first thaw out and revive, we wail for our dead, because many of us do not wake up from our winter sleep. Now you will cry in your turn as we did!"

True enough, the next spring the man's wife and children all died, and the man himself died too, in payment for his having been too curious to hear the frogs.

IBIS STORY

Y A M A N A

Once in the old days, as spring was drawing near, a man looked out of his lodge and saw an ibis flying by overhead. Joyously he cried out to the other lodges, "An ibis has just flown over my lodge. Come see!" The people heard him and came rushing out, crying loudly, "Spring has returned! The ibises are flying!" They leaped for joy and made much happy noise.

But the ibis is sensitive and easily irritated. She must be treated with respect. When she heard the commotion made by those men, women, and children, shouting on and on so raucously, she was highly provoked. In her anger she summoned forth a thick snowstorm with bitter frost and much ice. Snow fell and kept falling for an entire month. Snow fell incessantly, the whole earth was covered with ice, and it was agonizingly cold. The water froze in all the waterways. Many, many people died. They could not board their canoes or travel to get food. Nor could they leave their dwelling places to gather firewood. Heavy snow lay everywhere. More and more people died.

After a long time the snow stopped falling. Immediately the sun came out and shone so brightly that all the ice and snow melted. The earth had been covered with it, even up over the mountaintops. But now there was much water flowing in the channels and in the open sea. The sun grew so hot that the mountaintops were scorched—and remain bare to this day. The ice in both the broad and the narrow waterways was melted. Then at last the people could get down to the beach and board their canoes and go find food. But on the high mountain slopes and in the deep valleys the ice held fast—and still does. The sun was not hot enough to melt it. It can yet be seen, extending even out into the sea, so thick was the ice sheet that once lay over the earth. The bitterest of frosts and a dreadful snowfall: all of it was brought about by the ibis. Indeed, she is a touchy and irritable woman.

Since then the Yamana have treated the ibis with great reverence. When she approaches their lodges, the people keep still. They make no noise. They hush up the little children to keep them from shouting.

The Birth of the Hero

Kiowa Apache encampment.
Drawn by Titian Peale *circa*
1820, engraved by Young &
Delleker *circa* 1822   (*Private
collection*)

The ideal hero must be free from the taint of a sexual origin. Yet he must be conceived. The challenge is met in a variety of ways, amply demonstrating the ingenuity, and poetry, of myth.

UP FROM THE EARTH

MENOMINEE

Version A

The daughter of Nokomis, the Earth, is the mother of Manabush, who is also the Fire. The Flint grew up out of Nokomis, and was alone. Then the Flint made a bowl and dipped it into the earth; slowly the bowlful of earth became blood, and it began to change its form. So the blood was changed into Wabus, the Rabbit. The Rabbit grew into human form, and in time became a man, and thus was Manabush formed.

Version B

There was an old woman, named Nokomis, who had an unmarried daughter. The daughter gave birth to twin boys, one of whom died, as did also the mother.

Nokomis then wrapped the living child in soft, dry grass, laid it on the ground at the extreme end of her wigwam, and placed over it a wooden bowl to protect it. She then took the body of her daughter and the other grandchild and buried them at some distance from her habitation. When she returned to the wigwam, she sat down and mourned for four days; but at the expiration of the fourth day she heard a slight noise within the wigwam, which she soon found to come from the wooden bowl. The bowl moved, when she suddenly remembered that her living grandchild had been put under it. Upon removing the bowl, she beheld a little white rabbit, with quivering ears, and on taking it up said, "O my dear little Rabbit, my Manabush!"

OUT OF THE WIND

MENOMINEE

The variety of mythic thought, even within a single culture, is well displayed in this text from the Menominee and in the pair of Menominee fragments given above, each of which describes, in strikingly different terms, the birth of the hero Manabozho, called Manabush or Mánabus.

In the beginning, there was a lone old woman living on this island. Nobody knows where she came from, or how she got there, but it is true that she dwelt in a wigwam with her only daughter. Wild potatoes were the only food of the two women. Every day the old woman took her wooden hoe and went out to gather them. She packed them home and dried them in the sun, for in those days, there was no such thing as fire in that part of the world.

One day her daughter begged to go with her. "Mother, let me go and help you. Between us we can dig more potatoes than you can alone." "No, my daughter, you stay here," said the old woman. "I don't want you to go. Your place is at home caring for the lodge." "Oh dear! I don't like to stay here alone all day," teased the girl, "it's so lonely when you are gone! I'd much rather go with you. There is another old hoe here that I can use. Please let me go too."

At last the old woman consented to her daughter's pleading; the two armed themselves with their tools and set out. After a little journey they came to a damp ravine. "Here is the place where I always come to gather the potatoes," cried the mother. "You can dig here too. But there is one thing that I must warn you about: when you are digging these potatoes, I want you to face south. Be sure not to forget this. It was because I was afraid that you could not be trusted to remember that I never brought you here before." "Oh, that's all right, I won't forget," cried the girl. "Very well then, you stay right here and work, I am going to dig over there."

The girl set to work with a will, and enjoyed her task very

much. "Oh, how nice it is to dig potatoes!" she said, and kept up a running stream of conversation with her mother as she labored. As the time passed by, the daughter gradually forgot her promise and at last turned around and faced in the oppo- site direction as she dug. All at once there came a great rushing, roaring noise from the heavens and the wind swept down where she stood and whirled her round and round. "Oh, Mother! Help! Come quick!" she screamed. Her mother dropped everything and rushed to her aid. "Grab me by the back and hold me down!" cried the girl in terror. The old lady seized her with one hand and steadied herself, mean- while, by catching hold of some bushes. "Hold me as tightly as you can!" she gasped. "Now you see why I told you to stay at home! You are being properly punished for your disobedience."

Suddenly the wind stopped. The air was as calm as though nothing had ever happened. The two women hastily gathered up their potatoes and hurried home. After that the old woman worked alone. Everything went well for a while, and then one day the daughter complained. "I feel very strange and differ- ent, Mother, there seems to be something within me." The old woman scrutinized the girl narrowly, but made no answer, for she knew that her daughter was pregnant. At last she was brought to bed and gave birth to three children. The first of these was Mánabus, the second was a little wolf, Múhwase, and the last was a sharp flint stone. When the unfortunate mother gave issue to the rock, it cut her and she died. The old woman mourned her daughter greatly. In a paroxysm of rage and grief, she threw away the flint stone, but Mánabus and Múhwase she cherished and cared for until they grew to be children.

BORN FOR THE SUN

NAVAJO

With scrupulous attention to ceremonial detail, this typical Navajo story describes the conception and birth of the hero Nayénezgani ("Monster Slayer") and his alter ego, Tobad-zhistshíni ("Born for Water"). "Born for" is a Navajo expression meaning "fathered by."

. . . The people went their ways and left First Man and First Woman and their foster daughter to live by themselves. It happened soon after this that this holy girl wished for a mate. Every morning when the sun rose she lay on her back until noon, her head to the west and her feet to the east. From noon on, she went to the spring. She lay under the ledge and let spring water drip over her body. This took place each day for four days.

First Man said upon coming home one day: "Over to the east, at the foot of the mesa, there are two different kinds of grass. Their ripening seeds are plentiful." So First Woman and the girl went down to gather the seeds. But when they got there they began to think of the monsters who roamed about the country, and became frightened. Looking about them carefully, they hurriedly gathered only one kind of seed before they ran back to their home. When they reached their hogan the girl said, "Mother, I want to go back and collect the seeds from the other grass." First Woman said, "No, daughter, you cannot go there alone. Some monster might catch you." But the girl insisted. She promised to be careful and to look out for herself. After the request was made four times the old woman let her go, warning her to have great care.

The maiden went down the mesa as fast as she could and was soon busy gathering seeds from the grass. All of a sudden she heard something behind her. Looking around, she saw a great white horse with black eyes. He had a long white mane, and he pranced above the ground, not on the earth itself. She saw that the bridle was white too, and that the saddle was white. And there was a young man sitting on the horse. The young man's moccasins and leggings and clothing were all white. All was as for a bride.

The holy rider spoke: "You lay towards me each morning until noon. I am he whom you faced. When I am half over the center of the earth, you go to the spring. Your wish could not have two meanings." He continued:

"Go home and tell your father to build a brush hogan to the south of your home. Make ready a meal out of the seeds of the grasses that you have gathered. Put this meal into a white bead basket. Have the pollen from a pair of blue birds, and use this pollen to draw a line from east to west across the basket on top of the metal. Turn the hand and make a line from north to south, and a line must be drawn around the outer edge of the basket. Set the basket inside the brush hogan. You and your father must sit there late into the night. He will go home to his wife and you must stay there alone."

When the White Bead Girl returned home she told her mother of all that she had seen and all that she had heard. That night when First Man came home, his wife told him what the girl had related. First Man said, "I do not believe this thing. We are very poor. Why should we be visited by a Holy Being? I cannot believe what you tell me."

Now when the girl told her mother about her experiences, First Woman asked if she had acted according to this Holy One's directions each day. The maiden had said, "Yes." So the woman told her husband that indeed it was all true, and that he must go and prepare the brush shelter and not argue. When all was ready, First Man took the white bead basket filled with meal, and he and his foster daughter went into the brush shelter and sat there.

They sat there late into the night, then First Man went home to his wife and left the maiden there alone. The White Bead Girl returned early in the morning, and First Man asked her at once, "Who came last night?" The girl said, "No one came." First Man turned to his wife. "Did I not tell you that it is all a lie?" he said. But the girl said, "Wait, I thought that I heard someone, and this morning I found just one track, and some of the meal, that towards the east, had been taken." So First Man went with his daughter to the brush hogan and he saw the one track and also that the meal towards the east in the basket was gone.

That night they prepared another basket of meal, and again First Man took his daughter to the brush shelter, and again they sat there late into the night. He left the maiden there alone. In the morning the girl returned to the home and said, "There are two tracks of a man there now. The meal in the south of the basket is gone."

On the third night the same thing happened. In the morning when the maiden returned, First Man asked, "Who came?" And the girl said, "No one came." Then First Man became angry. "I told you that this thing is all a lie," he said. But the

maiden answered, "But, Father, there are three tracks, and
the meal towards the west is gone. And I thought that someone touched me last night."

The fourth night they went to the brush shelter as before,
taking with them fresh meal in a basket. They sat late into the
night, then First Man returned to his wife. When the girl
entered the home in the early morning, her father asked,
"Who came?" And the girl answered, "No one." First Man
was very angry and insisted that it was all a lie. "But,
Father," said the White Bead Maiden, "the meal towards the
north is gone, and there are four tracks. I thought that I was
moved by someone, and I was all wet when I awakened."

Now after the maiden was visited the fourth time by the
Holy Being, she lived with her foster parents for four days as
they had always lived. But at the end of the fourth day the
young woman said, "Mother, something moves within me."
First Woman answered, "Daughter, that must be your baby
moving." And it is at the end of the fourth month that a
woman feels life. After five more days had passed, twin boys
were born to the White Bead Woman. It is so that a woman
bears a child in the ninth month.

The Hero as Provider

Boy shooting fish. Drawn by Seth
Eastman, engraved by C. K. Burt,
published in Mary H. Eastman's
*The American Aboriginal
Portfolio,* 1853

*The hero's first task is to provide culture; that is,
food, utensils, clothing, and the other necessities of life.
One of the mysteries of the culture myth is that this new
life is sometimes an outgrowth of death, as in the Arapaho
myth given below. In the Tsimshian myth that follows,
it comes with expulsion from the nuclear family. In
the Anambé and Quechua myths that conclude this section,
it is directly associated with the onset of adult sexuality.*

THE MICE'S SUN DANCE

A R A P A H O

Nihansan was out on the prairie. As he was going along, he
came to a sun dance. He went up close; the drum was sounding softly, and he could hear the shouting. "Yah, let me look
at the dance," he said. The shouting came from inside an elk
skull lying there on the prairie. Then Nihansan shoved his
head through the hole in the skull. The mice that had been
playing inside all ran out, and Nihansan's head stuck fast in
the skull. He felt aimlessly about him. "What kind of a tree
are you?" he said to whatever he touched. "This is dog-
wood," it replied. Then he went on again. "My friend, what

kind of tree are you?" he asked. "This is bow wood." "Indeed!" Then he asked again, "My friend, what kind of tree
are you?" "This is Pawnee wood." "Well, I am getting close
to the river," he said. "My friend, what kind of tree are
you?" "I am praying bush." "Indeed!" Then he started on
again, feeling about him. "My friend, what kind of wood are
you?" "This is cottonwood," the tree said to him. "Well, I
am finally getting near," Nihansan said to himself, and he
continued on. "My friend, what kind of wood are you?"
"This is willow," it said to him. "Well, at last I have got
there," Nihansan said. He stepped on the sand and walked
over the bank, falling into the river. He floated down the
stream. Farther down some women were bathing. When he
came near them, he said, "Hit me right in the middle of the
head." Then indeed they struck him where he told them, and
cracked open the skull. "I will take it for my scraper," the
women said, as they seized the horns of the skull. "Nihansan
is always providing for us."

RAVEN

TSIMSHIAN

At one time the whole world was covered with darkness. At
the southern point of Queen Charlotte Islands, there was a
town in which the animals lived. Its name was Kúngalas. A

chief and his wife were living there, and with them a boy, their only child, who was loved very much by his parents. Therefore his father tried to keep him out of danger. He built for his son a bed above his own, in the rear of his large house. He washed him regularly, and the boy grew up to be a youth.

When he was quite large the youth became ill, and being very sick, it was not long before he died. Therefore the hearts of his parents were very sad. They cried on account of their beloved child. The chief invited his tribe, and all the animal people went to the chief's house and entered. Then the chief ordered the child's body to be laid out; and he said, "Take out his intestines." His attendants laid out the body of the chief's child, took out the intestines, burned them at the rear of the chief's house, and placed the body on the bed which his father had built for his son. The chief and the chieftainess wailed every morning under the corpse of their dead son, and his tribe cried with them. They did so every day after the young man's death.

One morning before daylight came, the chieftainess went again to wail. She arose, and looked up to where her son was lying. There she saw a youth, bright as fire, lying where the body of their son had been. Therefore she called her husband and said to him, "Our beloved child has come back to life." Therefore the chief arose and went to the foot of the ladder which reached to the place where the body had been. He went up to his son and said, "Is it you, my beloved son? Is it you?" Then the shining youth said, "Yes, it is I." Then suddenly gladness touched the hearts of the parents.

The tribe entered again to console their chief and their chieftainess. When the people entered, they were much surprised to see the shining youth there. He spoke to them.

"Heaven was much annoyed by your constant wailing, so He sent me down to comfort your minds." The great tribe of the chief were very glad because the prince lived again among them. His parents loved him more than ever.

The shining youth ate very little. He stayed there a long time, and he did not eat at all; he only chewed a little fat, but he did not eat any. The chief had two great slaves—a miserable man and his wife. The great slaves were called Mouth-at-Each-End. Every morning they brought all kinds of food into the house. One day, when they came in from where they had been, they brought a large cut of whale meat. They threw it on the fire and ate it. They did this every time they came back from hunting. Then the chieftainess tried to give food to her son who had come back to life, but he declined it and lived without food. The chieftainess was very anxious to give her son something to eat. She was afraid that her son would die again. On the following day the shining youth took a walk to refresh himself. As soon as he had gone out, the chief went up the ladder to where he thought his son had his bed. Behold, there was the corpse of his own son! Nevertheless, he loved his new child.

One day the chief and chieftainess went out to visit the tribe, and the two great slaves entered, carrying a large piece of whale meat. They threw the whale fat into the fire and ate of it. Then the shining youth came toward them and questioned the two great slaves, asking them, "What makes you so hungry?" The two great slaves replied, "We are hungry because we have eaten scabs from our shinbones." Therefore the shining youth said to them, "Do you like what you eat?" Then the slave-man said, "Yes, my dear!" Therefore the prince replied, "I will also try the scabs you speak about." Then the slave-woman said, "No, my dear! Don't desire to be

as we are." The prince repeated, "I will just taste it and spit
it out again." Then the male slave cut off a small piece of
whale meat and put in a small scab. Then the female slave
scolded her husband for what he was doing. "O bad man!
what have you been doing to the poor prince?" The shining
prince took up the piece of meat with the scab in it, put it
into his mouth, tasted it, and spit it out again. Then he went
back to his bed. When the chief and the chieftainess came
back from their visit, the prince said to his mother, "Mother,
I am very hungry." The chieftainess said at once, "Oh,
dear, is it true, is it true?" She ordered her slaves to feed her
beloved son with rich food. The slaves prepared rich food,
and the youth ate it all. Again he was very hungry and ate
everything, and the slaves gave him more to eat than before.

He did so for several days, and soon all the provisions in
his father's house were at an end. Then the prince went to
every house of his father's people and ate the provisions that
were in the houses. This was because he had tasted the scabs of
Mouth-at-Each-End. Now the provisions were all used up. The
chief knew that the provisions of his tribe were almost exhausted. Therefore the great chief felt sad and ashamed on
account of what his son had done, for he had devoured almost
all the provisions of his tribe.

Therefore the chief invited all the people in, and said, "I
will send my child away before he eats all our provisions and
we lack food." Then all the people agreed to what the chief
had said. As soon as they had all agreed, the chief called his
son. He told him to sit down in the rear of the house. As soon
as he had sat down there, the chief spoke to his son, and said,
"My dear son, I shall send you away inland to the other side
of the ocean." He gave his son a small round stone and a
raven blanket and a dried sea-lion bladder filled with all kinds

of berries. The chief said to his son, "When you fly across the ocean and feel weary, drop this round stone on the sea, and you shall find rest on it; and when you reach the mainland, scatter the various kinds of fruit all over the land; and also scatter the salmon roe in all the rivers and brooks, and also the trout roe; so that you may not lack food as long as you live in this world." Then he started. His father named him Giant.

Giant flew inland. He went on for a long time, and finally he was very tired, so he dropped down on the sea the little round stone which his father had given him. It became a large rock way out at sea. Giant rested on it and refreshed himself, and took off the raven skin.

At that time there was always darkness. There was no daylight then. Again Giant put on the raven skin and flew toward the east. Now Giant reached the mainland and arrived at the mouth of Skeena River. There he stopped and scattered the salmon roe and trout roe. He said while he was scattering them, "Let every river and creek have all kinds of fish!" Then he took the dried sea-lion bladder and scattered the fruits all over the land, saying, "Let every mountain, hill, valley, plain, the whole land, be full of fruits!"

THE HUNGRY OLD WOMAN

ANAMBÉ

The unwilling young man, "stung," or "bitten," by sexual desire, crosses the threshold from childhood to maturity and becomes a woman's provider—all the while fleeing until, at last, he escapes to a disembodied womb (symbolized by the monkeys' pot and by the snakes' burrow). From the womb he is reborn as a child and delivered (by the stork) to his own mother, who evidently will chase away sexual temptation (symbolized by the agouti) and provide him with food from her garden. And yet, though a child, he is also old (white-haired). It may be said that he has expressed his dilemma, or, alternately, achieved his ideal.

A young man perched in a tree was fishing in the waterway below, when the hungry old woman came by with her net. She saw the young man's reflection in the depths of the stream and tried to scoop him up with the net. But the net remained empty. At this the young man laughed from up in his tree. Said the hungry old woman, "So there you are! Come down, my grandson."

"Not I," he said. "Watch out, or I'll send wasps to get you," she said. And she did. But the young man broke a little branch and killed all the wasps.

Then the old woman said, "Come down, my grandson, or I'll send stinging ants." Still he did not come down. Then she did as she'd warned, and the ants drove the young man into the water.

The old woman threw her net over him, wrapped him up in

it, and carried him off to her house. When she got there, she laid him on the ground and went to look for firewood. Presently, her daughter came out, saying, "Mother always tells me what she's killed when she comes back from hunting. But today she said nothing. Let me see what it is."

She opened the net and there was the young man. He said to her, "Hide me." So the young woman hid him. Then she went and got the mortar and, smearing it with resin, placed it in the net where the young man had been.

The old woman came out of the woods, put the net with its contents on the buccan, and kindled a fire. The mortar began to warm up. The resin melted and the old woman saw that she had been deceived. Then, as the fire burned through the net and the mortar appeared, she said to her daughter, "Where is my dinner? Give it to me or I'll kill you."

The girl was frightened. She told the young man to cut some assai palms so that baskets could be made—these baskets to be changed into various animals. Then the two took flight, with the old woman close behind them.

When she had overtaken them, the young man told the baskets to turn into tapirs, deer, peccaries, and every other kind of game. And so it was done, and the hungry old woman ate it all.

When the young man saw that the meal was too small, he ran on. Then he made a fish weir, and many fish were captured there. Then the old woman arrived and stepped into the weir. As she was eating the fish, the young man cut a stick of marajá, struck her with it, and fled.

Now the girl said to him, "When you hear a bird singing 'kaw-kaw kaw-kaw kaw-kaw,' you will know that my mother is not far behind."

The young man walked on and on and on. When he heard

the "kaw-kaw," he started to run. He came to where monkeys were gathering honey. He said to them, "Monkeys! Will you hide me?" The monkeys put him into an empty pot. The old woman arrived; she did not see the young man. She went on.

Now the monkeys told the young man he could go. On and on and on he walked. Again he heard "kaw-kaw kaw-kaw kaw-kaw." By now he had reached the house of the bushmaster, and he asked him to hide him.

So the bushmaster hid the young man. The old woman arrived; she did not see him. Again she went on.

In the evening he heard the bushmaster and his wife conversing: they were planning to set up a buccan and eat the young man. But while they were making the buccan, a makauan sang out; and the young man said, "O makauan, my grandfather! Come let me speak with you." The makauan heard him and came, asking, "What is it, my grandson?"

"There are two bushmasters who want to eat me."

"How many burrows do they have?"

"Only one."

Then the makauan ate the two bushmasters, and the young man went on and came out of the forest; he came to a stork, who was catching fish and dropping them into a hamper. He asked him to take him with him. And so, when the stork was done with his fishing, he told the young man to get into the hamper. Then he flew with him as far as the branch of a big tree, where he left him, for he was unable to carry him farther.

From up in the tree the young man could see a house. He climbed down and started toward it. As he reached the dooryard, he heard a woman scolding an agouti who had been eating her manioc.

The woman led the young man to her house and asked him

where he came from. He told her everything, how he had been watching for fish at the edge of the water and how the hungry old woman had taken him home. He had been young then, but now he was old. His hair was white.

The woman recognized him and knew him to be her son. Together they entered the house.

CONIRAYA AND CAHUILLACA

QUECHUA

In order to call attention to the structure of the following "double myth," I have divided it into two parts. In part 1 the story is told essentially from a woman's point of view; in part 2 it is retold from the point of view of a man. The reiterative separation of good and evil that begins part 2 corresponds to the creation of villages, fields, and aqueducts mentioned at the beginning of part 1. Each of these beginnings exemplifies the mythic theme I have called "setting the world in order." But in each case the story ends in a reversal, a flight from sexuality. The rather poorly developed "provider" theme is represented in part 1 by the woman's weaving, in part 2 by the man's filling the ocean with fish.

1

In the old days Coniraya Viracocha used to travel about in human form, but as though he were very poor: his cloak and his tunic were rags. Nobody recognized him. People cried, "You louse-ridden wretch!"

Yet it was he who created all the villages. All the fields, all the beautifully terraced hillsides: he spoke them into existence with merely a word. It was he who taught the use of aqueducts; and he made the water flow by letting fall to the ground a single blossom of the reed called pupuna. As he went along, he made all sorts of things. And in his wisdom he disdained the other, local gods.

Now in those days, there was a woman called Cahuillaca. She too was a god, this Cahuillaca, and yet a virgin, though she was pretty. The gods and spirits all wanted to sleep with her; they desired her. But she would have none of them.

One day as this woman, whom no man could touch, sat weaving beneath an eggfruit tree, Coniraya, in his wisdom, changed himself into a bird and went and perched in the eggfruit tree. Placing his semen inside a ripe eggfruit, he let it fall beside the young woman. The woman was pleased and she ate it at once.

In this way and no other, they say, she grew pregnant, untouched by a man. And in nine months' time, just as all women give birth, so did she, though a virgin, give birth. Then for a year she nursed the child at her breast, asking, "Whose little boy can this be?"

When the boy was a full year old, crawling on all fours, she summoned the gods and spirits to determine which of them might be the father. Hearing the summons, the gods were well pleased. They put on their good clothes and arrived, each thinking, "Only me will she love, only me."

They met at the place where she lived, called Anchicocha.

When all the gods and spirits were seated, the woman spoke: "You men, you lords, behold this child! Which of you gave him to me?" Then she asked each in turn, "Was it you? Was it you?" But no one answered "It was I."

Coniraya Viracocha sat at the very end—nothing but a pauper. She scorned to question him, thinking, "How could my son be the child of this beggar?"

Inasmuch as so many lordly men were sitting there, and yet none would say "He is mine," she said at last to her little boy, "Go, find your father yourself!" Then she said to the gods, "Whichever of you is the father, the child will climb up on you."

Then the boy began at one end, crawling on all fours without stopping until he reached the other end, where his father sat. When he got there, he was filled with joy and crawled up at once on his father's thigh.

Seeing this, the mother flew into a rage, crying, "Can such a miserable wretch be my husband?" Then she picked up her child and ran in the direction of the sea.

"Now she will love me!" cried Coniraya Viracocha, and he threw on his robe of gold, terrifying the other gods. "Sister Cahuillaca, look! See how beautiful I am!" And as he rose up, the earth was suddenly bathed in light. But the goddess did not look back. She ran on, continuing her flight to the sea. Having given birth to the son of so hideous and crude a man, so she thought, she wished that she might disappear. Then she arrived at the Pachacamac Sea, where she and her son were changed to stone. They can still be seen there today: two rocks like human beings.

2

Far in the distance Coniraya pursued her, thinking each moment that she would appear and look back. He called out. He kept crying her name.

As he went along, he met a condor, and he asked it, "My brother, have you seen a woman?" The condor replied, "You will find her close by." Then the god spoke these words: "You shall live the longest of all the animals. When the guanaco dies, you alone shall eat its flesh, also the flesh of the vicuña and all the other game. If any man kills you, he himself shall be doomed to death."

Then he came to a skunk, and he asked her, "Sister, have you seen a woman?" She answered, "You will never find her. Already she is far away." Hearing this, he sentenced her severely, saying, "Because of what you tell me, you shall go about by night, not by day. Men shall scorn you, and you shall have an evil stench."

Then he met a puma, who told him, "She is close by, you will shortly overtake her." And the god answered, "You shall be venerated. You shall kill and eat the llama, especially the evil man's llama. Dancers shall wear your hide at sacred feasts and in this way you shall dance. They shall come to fetch you once a year, sacrificing llamas in your honor; and indeed you shall dance."

Then he met a fox. But the fox said, "She has gone far away, you will never find her." And the god answered, "As you travel along in the distance, men shall speak of you contemptuously, saying, 'There's a fox. The rascal!' And if someone kills you, he shall leave your pelt behind, for it shall be worthless."

Next he met a hawk. The hawk said, "She is yet close by.

You will find her." Then the god replied, "You shall have much joy; and when you eat, your food shall be the hummingbird and other birds as well. And when you are killed, the man who has killed you shall honor you by sacrificing one of his llamas; when he dances, he shall place you upon his head so that you shall be his ornament."

Then he met some parrots. But the parrots said to him, "Already she is far away. You will see her no more." And Coniraya replied, "As you fly about, you shall screech. And as you look for your food, men shall hear your screeching and capture you with ease. You shall be miserable. You shall be despised."

And so he went on, predicting good fortune to whomever he met who would give him a good report. All others he cursed.

When he got to the seashore, he turned toward the place called Pachacamac, soon arriving at the home of the god Pachacamac's two unmarried daughters, who were guarded by a serpent.

Now the mother of these two maidens had shortly beforehand gone out to the sea, looking for Cahuillaca; and the mother's name was She-Who-Gives-Birth-to-the-Dove. While she was out, Coniraya approached her elder daughter; he made her sleep with him. Then he tried to sleep with the younger one, too. But she changed herself into a dove and flew away. This, then, is why her mother was called She-Who-Gives-Birth-to-the-Dove.

Now, at that time, there was not even one little fish in the sea. She-Who-Gives-Birth-to-the-Dove kept them all in a very small tank in her home. Coniraya was angry, thinking, "Why has she gone to the shore, seeking this woman named Cahuillaca?" In his anger he threw the fish into the sea, and indeed the sea ever since has been teeming with fish. Then he left and went walking along the coast.

When She-Who-Gives-Birth-to-the-Dove returned, her daughter reported, "He slept with me!" Then filled with anger, she set out to find him. She ran after him, calling his name, until finally he answered her, "Yes!" and waited.

Then she said to him, "Con, my dear, let me pick the lice from your hair." And so she loused him.

But as she was lousing him, she caused a great rock to grow up beside him, intending to tip it over and kill him. But Coniraya, in his wisdom, guessing what she had in mind, merely said, "I'll be back in a moment, dear sister. I have to urinate." And with that he escaped to these upland villages.

And here for a long while he remained and played pranks and made fun of many towns and many men.

The Hero as Deliverer

"Killing Alligators." Southeastern
United States. Painted *circa*
1565 by Jacques Le Moyne,
engraved *circa* 1590 by Theodore
De Bry   (*Picture Collection,*
New York Public Library)

If the hero provides culture, he must also deliver the world from the evils that culture entails. The principal evil, death, is treated elsewhere in this collection (especially in the concluding section). Here the choices are limited to four myths whose common theme is aggression, the crime of "eating" others.

THE CANNIBAL DWARFS

ARAPAHO

A man was traveling along the river in search of game. He went up a hill to look for some kind of animal, but he saw that the atmosphere was smoky in the timber. So he walked to the place, and found a tepee by itself. "Somebody is coming, somebody stops at the door, somebody walks from the door, somebody is walking around the tepee, somebody stops at the door and waits for admittance," said someone inside. So this hunter went in and saw a small man sitting alone, and he was blind. "Well! Well! You are the only good person bringing yourself for food," said the dwarf, moving himself and looking up in the air. "Well, yes, I came to deliver myself to you. I am very fat and I know that you will relish the meat with your folks," said the man. "Thank you! that is what I need," said the dwarf. "I suppose you are hungry and ready to take me," said the man. "Oh, no! You may wait until my relatives return," said the dwarf. "All right, I shall wait patiently, but excuse me for a short time," said the man, going out.

This man went and cut a stick, which he sharpened at one end, and went into the tepee with it. "Now, partner, what are these things suspended to the tepee poles?" said the man. "Well, young man, those are hearts belonging to my relatives," said the blind dwarf. "Well, then, partner, can you tell whose heart this is?" said the man, with his sharp stick pointing to one. "That is my father's heart," said the dwarf. The moment he told it to the man, the man punched it with the stick.

The relatives of the dwarf were out after food. When they left him, they cooked the head of a human being for him to eat. When the hunter went in, this dwarf was sitting at the bowl, which had a head, well boiled, with a little soup in it. The dwarf was relishing the soup. The father dropped dead as the visitor thrust the stick into his heart, while they were still away from the tepee looking for human food. It was a very hard blow to the family.

After this man had struck the heart of the father, and so killed him, he then asked the dwarf to whom the next heart belonged. The dwarf said that it belonged to his mother. After the dwarf had spoken the word, the man punched it with a sharp stick; the owner of it dropped, being out and away from the tepee. This man asked the dwarf who were the owners of the different hearts, and pierced them with the sharp stick, until he came to the last one at the door. "Whose heart is this, partner?" said the man. "Well, that is my own heart, partner," said the dwarf. The man pierced it, and the dwarf gave up suddenly and died.

Thus these small people who left their hearts at home while they were out doing mischief were exterminated. They were dwarfs, and their appearance was cruel, and their speech was like that of children.

TWO FRIENDS

GREENLAND ESKIMO

Two friends loved each other very dearly. From childhood they had been constant companions. One lived at one of the outermost islands, and the other had his abode far up, at the head of a fiord. They very often visited each other, and when they had been parted for some days, they felt a mutual longing to meet again.

In the summer the man from the fiord used to go out reindeer hunting in the interior; but before he went back to the place where he lived, he always took a whole reindeer, choosing one of those with velvety horns and leaving all the tallow in it, to regale his friend with. The islander, on his part, saved and laid by large quantities of seals: and when the reindeer hunter returned, he immediately visited his friend and was regaled with nicely dried seal flesh; but in the evening, when the room grew heated, the frozen meat was produced and set before his friend as a cold dish. The guest then praised it very much, and they gossiped till late in the evening. The next day the reindeer hunter usually had a visit from his friend, but now they ate only reindeer flesh, and especially the tallow. The friend found it extremely delicious, and ate till he was ready to burst; and at his departure next day he was presented with some dried meat and tallow.

One autumn the hunter lingered in the interior longer than usual. At length the earth was quite frozen over, and still he did not return. At first the friend longed for him very much, but after a while he grew angry with him; and when the first of the preserved seals began to spoil, they commenced to eat away at the whole lot. Later on, when he heard that the hunter had returned, he went out to a grave and cut a bit of fat from a dead body, and with this he rubbed certain parts of a seal he intended to treat his friend with, in order to do him an evil turn on his arrival.

Shortly afterwards he came to pay his visit. The meeting was very pleasant, and as usual he was regaled with various delicacies; and the hunter now told that he had had small luck in getting the reindeer with velvety horns, and this was the reason why he had stayed away so long; and his friend answered, "I was expecting thee very anxiously for some time, but when my first preserved seals began to rot, we ate them all up"; and he added, "Let us have the one that was last put by; we will have it for a cold dish." It was accordingly brought in and nicely served up, and the host laid the piece that had been rubbed over with the bit of fat uppermost, and set it before his friend, at the same time begging him to partake of it; but just as the visitor was in the act of helping himself to a piece, something from beneath the ledge gave a pull at his leg. This somewhat puzzled him; however, he was going to commence a second time when he got another pull, upon which he said, "I must go outside a little," and rose up at the same time and went.

Being an angakok, he now heard the voice of his guardian spirit warning him, saying, "Thy friend regales thee with a base design; turn the piece over when thou goest back and eat of the opposite part; if thou eatest of the part that is now uppermost, thou wilt be sure to go mad." Having again seated himself, he turned the meat over; but his host thought it might be a mere accident. When the guest had eaten sufficiently, he felt a pain in his stomach—he had probably touched some of the poisoned flesh; but he soon recovered, and on taking leave, he asked his friend to return the visit soon.

When he came home he took a reindeer with velvety horns and treated it in the same manner as his friend had done the seal—rubbing it well with some fat from a dead body; and when his guest came, he instantly regaled him with dried meat and tallow, and never before had the visitor found it so much to his taste. At night the reindeer was set before them with the poisoned side turned up, and putting the knife into it, he said, "There, we have got some cold meat; I have kept it for thee this long while." The friend ate away at it, and several times exclaimed, "This is really delicious!" and the host answered, "Yes, that is because it is so very fat."

When the meal was over, the guest felt a pain in his stomach, and looking hard at everyone present, he got up and went outside, but the pains were not relieved. Next day he took his leave, and it was a long time before his friend saw him again; when he went out kayaking he never met him as he had done formerly. At length, when the ice began to cover the waters, a boat was seen to put into the firth from the sea, and was recognized as being the boat of the friend; but finding that he himself was not of the party, he asked, "Where is your master?" "He is ill, and has turned raving mad; he wanted to eat us, and therefore we all took flight."

On the very next day the hunter went out to visit his friend. Nobody was to be seen about the house; but creeping through the entry and looking over the threshold, he beheld his friend lying on his back, with eyes staring wildly and his head hanging over the edge of the couch. He went up to him and asked him how he did, but no answer was given. After a short silence he suddenly started up and shouted with all his might, "Because thou hast feasted me basely, I have eaten up all the inmates of my house, and I will now devour thee too"—and he bounded towards him; but the other escaped through the entry, and quickly made for his kayak. He only succeeded in pushing off as his pursuer was in the very act of seizing hold of him. The madman now continued running along the shore and crying, "I feel much better now; do come back. When I have not seen thee for a day or two, I am longing dreadfully for thee." On hearing him speak quite sensibly the friend believed him, and put back again. As soon as he reached the shore, however, the former made a rush at him; but happily, observing this, he pushed off in time.

At home he never spoke or ate, out of grief for his friend, and his housemates thought him much altered. Towards night he commenced talking to them of his own accord, and told them how he had fared; but the others advised him not to return any more, being sure the madman would eat him too, if he had the chance. Nevertheless, he paddled away the very next morning *as if compelled to do so*. Then it all happened just as on the former day. The madman pursued him right into the house, and fastened the door, so that he was obliged to get out through the window, and he barely escaped to his kayak.

The day after, they again tried to detain him; but he was bent upon going. He entered his friend's house and found him worse than before: this time he was lying with his head on the floor and his heels resting on the edge of the bench; his eyes were far protruded and staring wildly, and the bone of his nose as sharp as a knife's edge. When his former friend approached, he started up and pursued him around the room, always crying, "I am starving; I must have thee for food." At last the friend succeeded in jumping out of the window, and reached his kayak; but no sooner had he got clear of the shore than he saw the madman walking on the surface of the water, ready to seize hold of the prow of his kayak. He now began swinging to and fro in his kayak, and by this means ripples were formed, so that the madman could not steady himself but was very nearly falling. Thus he once more escaped him.

The day after, his housemates again wanted to detain him, but he answered them, "When I have not seen my friend for a whole day, I am ready to die with longing, and cannot desist from going to him." Having arrived at the house of his friend, he found it to be deserted; he searched about everywhere, but did not find him. Outside he observed some footprints winding up hills, and following them, he stopped at a cave in the rock. Here his friend was sitting bent together and much shrunk. As he did not move, his friend went up to him and, on trying to lift him up, found him to be quite dead and his eyelids filled with blood. He now carefully covered and closed up the entrance of the cave, and was henceforth friendless.

HOW THE FOG CAME

SMITH SOUND ESKIMO

Again, in a tiny myth from northern Greenland, eating is equated with aggression; and in the Seneca legend that follows it, the verbs "to eat" and "to make war" are used interchangeably. But it must be noted that eating has other symbolic meanings, which, if related, are related only distantly. In the story of Raven (p. 168), uncontrollable eating is associated with starvation; in "The Buffalo Wife" (p. 209), eating, as in so many myths, is equated with coitus; in "The Hungry Old Woman" (p. 173), it becomes the symbolic manifestation of a "devouring" woman, with overtones of dangerous maternal sexuality. Here, in the second half of a myth that begins with a too-aggressive father (who "eats" people), the dangerous mother returns, this time in a variant of the classic "magic flight," in which the three obstacles (the hills, the water, and the tip of the garment) are remotely reminiscent of the female genitalia. Having rid himself of the father, the hero finds that the mother is available. If he desires her, he also fears her. He flees—and escapes.

There was a Mountain Spirit that stole corpses from their graves and ate them when it came home. And a man, wishing to see who did this thing, let himself be buried alive. The Spirit came, and saw the new grave, and dug up the body, and carried it off.

The man had stuck a flat stone in under his coat, in case the Spirit should try to stab him.

On the way, he caught hold of all the willow twigs whenever they passed any bushes, and made himself as heavy as he could, so that the Spirit was forced to put forth all its strength.

At last the Spirit reached its house, and flung down the body on the floor. And then, being weary, it lay down to sleep, while its wife went out to gather wood for the cooking.

"Father, Father, he is opening his eyes," cried the children, when the dead man suddenly looked up.

"Nonsense, children, it is a dead body, which I have dropped many times among the twigs on the way," said the father.

But the man rose up, and killed the Mountain Spirit and its children and fled away as fast as he could. The Mountain Spirit's wife saw him and mistook him for her husband.

"Where are you going?" she cried.

The man did not answer, but fled on. And the woman, thinking something must be wrong, ran after him.

And as he was running over level ground, he cried: "Rise up, hills!"

And at once many hills rose up.

Then the Mountain Spirit's wife lagged behind, having to climb up so many hills.

The man saw a little stream, and sprang across.

"Flow over your banks!" he cried to the stream. And now it was impossible for her to get across.

"How did you get across?" cried the woman.

"I drank up the water. Do likewise."

And the woman began gulping it down.

Then the man turned round towards her, and said: "Look at the tail of your tunic; it is hanging down between your legs."

And when she bent down to look, her belly burst.

And as she burst, a stream rose up out of her, and turned to fog, which still floats about to this day among the hills.

HIAWATHA

SENECA

In other versions of this famous story, Deganawidah is the thinker, Hiawatha the doer. Here the roles are reversed (Hiawatha and Deganawidah are twin aspects of a single personality), and the cannibal motif, employed in at least one variant, is replaced by an equally vivid image: the human mind as a nest of snakes.

Where the Mohawk River empties into the Hudson, in ancient times there was a Mohawk village. The people there were fierce and warlike and were continually sending out war parties against other settlements and, returning, would bring back long strings of scalps to number the lives they had destroyed. But sometimes they left their own scalps behind and never returned. They loved warfare better than all other things and were happy when their hands were slimy with blood. They boasted that they would eat up all other nations, and so they continued to go against other tribes and fight with them.

Now among the Mohawks, there was a chief named Deganawidah, a very wise man, and he was very sad of heart because his people loved war too well. So he spoke in council and implored them to desist lest they perish altogether, but the young warriors would not hear him and laughed at his words; but he did not cease to warn them until at last, despairing of moving them by ordinary means, he turned his face to the west and wept as he journeyed onward and away from his people. At length he reached a lake whose shores were fringed with bushes, and being tired he lay down to rest. Presently, as he lay meditating, he heard the soft spattering of water sliding from a skillful paddle, and peering out from his hiding place, he saw in the red light of sunset a man leaning over his canoe and dipping into the shallow water with a basket. When he raised it up, it was full of shells, the shells of the periwinkles that live in shallow pools. The man pushed his canoe toward the shore and sat down on the beach, where he kindled a fire. Then he began to string his shells and, finishing a string, would touch the shells and talk. Then, as if satisfied, he would lay it down and make another until he had a large number. Deganawidah watched the strange proceeding with wonder. The sun had long since set, but Deganawidah still watched the man with the shell strings sitting in the flickering light of the fire that shadowed the bushes and shimmered over the lake.

After some deliberation he called out, "Kwa, I am a friend!" and, stepping out upon the sand, stood before the man with the shells. "I am Deganawidah," he said, "and come from the Mohawk."

"I am Hiawatha of the Onondaga," came the reply.

Then Deganawidah inquired about the shell strings, for he was very curious to know their import, and Hiawatha answered, "They are the rules of life and the laws of good government. This all-white string is a sign of truth, peace, and good will; this black string is a sign of hatred, of war, and of a bad heart; the string with the alternate beads, black and white, is a sign that peace should exist between the nations. This string with white on either end and black in the middle is a sign that wars must end and peace be declared." And so Hiawatha lifted his strings and read the laws.

Then said Deganawidah: "You are my friend indeed, and the friend of all nations. Our people are weak from warring and weak from being warred upon. We who speak one tongue should combine against the Hadiondas instead of helping them by killing one another, but my people are weary of my advising and would not hear me."

"I, too, am of the same mind," said Hiawatha, "but Atotarho slew all my brothers and drove me away. So I came to the lakes and have made the laws that should govern men and nations. I believe that we should be as brothers in a family instead of enemies."

"Then come with me," said Deganawidah, "and together let us go back to my people and explain the rules and laws."

So when they had returned, Deganawidah called a council of all the chiefs and warriors and the women, and Hiawatha set forth the plan he had devised. The words had a marvelous effect. The people were astonished at the wisdom of the strange chief from the Onondaga, and when he had finished his exposition, the chiefs promised obedience to his laws. They delegated Deganawidah to go with him to the Oneida and council with them, then go onward to Onondaga and win

over the arrogant, erratic Atotarho, the tyrannical chief of the
Onondaga. Thus it was that together they went to the Oneida
country and won over their great chief and made the people
promise to support the proposed league. Then the Oneida
chief went with Hiawatha to the Cayugas and told them how,
by supporting the league, they might preserve themselves
against the fury of Atotarho. So when the Cayugas had promised allegiance, Deganawidah turned his face toward Onondaga and with his comrades went before Atotarho. Now when
Atotarho learned how three nations had combined against
him, he became very angry and ran into the forest, where he
gnawed at his fingers and ate grass and leaves. His evil
thoughts became serpents and sprouted from his skull and,
waving in a tangled mass, hissed out venom. But Deganawidah did not fear him and once more asked him to give his
consent to a league of peace and friendship; but he was still
wild until Hiawatha combed the snakes from his head and
told him that he should be the head chief of the confederacy
and govern it according to the laws that Hiawatha had made.
Then he recovered from his madness and asked why the
Seneca had not been visited, for the Seneca outnumbered all
the other nations and were fearless warriors. "If their jeal-
ousy is aroused," he said, "they will eat us."

Then the delegations visited the Seneca and the other
nations to the west, but only the Seneca would consider the
proposal. The other nations were exceedingly jealous.

Thus a peace pact was made and the Long House built;
and Deganawidah was the builder, but Hiawatha was its
designer.

Now, moreover, the first council of Hiawatha and Deganawidah was in a place now called Albany at the mouth of a
small stream that empties into the Hudson.

Comedy of Horrors

"Hunting Signal of the
Assiniboins." Painted in
1833 by Karl Bodmer, engraved
circa 1840 by Karl Vogel
(*Kennedy Galleries, New York*)

In these harsh little trickster tales, the hero becomes an anti-hero and the narrator permits himself to smile at sadistic impulses:

THE FOX

BLACKFOOT

One day Old Man went out hunting and took the fox with him. They hunted for several days, but killed nothing. It was nice warm weather in the late fall. After they had become very hungry, as they were going along one day, Old Man went up over a ridge and on the other side he saw four big buffalo bulls lying down; but there was no way by which they could get near them. He dodged back out of sight and told the fox what he had seen, and they thought for a long time, to see if there was no way by which these bulls might be killed.

At last Old Man said to the fox: "My little brother, I can

think of only one way to get these bulls. This is my plan, if you agree to it. I will pluck all the fur off you except one tuft on the end of your tail. Then you go over the hill and walk up and down in sight of the bulls, and you will seem so funny to them that they will laugh themselves to death."

The fox did not like to do this, but he could think of nothing better, so he agreed to what Old Man proposed. Old Man plucked him perfectly bare, except the end of his tail, and the fox went over the ridge and walked up and down. When he had come close to the bulls, he played around and walked on his hind legs and went through all sorts of antics. When the bulls first saw him, they got up on their feet and looked at him. They did not know what to make of him. Then they began to laugh, and the more they looked at him, the more they laughed, until at last one by one they fell down exhausted and died. Then Old Man came over the hill, and went down to the bulls, and began to butcher them. By this time it had grown a little colder.

"Ah, little brother," said Old Man to the fox, "you did splendidly. I do not wonder that the bulls laughed themselves to death. I nearly died myself as I watched you from the hill. You looked very funny." While he was saying this, he was working away skinning off the hides and getting the meat ready to carry to camp, all the time talking to the fox, who stood about, his back humped up and his teeth chattering with the cold. Now a wind sprang up from the north and a few snowflakes were flying in the air. It was growing colder and colder. Old Man kept on talking, and every now and then he would say something to the fox, who was sitting behind him perfectly still, with his jaw shoved out and his teeth shining.

At last Old Man had the bulls all skinned and the meat cut

up, and as he rose up he said: "It is getting pretty cold, isn't it? Well, we do not care for the cold. We have got all our winter's meat, and we will have nothing to do but feast and dance and sing until spring." The fox made no answer. Then Old Man got angry and called out, "Why don't you answer me? Don't you hear me talking to you?" The fox said nothing. Then Old Man was mad, and he said "Can't you speak?" and stepped up to the fox and gave him a push with his foot, and the fox fell over. He was dead, frozen stiff with the cold.

JUAN TUL

MAYA

The flavor of this tale is unquestionably indigenous, even though some or all of its incidents may have been borrowed from Old World lore.

Squirrel Woman was passing through the woods one day when she heard moans issuing from the depths of a cave. Wondering what poor creature might be in need of help, she went inside and found Juan Tul standing on his hind legs, holding up the roof of the cave with his forepaws.

"What is it?" she asked.

"Oh, Mother! The roof of the cave is about to fall. If I let go, I'll be crushed to death. But if I stand here much longer, I'll die of hunger. Oh, if only you knew how weary I am!"

The squirrel was compassionate.

"Mother, your heart is good. Pity me, and take my place for only a few minutes while I rest."

Squirrel Woman agreed and, placing her hands above her head, began holding the roof.

"Mother, thank you! Now let me go out for a moment and get something to eat. I'll be right back. Remember to keep the roof up, or it'll fall and kill you."

The squirrel stood fast, and as the rabbit turned to leave she urged him to come back with a few sticks so that together they might prop the roof and both be free. The rabbit promised to do so. But as it happened, he did not return.

Squirrel Woman grew tired and at long last, thinking how she might have been tricked, gradually relaxed her hold. Perhaps a little dust sifted down. Nothing more. Angrily she left the cave in search of the rabbit, intending to berate him for having treated her so badly. She walked and walked, and after a while she met him again, this time lazing in a patch of high grass. He tried to hide, but didn't have time.

"So I've found you," said the squirrel, and she began to berate him.

"Mother, you must be mistaken. You're thinking of someone else. I never stray from home, and I know nothing about a cave. At the moment I'm trying to get together some thatch for my master's new roof, but if I ever catch this other rabbit you're talking about, I'll give him the beating he deserves."

The squirrel hesitated, but after she had thought about it, she realized that it was indeed possible to confuse one rabbit with another. Meanwhile, Juan Tul had piled up a big bundle of grass. When he went to lift it, he pretended he couldn't.

"Heavy!" he cried. Then, calling out to the squirrel: "You're a good woman. You won't mind giving me some help. Come, we'll split this bundle in half. My master will be grateful to you. He's a decent man. You'll get a reward."

The squirrel consented. Then Juan Tul put half the bundle on her shoulders, set fire to it, and ran away.

Squirrel Woman cried for help, but no one came. She wished she had never listened to the rabbit, for now she could have no doubt as to who he was. At last she succeeded in putting out the fire. Then she went on her way, sore from her burns, thinking how she would punish Juan Tul if she ever met him again.

And she did meet him again. There he was, hanging on to the end of a vine, going up and down, up and down.

"Devil vine, shrink!" he would say, and the vine would shorten, pulling him up to the top of the tree. "Devil vine, stretch!" And then it would lengthen and carry him back to the ground. He pretended not to notice Squirrel Woman and went on with his game.

The squirrel was angry. "You won't fool me again, rabbit. As soon as I catch hold of that vine, you're going to get a whipping."

"Oh no, you have the wrong rabbit!" he cried. But the squirrel would not be dissuaded. The moment the end of the vine touched the ground, she seized it and started to yank it loose to make a whip. But Juan Tul quickly jumped off and gave the order "Shrink!"

At once the poor squirrel was drawn to the top of the tree by the shrinking vine. Not knowing the words to command it, she was unable to make it descend. The rabbit ran and hid.

At last she climbed down. Then she set out in earnest to get her revenge.

Juan Tul was watching from not far away. He ran on for some distance, then allowed himself to be seen. The squirrel pursued him. But he ran faster than she. Again he showed himself. Again she pursued. And again and again.

Squirrel Woman was tired and thirsty. Then Juan Tul hid once again and made her something to drink. He made balche. He poured it into a gourd and, smearing his face with balche leaves so as not to be recognized, he stepped back onto the path and waited.

Squirrel Woman came along. She did not recognize him disguised. She said, "Tell me, my friend, have you seen Juan Rabbit? Has he come this way?"

"Oh, I wouldn't know. I don't know any rabbit by that name. This is the first I've heard of him."

Squirrel Woman was exhausted and nearly dying of thirst. She saw the drinking gourd and begged for water.

"I haven't much left but—here, I can't bear to see you suffer."

The squirrel raised it to her lips and began to gulp. She immediately realized that what she was drinking was not water. But it was too late. She had swallowed the balche and now it was making her drunk. Then the rabbit wiped the disguise from his face and mocked her, saying, "Come, my dear, punish me if you can."

The squirrel could barely stand. Moments later she fell to the ground in a drunken sleep. When she awoke, Juan Tul had disappeared.

Unwilling to admit defeat, Squirrel Woman set out once again in pursuit of the rabbit, who meanwhile had come to a pool where the water was cold and sweet. Climbing to the top of a post near the water's edge, he settled himself and waited. It was not long before Squirrel Woman arrived.

Without looking up, and so failing to notice Juan Tul, she went straight to the pool to drink. But there in the water she saw his reflection, and mistaking it for the rabbit himself, she cried, "You won't escape me now!" and she jumped in after him.

But he wasn't there. Then she thought he must have dived to the bottom. Quickly she calculated that if the rabbit could do it without drowning, she could do it too. She plunged to the bottom. But the depth was too great.

Squirrel Woman drowned as Juan Tul laughed from the top of his post. Then at last she was dead.

HOW HE GOT TONGUE

CHEYENNE

Wihio was living in his home, and not far away was a camp of people. One day he had nothing to eat, and no way to kill anything; so he paid a visit to one of his neighbors, hoping that he would be asked to eat with him.

When Wihio stepped into the lodge he saw that there was plenty of food there—dried meat and back fat and tongues. Every time the man went out he killed an elk, and when he did so he took the tongue out and saved it, and tongues hung all about his lodge. Wihio longed for the tongues, but the man did not offer him any; he just gave him some dried meat.

As Wihio was returning to his lodge, he saw a coyote not far
off, and called to him asking him to come in.

When the coyote had sat down, Wihio told him about what
he had seen in the man's lodge, and he asked the coyote to go
there with him again, so they might eat there.

The coyote thought the man would not let him come in,
because everyone knows that coyotes always steal meat.

"Well," said Wihio, "let us arrange some plan by which
you can come. What can we do? How can we get in?" The
coyote thought for a long time, and at last he told Wihio how
they might do what they wished to. The coyote said, "You
dress up like a woman, and tie me up like a baby, and carry
me there. Give me good things to eat when you get the meat."

"Ah," said Wihio, "it is good. I will give you a part of
everything that is given to me." Then he began to tie up the
coyote like a baby, so that he could carry him. After he had
done so, he took up the coyote on his arm like a baby, and
went back to the lodge and said to the man, "My child is
crying for food." Wihio whispered to the coyote to cry for
tongue, and he did so. The man asked Wihio what the baby
wanted, and Wihio said, "He is crying for tongue." The man
took a tongue and put it in the water and boiled it.

After the tongue was cooked the man gave it to Wihio, who
began to eat, and gave the coyote only just a taste of it.
Wihio ate all he could, for he was hungry. The coyote kept
whispering to him, "Give me some too, I am hungry"; but
Wihio continued to eat, and just dipped his fingers in the
soup and let the coyote lick them. At last the coyote grew
angry and said, "I am going to tell him about you, that you
have dressed me up like a baby in order to get some
tongue."

Wihio kept on eating very fast, and gave the coyote none

of the tongue, and at last went out of the lodge, carrying the baby. He went to the river, and said to the coyote, "You were going to tell about me, were you? You ought to keep quiet when I am eating; you trouble me too much." Then he threw the coyote, all tied up, into the river, and he floated down the stream.

THE BUFFALO WIFE

OKANAGON

This tale is a parody of the widespread culture myth, known through countless variants, in which a hero brings food to his people by making the food animal his bride. Rather than "setting the world in order," this anti-hero sets the world in disorder, causing the buffalo to be unequally distributed.

Coyote was traveling about, and went northward from the Salish to the Blackfoot country. He found the skeleton of an old buffalo bull. He urinated on the skull and passed on. Presently he heard a noise like wind behind him. He looked back, but saw nothing. The noise grew louder, and he looked again. He saw a buffalo bull approaching at full speed.

It was the bull whose skull he had insulted. Coyote ran away, but the buffalo gained on him. He saw a large boulder and ran for it. He ran round and round the stone, the buffalo at his heels. Coyote was exhausted, and shouted, "Why do you chase me?" The buffalo replied, "Because you urinated on my head while I was dead."

Coyote said, "What killed you?" Buffalo answered, "I became old, and a younger bull killed me. My horns were dull." Coyote said, "If you will promise not to hurt me, I will sharpen your horns after I have had a rest."

Buffalo stopped. Coyote gathered pitchy roots of the yellow pine, which have sharp points, and attached them to the ends of Buffalo's horns. Then he told him to go to an old log and toss it. He said, "Go and try that old log; and if you can toss it without breaking the points of your horns, they are strong enough. If they break, I will make them over."

Buffalo did as directed, and his horns stood the test. He was very glad, and said to Coyote, "I will be your friend. I have been dead a long time. My *snahauq,* who took my wives, is somewhere around. Let us go and find him! I will kill him and take back the women, and will give some of them to you."

Coyote was glad, and agreed to go with him. On the plain they found Buffalo's enemy surrounded by a band of women. Buffalo said, "That is he, and these are all my wives. Hide here, and I will go and fight him. If he overcomes me, you must run away, for he will kill you if he sees you. If I vanquish him, then come to me."

Buffalo ran forward, and attacked the bull and tore him in two. Coyote went to Buffalo, who said, "Friend, pick out one of these women, whichever you like." Coyote replied, "Pick out a fat one for me. My home is far away, and she will get thin while traveling with me." Buffalo picked out a very fat one, and said, "This one will be your wife. You must not sleep with her for three nights. After that everything will be well, and you may do as you wish."

Coyote started homeward with his new wife. The second night he said to himself, "The time that he named is too long. No one since the beginning of the world has had a wife for three nights without sleeping with her." He seized his wife, and would have had connection with her, but she became invisible and returned to her band.

Coyote thought she must have gone home, so he went back. He found Buffalo-Bull, and said to him, "My wife did not like me; the second night she ran away." He did not tell Buffalo that he had disobeyed his orders. Buffalo was angry and said, "Your wife is here. You did not treat her right. You did not do what I told you. However, since you are my friend, I will give her back to you. Now, you must remember, three days." This time was sufficient to cross the mountains. Coyote was going to the Upper Kutenai or Pend d'Oreille country. He abstained for three nights; then he lay with his wife, and was glad.

On the succeeding day he was hungry. He looked at his wife, and thought how fat she was. He said to himself, "My wife is only a trouble to me. I will kill and eat her." He said to her. "Go up that defile. I will go around the other way hunting." Coyote ran around the hill, and met his wife as she came up the defile. From above he shot her twice, and killed her.

Now, he cut her up, and found that she was very fat. He spread out the skin, and thought what a fine robe it would make. He felt like defecating, and went off some little distance. He tried, but could not do so. He tried hard, and thought he would burst, but nothing came. He felt of himself, and noticed that his anus was swollen. He was seized with violent pains and could not stand up. Then Magpie came, and alighted on the carcass of the buffalo cow.

Coyote called Magpie bad names, but he paid no attention. Then Eagle, Buzzard, and Raven came, and all the other birds that eat meat. Wolf came, and all the animals that eat meat, and they ate the buffalo cow. Coyote could not defend himself. He only called them nasty names. The birds and animals picked the bones clean and scattered them. Then Wolverine came, stuck his head into the pelvic bones, and ran away with them.

Now Coyote defecated dung about one third the length of a finger. He was angry at his excrement, put it on a rock, and beat it flat with a stick. He said, "You have done this. You have made me lose all the fine meat." He looked for the skin and scraps, but not a bit was left. He looked for bones, but there were none. He followed the animals' tracks and found some bones. Then he made a fire, and cooked and broke the bones. He had found his wife's bladder, and put the marrow into it. There was just enough to fill it. He tied it up and set it aside to cool off. He lay down and said, "I will watch it; and when it has cooled off, I will eat it."

Three or four times he got up and looked at it, but it had not cooled off yet. He said, "I will put it into water." He took it to a small lake, and put it into the water, but it would not stiffen. He saw a muskrat swimming about. He said to it, "Take hold of the mouth of this bladder and swim with it to deep water, so that it cools, and the fat sets." He put his foot down suddenly, and scared Muskrat, who ducked his head under water. He thought this was great fun, and said, "When he comes back, I will have some more fun."

When Muskrat returned, he stamped his foot again. Muskrat ducked his head suddenly and tore the bladder. All the marrow ran out.

Coyote ran into the water to catch the marrow with his hands and eat it, but he caught only water. He became angry, took a stick, and jumped into the water to punish Muskrat; but the latter ran into his house, and Coyote could not catch him. The foolish Coyote had lost both his wife and his meat.

Had he been wise and carried his wife home, there would now be buffaloes all over the Okanagon country, and probably throughout the Thompson and Shuswap countries as well.

Buffaloes do not go farther west than the place where Coyote killed his wife. When the western Indians wanted buffalo, they had to go east and hunt them. Otherwise they had to buy robes. Buffaloes were plentiful in the Salish country, but hardly ever went as far west as the country of the Coeur d'Alène and Kalispel. Since the marrow was spilled on the water, some lakes have on their surface oil, or something that appears like oil.

Jaguar and Fox

Jaguar. Drawn and engraved by
C. G. Specht, from John George
Wood's *Our Living World*, 1885,
Vol. 1

Tales of the following sort have often been published in Latin—or have not been published at all—in order to prevent them from falling into the hands of the merely curious. In the words of a native informant, "A man is careful when he tells these stories, and if he sees that his sister is present, he skips this kind."

OLD-MAN-COYOTE AND THE STRAWBERRY

CROW

One day Old-Man-Coyote came down to the river valley and was eating wild strawberries from a bush, when he saw four women coming toward him. He quickly transferred himself under the earth, beneath the strawberry bush, and caused his penis to project up into the bush among the strawberries.

When the women came along to the bush where Old-Man-Coyote was concealed, they began to pick and eat the strawberries. One of them tried to pick the head of the penis for a strawberry, and as she could not pluck it, she stooped over and tried to bite it off. She called out to her companions, who also tried to pluck it but could not. So they determined to cut it off and take it home, and began to hunt for a sharp piece of flint. But when they got back to the bush, the strawberry had disappeared. Then they declared it to have been Old-Man-Coyote who had done this.

They then agreed to retaliate and watched Old-Man-Coyote all the time, until one day they saw him coming through the woods. Then they quickly disrobed and made their noses bleed by hitting themselves, and took the blood and smeared it over their bodies to make it appear as though they had been murdered, and laid themselves down on the grass, all spread out.

Old-Man-Coyote soon found them in this condition and exclaimed, "How came they here, these pretty things!" and then went over and touched their breasts and felt all over them and put his hand on their vulvas to find out, by smelling, how long they had been lying there, and he said, "They must have been dead for a long time, because they smell so badly." Then he turned away, and had gone but a short distance when the women got up and laughingly told him they had retaliated for what he had done to them.

OLD-MAN-COYOTE AND THE MOUSE

CROW

The young women were dancing, and the young men were looking on. There was a good-looking young woman. She said, "Young men, expose your penises!" She wished to marry the one with the smallest penis.

Old-Man-Coyote heard this and started to come over. He met a little mouse. "My dear younger brother, give me your little penis." He took it: he put on the mouse's and gave the mouse his own. Then all the young men removed their loincloths and stood toward the young woman, who saw them all. Old-Man-Coyote's penis was very small. The young woman said, "That one is very small. I'll marry him." "Very well," they said.

Then they said, "Say! This person's penis is enormous! Look at it!" Then they all turned around. The mouse was dragging along Old-Man-Coyote's penis, covered with dust. They asked him, "How can this be? Your penis is huge, but your body is small. Your penis is bigger than you are." They teased him endlessly. They poked at his penis. He felt like running away. "But this isn't mine!"

"Whose is it, then?"

"It's First-Worker's. He took mine off with him. This is his. I'm trying to walk with it, but it's no use. I can't even drag it."

They called out, "Hey, First-Worker! Little-Penis! You wanted to get married, didn't you! Come now, this is your penis."

He came; he came on over. There was his penis, covered with dust. It was huge. Then he said to the mouse, "Let's go!" They went to a little gully, and there he took back his penis. Then he knocked down that little creature and killed it; it lay there shivering.

The young women learned about it. They ran off in different directions. Then Old-Man-Coyote ran away again.

JAGUAR AND FOX

MUNDURUCÚ

A jaguar met a fox carrying a vine. He asked him where he was going, and the fox replied, "A storm is coming up. I'm looking for someone who will tie me to a tree so I won't be blown away." Then the dull-witted jaguar said, "Tie me up first!" So the fox tied him up, tying his hand to his anus, just to be mean, and walked away.

A wasp flew by. The jaguar begged to be set free, but the wasp, though he tried, was unable to bite through the vine. His teeth were not sharp enough.

Then along came a squirrel, who succeeded where the wasp had failed. When he had freed the jaguar, he said to him, "Now you must eat the fox. He likes to sleep in a hollow tree or in among bushes. You'll catch him there." So the jaguar set out.

He came to a hollow tree and hid inside it. But the fox was wary. He was on the lookout. He came up slowly and called out twice, "Hollow tree!" But neither the first time nor the second time did the tree give any answer. "Now I know someone's there," said the fox. "When it doesn't answer, it means someone's inside. It only answers when no one's there." He called once more, and the dull-witted jaguar answered, "What is it?" Then the fox ran away.

The next day the jaguar hid himself in the bushes. The fox came along in the afternoon, and to see if anyone was lying in wait for him, he called out, "Bushes!" No answer. He called again. Again no answer. "Now I know someone's hiding in the bushes," said the fox. "When they don't answer, it means someone's inside. They only answer when no one's there." He called once more, and the dull-witted jaguar answered, "What is it?" Then the fox ran away.

Now the jaguar thought he would catch the fox at his drinking place. So he hid himself there. But, as always, the fox was wary. He had been eating honey and he smeared himself with it and rolled on the ground until he was all covered with dry leaves.

He went to the stream. Slowly he approached. The jaguar caught sight of him and marveled. "This must be a chief of the Leafy Beasts," said the jaguar. "My grandfather used to tell stories about them."

The fox slaked his thirst. Then he jumped into the water and ducked under and the leaves came off his coat. When he came back up, the jaguar recognized the fox. He started after him, but couldn't catch him.

"I'll never catch the fox," said the jaguar. Then the other animals advised him to play dead. He did, and the animals wailed and called out to others, so they could weep too. The fox was among them.

Slowly he drew near. "Is the jaguar really dead?" he asked. "Yes," they said. But the fox wouldn't believe it, and he said to himself, "Just before he died, my grandfather blew one last fart." Then the others whispered in the jaguar's ear, "Blow a fart." The jaguar farted and the fox ran away.

And so the dull-witted jaguar was never able to catch the crafty fox.

TURTLE AND FOX

ANAMBÉ

One day as Turtle was playing his flute, Fox came close to listen.

"Lend me your flute," he said.

"No," said Turtle, "you'd keep it."

"Well, then let me hear you play."

Turtle began to play: [narrator sings in a mocking voice] "fah-fah-coulo-faw-fah."

"Turtle, you play beautifully! Now can't I try?"

"Here," said Turtle, "but don't run off with it. If you do, you'll be sorry."

Fox took the flute, tried it, and began to dance. Delighted, he ran off with it.

Turtle started after him but stumbled and flipped over on his back. "Just wait!" he said. "I'll catch up with you by and by!"

Then Turtle went off through the forest and came to the edge of a river. He cut some wood, built a bridge, and on the opposite bank felled a tree that had a nest of bees in it. He took out the honey and went back and positioned himself along Fox's path. He hid his face in the leaves and daubed his anus with the honey. Soon Fox came along.

·"Uh-oh! What's this?" he said, seeing the honey shining there. He stuck his finger in and tasted it. "It's honey!"

Just then another fox, who happened to be passing by, cried, "Come now! That's Turtle's anus!"

"No, no. It's honey. It really is." Then he greedily stuck in his tongue—and Turtle squeezed his anus shut.

"Turtle! Let go of my tongue!" cried Fox.

"So!" retorted the other fox. "Wasn't I right? I told you what it was, but you kept saying 'No, no. It's honey.' "

"Aha!" said Turtle. "What did I tell you? I've got you now, haven't I! And you so clever! Now, where is my flute?"

"Turtle, I haven't got it!"

"You lie. Give me my flute, now! Or I'll squeeze harder."

Then Fox gave Turtle his flute.

COYOTE AND WREN

UPPER COWLITZ

Though a small bird, the wren has a rather long bill (and a melodious call). For this reason mythmakers occasionally give Wren the role assigned to the flute-playing turtle in the preceding story. In the tale that follows, Wren's special attribute appears in a somewhat different guise.

A number of people were living there. They gathered food, they did it well, the women felt proud. They went down to the water, because it was a warm day. The sun was shining, they went into the water, the five unmarried girls went into the water for a swim.

Coyote himself traveled in that direction. As he was going along, he saw the women in swimming, from the opposite side. He stepped upon and made a hole in a large rock. He thrust his penis across the stream towards the women, but it was too short, not long enough, he was unable to do it, he gave it up.

He went on, he went on and saw Wren, he reached him. Wren said, "How are you, younger brother? What are you doing? What do you want?"

"I want to borrow that soft basket with your long penis coiled up in it. I would like to take it here and there today."

Wren said, "No. You would make my penis hungry."

"Oh no. I would give it food."

Wren said, "Very well then," and he gave it to Coyote, he loaned it to him.

The brave Coyote carried it away, he reached the place where he had been. "The unmarried girls are bathing there now," he said. He sat down, he thrust it across the stream there to the eldest of the women. He did it: now that was how it became tight in her.

When she took it, the woman said, "Oh, it's become nice in the water." But after an hour she became tired and cold. The people told her to cut it off. Someone went, obtained a knife, and cut at it. It was a bad knife, it did not cut through at all. A bird flew by and told them to cut it off with sharp grass. Then someone went and cut it through with sharp grass. Part of it shrank back toward Coyote, part of it in the other direction. The woman pulled it out of the water, she carried it towards home.

Coyote himself went on. He returned it to Wren's soft basket. Wren said, "This penis of mine has become hungry." Wren went on, he took an axe, he chipped off small pieces of bark from medium-sized fir trees, he fed them to it, but it would not eat. He said, "The rascal, Coyote! He has killed my penis!" He looked at it, he examined it closely. It had been cut through, it was dead.

Ghosts

"Chinook Burial." Painted by
J. M. Stanley, engraved by J. D.
Smillie, published in Henry Rowe
Schoolcraft's *Indian Tribes*,
Vol. 6, 1857

The dead are lamented, but they are also feared. Their power is to be avoided, yet it must be utilized. The various possibilities are explored in five quite different tales, all from North America.

THE TWO JEEBI-UG

CHIPPEWA

There lived a hunter in the North who had a wife and one child. His lodge stood far off in the forest, several days' journey from any other. He spent his days in hunting and his evenings in relating to his wife the incidents that had befallen him. As game was very abundant he found no difficulty in killing as much as they wanted. Just in all his acts, he lived a peaceful and happy life.

One evening during the winter season, it chanced that he remained out later than usual, and his wife began to feel uneasy, for fear some accident had befallen him. It was already dark. She listened attentively and at last heard the sound of approaching footsteps. Not doubting it was her husband, she went to the door and beheld two strange females. She bade them enter, and invited them to remain.

She observed that they were total strangers in the country. There was something so peculiar in their looks, air, and manner that she was uneasy in their company. They would not come near the fire; they sat in a remote part of the lodge, were shy and taciturn, and drew their garments about them in such a manner as nearly to hide their faces. So far as she could judge, they were pale, hollow-eyed, and long-visaged, very thin and emaciated. There was but little light in the lodge, as the fire was low, and served by its fitful flashes rather to increase than dispel their fears. "Merciful spirit!" cried a voice from the opposite part of the lodge, "there are two corpses clothed with garments." The hunter's wife turned around, but seeing nobody, she concluded the sounds were but gusts of wind. She trembled, and was ready to sink to the earth.

Her husband at this moment entered and dispelled her fears. He threw down the carcass of a large fat deer. "Behold what a fine and fat animal," cried the mysterious females, and they immediately ran and pulled off pieces of the whitest fat, which they ate with greediness. The hunter and his wife looked on with astonishment, but remained silent. They supposed their guests might have been famished. Next day, however, the same unusual conduct was repeated. The strange females tore off the fat and devoured it with eagerness. The third day the hunter thought he would anticipate their wants by tying up a portion of the fattest pieces for them, which he placed on the top of his load. They accepted it, but still appeared dissatisfied, and went to the wife's portion and tore off more. The man and his wife felt surprised at such rude and unaccountable conduct, but they remained silent, for they respected their guests, and had observed that they had been attended with marked good luck during the residence of these mysterious visitors.

In other respects the deportment of the females was strictly unexceptionable. They were modest, distant, and silent. They never uttered a word during the day. At night they would occupy themselves in procuring wood, which they carried to the lodge, and then, returning the implements exactly to the places in which they had found them, resume their places without speaking. They were never known to stay out until daylight. They never laughed or jested.

The winter had nearly passed away, without anything uncommon happening, when, one evening, the hunter stayed out very late. The moment he entered and laid down his day's hunt as usual before his wife, the two females began to tear off the fat, in so unceremonious a way that her anger was excited. She constrained herself, however, in a measure, but did not conceal her feelings, although she said but little. The guests observed the excited state of her mind, and became unusually reserved and uneasy. The good hunter saw the change, and carefully inquired into the cause, but his wife denied having used any hard words. They retired to their couches, and he tried to compose himself to sleep, but could not, for the sobs and sighs of the two females were incessant. He arose on his couch and addressed them as follows:

"Tell me," said he, "what is it that gives you pain of mind, and causes you to utter those sighs. Has my wife given you offense, or trespassed on the rights of hospitality?"

They replied in the negative. "We have been treated by you with kindness and affection. It is not for any slight we have received that we weep. Our mission is not to you only. We come from the land of the dead to test mankind, and to try the sincerity of the living. Often we have heard the bereaved by death say that if the dead could be restored, they would devote their lives to make them happy. We have been moved by the bitter lamentations which have reached the place of the dead, and have come to make proof of the sincerity of those who have lost friends. Three moons were allotted us by the Master of Life to make the trial. More than half the time had been successfully passed when the angry feelings of your wife indicated the irksomeness you felt at our presence, and has made us resolve on our departure."

They continued to talk to the hunter and his wife, gave them instructions as to a future life, and pronounced a blessing upon them.

"There is one point," they added, "of which we wish to speak. You have thought our conduct very strange in rudely possessing ourselves of the choicest parts of your hunt. *That* was the point of trial selected to put you to. It is the wife's peculiar privilege. For another to usurp it, we knew to be the severest trial of her, and consequently of your temper and feelings. We know your manners and customs, but we came to prove you, not by a compliance with them, but by a violation of them. Pardon us. We are the agents of him who sent us. Peace to your dwelling, adieu!"

When they ceased, total darkness filled the lodge. No object could be seen. The inmates heard the door open and shut, but they never saw more of the two jeebi-ug.

The hunter found the success which they had promised. He

became celebrated in the chase, and never wanted for anything. He had many children, all of whom grew up to manhood; and health, peace, and long life were the rewards of his hospitality.

THE GHOST COUNTRY

KWAKIUTL

The ghosts live in four houses, each one deeper than the preceding one. A Koskimo woman was crying on account of her dead father. They buried him and she was crying under the grave for four days. The people called her but she refused to leave. On the fourth day she heard somebody come who called her. "I call you downward, Crying Woman."

Then she jumped up and the ghost said, "Follow me." He went downward and she followed him. They came to a house called Hemlock-Leaves-on-Back. They entered the house and an old woman was sitting near the fire. She said, "Ah, ah, ah, ah. Sit down near the fire." They took poles to take down dry salmon and prepared to roast it. They placed it on a small food mat and broke it up and gave it to Crying Woman.

Just when she was about to take it, a person came in and invited her into another house called Maggots-on-Bark-on-Ground. Then the woman who lived in the first house said,

"Ah, ah, ah, ah. Go with her. They are higher in rank than we are." She followed the person who had invited her and entered the next house. She saw an old woman sitting by the fire and she seemed to be the same one whom she had seen first. She prepared food in the same way, giving her something to eat.

Just when she was about to eat, another woman came to her and invited her into her house, which was called Place-of-Mouth-Showing-on-Ground. The woman in the second house said, "Go with her. They are higher in rank than we are." When she entered, the same old woman seemed to be sitting by the fire. Again they prepared something for her to eat.

When she was just about to begin, she was called by another person into the fourth house, called Place-of-Never-Return. Again the woman said, "They are higher in rank than we. Go." When she entered she saw her father sitting at the end of the house. And when he saw her he became angry and said, "Why do you come here? This is the place from which nobody ever returns. Whoever enters the first three houses may return. But if you come here, you must stay. Do not eat what is offered to you and go back."

Then he called the ghosts to take her back. She was lying under the grave tree like one dead. The ghosts came back singing the following song:

hama yahahaha

She was like one dead when she came back. When her father spoke to her he had said, "When we take you back we will sing so that the Koskimo may hear our song." They brought her up alive on a board. The people heard the song, but they did not see anyone. Then they took the board into the winter-dance house. This song belongs originally to the Koskimo and was carried from there to the Newettee and to the Nákwado.

THE DEAD WIFE

ALABAMA

The wish to murder one's wife is balanced by the knowledge that one cannot live without her.

A man and his wife were going along a trail, when the man picked some berries of the button snakeroot and threw them gently at his wife, who was ahead of him. They passed through her body and she died. Then the woman's relatives took her and buried her, and her husband with her, although he was alive.

When night came, she went to a dance. The next night she was gone again. She came back covered with sweat. Then she said to her husband, "You have nothing to do here but lie still and be sad. Get on my back." So he got on her back; she jumped up and put him down outside, going through the earth with him. And when he reached his house and the people saw him, they said, "He has broken through the earth." They set out for the place and, when they got there, looked all about, but nothing was disturbed.

THE VAMPIRE SKELETON

ONONDAGA

The married couple encounters death; the child avoids it. To make the point more emphatic, the mythmaker has the skeleton reappear as a fox, which the Onondaga recognize, or at one time recognized, as a symbol of sexual love. Here again is the familiar anguish of the culture myth: love breeds death. Or, to put it another way, death is the price of love. As the mythmaker reminds us, there is only one escape: to remain a child.

In old times the Onondagas lived on a much larger reservation than now—a great land—but they made hunting parties to the Adirondacks. A party once went off in which there were an old man, his daughter and her husband, and their little boy. They went one day and camped, and another day and camped, and then separated. The old man, his daughter, and her husband turned one way, but the little boy accidentally went the other way with his uncle.

The three kept on, and late in the day found an empty cabin in a clearing. There was an Indian bedstead on each side within, and as no one seemed to live there, they resolved to stay for the night. They gathered plenty of fuel, stripping long pieces from the shagbark hickory, built a fine fire, spread their deerskins on the bedsteads, and then went to sleep—the old man on one side, and the man and his wife on the other.

When the fire became low and it grew dark in the cabin, the young people were awakened by a sound like a dog gnawing a bone. They stirred about, and the noise ceased, but was followed by something like rattling bones overhead. They got up and put on more fuel, and were going back to bed when they saw something like water flowing from the other couch. It was blood, and the old man was dead. His clothes were torn open and his ribs broken and gnawed. They covered him up and lay down again. The same thing happened the second time, and this time they saw it was a terrible skeleton, feeding on the dead man. They were frightened and in whispers devised a plan of escape. They made a great fire, and the wife said, "Husband, I must go to the spring and get some water; I am so thirsty." She went out quietly, but a little way off ran with all her might toward her own country.

When her husband thought she had a good start, he made a very big fire, to last a great while, and then he said, "What has become of my wife? I am afraid she is drowned in the spring. I must go and see." So he went out, and a little way off he, too, ran with all his might, and when he overtook his wife he caught her by the arm and they both ran on together. By and by, the fire went down, the skeleton came again, and when he found both were gone he started to give chase. Soon they heard him howling terribly behind them, and they ran faster.

It happened that night that the Onondagas were holding a feast, and it now drew near morning. The man and woman heard the drum sounding far off, tum-tum, tum-tum, and they ran harder, and shouted, but the skeleton did the same. Then they heard the drum again, TUM-TUM, tum-tum, and it was nearer, and they shouted again. Their friends heard the distress cry, and came to their rescue with all their arms. The skeleton fled. The fugitives fell down fainting, and did not regain their senses for four hours; then they told their story.

A council was held, and the warriors started for the dreadful spot. They found the hut and a few traces of the old man. In the loft were some scattered articles, and a bark coffin. In this was the skeleton of a man left unburied by his friends. They determined to destroy everything, and fuel was gathered on all sides and fire applied. The warriors stood around with bent bows and raised hatchets. The fire grew hot, the cabin fell in, and out of the flames rushed a fox with red and fiery eyes; it dashed through the ranks and disappeared in the forest. The dreadful skeleton was seen no more.

"But what had the little boy to do with all this?"

"Oh, that is to show it was well he went the other way."

FORTY DEAD MEN

MAKAH

At Ozette two brothers undertook whaling, although their father had not been a whaler. The elder was unsuccessful, but the younger killed several whales the first season. Thereafter he was always lucky, while his brother always failed. The elder often asked how he got his power, but the young whaler told nothing.

The younger brother often lay all day with his back to the

fire, and he slept there at night. He seldom ate, and then only a little. The way he obtained his power was this: He dreamed of forty ghosts, and then cleared a place in the woods back of the village. Around it was a thick jungle of crab trees, which he made impenetrable by interweaving trees and brush he had cut down, leaving only a narrow entrance. In the clearing he arranged some brush and small poles in the form of a canoe and four whales in a row. The whales were so large that he could place two corpses under them. Around the edge of the clearing he placed boards so as to make a shelf about two feet from the ground, and on it, bound to upright stakes, he stood forty dead bodies. Each held a stick in its right hand, and he arranged a rope so that by pulling it he caused all of them to strike with their batons the board on which they stood. Another line raised the left arms of the corpses at the will of the whaler. In the brush canoe he had a full crew of seven dead men, and by means of ropes he made them paddle when he gave the order. In visiting this place the whaler always rested four times after leaving the burial ground, and on reaching the clearing he walked around it four times in-side the line of corpses.

One day a son of the elder brother died, and the body was placed in a hole and covered with stones. On the fourth night the younger brother left the house. The other heard him, and softly followed him to the new grave, and silently watched him remove the stones, take out the body, and fill the hole with stones. With the body on his back, and walking in the fashion of whalers at such times, the young man went along the beach and then turned into the woods. The elder brother cautiously followed, pausing when the other rested. Whenever the whaler stopped he screeched like an owl, and prayed, "May I be given a chance to spear a whale, and may the people say it was I that did it!" When finally they reached the clearing, it was dawn.

The whaler threw the body beside the first whale, and made the dead men strike the boards with their sticks. Then he stood the new body beside a stake and lashed it there. He slowly got into the canoe, took up a harpoon, and hurled it at the first brush whale. At that instant his brother sprang through the hedge. The whaler fell unconscious, and the elder leaped upon him. When the whaler opened his eyes, he begged, "Spare my life, and I will show you how to do everything! I will let you use all this, and tell you the best places to wash!"

"Why did you not let me have this when I asked you?" demanded the elder man. "The people have been laughing at me long enough! I asked you this many years ago, but you told me nothing. Now I can take everything you have. If you had told me, this would never have happened. And you took my dead son so soon after I buried him! Though you are my brother, I cannot spare your life!" He stabbed him, but did not kill him. Still the whaler pleaded, "Let me go! Whatever I have shall be yours! If you kill me, you will have no good from these things, because you will not know how to use them. If you try to use them by yourself, you will die soon!" But the elder brother stabbed him to death. Then he lashed the warm body to the other side of the stake that supported his own son. It was now broad daylight, and the man went home and told his wife all.

Four or five days later he returned to the clearing. He pulled on the rope, and the sticks struck the boards. Then he prayed as he had heard his brother do. He got into the brush canoe, threw the harpoon at the first whale, and said, "I have forty dead men for my power! May I spear a whale, and may the people say it was I that speared it!" He heard a sound from his dead brother, then the words: "You ought to be ashamed! You are not doing it the right way!" Then he went home feeling very ill, and that night he died.

Tales of the White Man

"Execution of the Inca of Peru
by Pizarro." Painted in 1869 by
Alonzo Chappel. Unsigned
engraving published in 1870
(*American History Division, New
York Public Library*)

The deterioration of native American culture, a process that has recently been arrested in some localities, is due in part to the Indian's ambivalent—one might indeed say philosophical—attitude toward the white man.

THE LAND SALE

QUILEUTE

A long time ago a big steamer ran ashore on a rock at James Island. There were many white people on the steamer that grounded on the rock. Many things were washed ashore from the steamer, and the Indians picked up everything. As they did not know what forks were, they used them in order to brush the dog blankets, and they used the "hardtacks" by rolling them about on the beach.

But the Quileute took care of the white people, feeding them and giving them a place to sleep. They even gave one white man a pretty woman for a wife while he was here. The

white people stayed a long time in Quileute land. Some of
the white people learned to speak the Quileute language, as
they were unable to talk to the Quileute, because none of them
could speak the language of the white people. Only Hauwiyal
knew how to speak Chinook. Hauwiyal was treated very well
by the white people when they grounded on the rock.
Hauwiyal took good care of the white people. That is why the
captain gave them much canvas. Then Hauwiyal paid a little
for the canvas. How much he paid I shall not say what it was.
Every day the white people were at Lapush rocking in swings
with the girls. Then Hauwiyal sent one of his men to take the
white people to Neah Bay, when the white people wished to
go away.

Before they went away the white people tried to pay
Hauwiyal, because they were well taken care of. But
Hauwiyal did not wish to be paid, because he was good-
hearted. The Quileute did not like Hauwiyal, but they were
proud that he was a good-hearted man.

Then, not many years after, one white man came to Quileute land, as the white people who had formerly arrived at the
beach had been well taken care of. All the Quileute knew the
name of the good white man. All called him Stimin [Stevens].
He assembled the Quileute in order to talk to them, and paid
the Quileute because they had taken good care of the white
people that had formerly drifted ashore. Then Stevens gave
the Quileute axes, and tools to hit the ground with, and tools
to cut wood with, and shovels. Then Hauwiyal spoke to
Stevens, being glad that Stevens had been good to them.
Then Stevens stood up and spoke to the Quileute men, saying: "Every time you see a white man drifted ashore take
good care of him. The reason I have given you the white
people's working tools is that you have taken care of the

white people when they needed care." This time Hauwiyal alone was talking to Stevens when they had been assembled, because only one was able to talk to the white people, as only one knew Chinook. Then Stevens went south. All the Quileute were happy with the working implements given to them by Stevens when they took care of the white people that had drifted ashore.

Then not long afterward a white man came to Quileute land. It was again Stevens who came. Then he again assembled the Quileute people. Ever since then, when they were told by Stevens to take good care of the white people when they needed care, they took good care of the white men even if they did not need care. Then, when the Quileute were again assembled by Stevens, once more they were told what they had been told before: to take care of the white people when they needed care. This time the Quileute began to eat the white people's food given them by Stevens—flour and a little of everything.

He did not tell them then that he was buying land from the Quileute. Stevens only asked Hauwiyal how big a land the Quileute had. Then Hauwiyal said. "If you wish to know, accompany me. I will show you how big our land is." Then Stevens said, "I will go with you. Let us go tomorrow." Then the next day Hauwiyal took Stevens to show him his land in the middle of the Lower Prairie and above the Upper Prairie. Then Hauwiyal showed Stevens the digging place from which were gotten the fern roots which the Quileute ate. Then Hauwiyal returned with Stevens. Then again the next day Stevens went south.

Then not many years afterward the white people began to arrive, and were taking the land away from the Quileute at the Lower Prairie and at the Upper Prairie. The Quileute were unable to talk about their land, they were told by Stevens not to get angry at the white people. Then not many years afterward the white people came to where the Quileute used to live. They drove away the Indians, forbidding them to live where they used to live. Then the Quileute came finally here where we are all grouped. They were deprived of all their land by the white people.

So much for that, because I do not know much about it.

THE PONGO'S DREAM

QUECHUA

This European-style tale was collected in the Quechua language by the Peruvian poet-novelist José María Arguedas.

A little man was making his way toward the great house of the hacienda owner. He was a peon, coming to serve as a menial, a pongo, in the mansion of his patrón. He was small, miserably made, poor in spirit—wholly deplorable. His clothes were worn-out.

The great master, the patrón, of the hacienda could not keep from laughing when the little man greeted him in the long gallery. In the presence of all the men and women who served him, he demanded, "Are you human? or something else?"

The pongo bowed his head and made no answer. Terrified, he remained standing, his eyes frozen.

"I have my doubts," continued the patrón, "but at least we'll see if he scrubs pots, or whether or not he can hold a broom with those impossible-looking hands of his." Then to his foreman he gave the order: "Here, take this filth!"

Dropping to his knees, the pongo kissed his master's hands; then, crouching, he followed the foreman to the kitchen.

Small as he was, his abilities were equal to those of an ordinary man. Whatever he was asked to do, he did well. Yet there remained a touch of fear in his face. Noticing this, some of the peons would laugh. Others were sympathetic. "Orphan of orphans, child of the wind," said the mestizo cook when she saw him. "Those freezing-cold eyes must have come from the moon. A soul of pure misery!"

The little man spoke to no one. He worked without making a sound and ate in silence. He obeyed every order. "Yes, dear papa," or "Yes, dear mama," was all he would say.

Owing perhaps to a certain fearfulness in his face, and because of his tattered clothing, and perhaps, moreover, on account of his unwillingness to speak, the patrón conceived a particular scorn for the little man. At nightfall, when the peons assembled in the gallery of the great house to say the Ave Maria, without fail the patrón would torment the pongo in front of all the others; he would pick him up and shake him like a hide.

He would give him a push on the head and make him fall to his knees, and as he knelt he would slap him lightly across the face.

"I believe you're a dog. Bark!" he would say.

The little man was unable to bark. So the order would be

changed: "Then get down on all fours!"

And he would obey, scurrying to and fro.

"Run sideways!" the master would say.

Then the pongo would run sideways, imitating the little dogs of the high plains. And the patrón would laugh heartily, his whole body shaking with laughter.

"Turn around!" he would cry, when the little man had reached the far end of the gallery. And the pongo would turn around and run back, veering just a little to one side. When he had finished he would be all tired out.

Meanwhile, a few of his fellow peons would be reciting the Ave Maria. Very slowly they would recite it, like a sigh from within the heart.

"Prick up your ears, viscacha! You're a viscacha now!" the master would cry to the tired-out little man. "Sit up on your hind legs! Put your hands together!"

And just as if in his mother's womb he had felt the influence of a viscacha, the pongo would now give a perfect imitation of that little creature—the way it sits up on a rock, motionless, listening—though of course he was unable to prick up his ears. A few of the peons would always burst out laughing.

Without kicking him too hard, the patrón would strike the little man with his boot, sending him sprawling on the brick pavement of the gallery.

Then to his Indians, who were lined up waiting, the patrón would say, "Let us recite the Paternoster." And presently the pongo would rise to his feet, but he would not be able to recite because he would not be in his proper place. Nor did such a place exist.

In the growing darkness the peons would step down from the gallery and into the patio and begin making their way toward the little cluster of living quarters.

Then the patrón would turn to the pongo: "Out of here, you paunchy runt!"

And so every day the patrón would make his new pongo grovel in front of the entire household. He would command him to laugh, or make him pretend to cry. He delivered him up to the ridicule of the other peons who were his equals.

But one evening, at the vesper hour, when the gallery was overflowing with all the hacienda folk, and when the patrón had just begun to notice the pongo with those solid eyes of his, the little man suddenly spoke up loud and clear. His face retained just a trace of fear.

"Sire," he said, "may I have your permission? My dear father, I wish to speak with you."

The patrón could not believe his ears.

"What? Was it you who spoke, or someone else?" he asked.

"Your permission, dear father, to speak. With you. I wish to speak with you," repeated the pongo.

"Speak—if you can," said the master.

"My father, my lord, my soul," began the little man, "last night I dreamed we were dead, you and I. We were together in death."

"With me? You? Let's hear the rest of it, Indian!" said the great patrón. "Come, let's hear it!"

"We were dead, my lord. And it seemed we were naked, the two of us, together. Naked before our great Father, St. Francis."

"And then what? Speak!" commanded the patrón, torn between anger and curiosity.

"There we were, dead, and naked, standing side by side, and our great Father, St. Francis, was searching us with those eyes of his that can see farther than anyone knows. He searched us both, you and me, and I believe he was weighing our souls, judging us for what we had been and what we were. And you, being rich and great, you looked straight into those eyes, my father."

"And you?"

"I know not what I am, sire. I have no way of judging my own worth."

"True. Go on."

"Then, after that, our Father opened his mouth and spoke: 'Let the most beautiful of all the angels appear. And let this incomparable one be accompanied by another, little, angel, who likewise shall be the most beautiful of all. Let the little angel bring a gold goblet, filled with the sweetest, clearest honey.' "

"And then?" asked the patrón.

All the Indians were listening to the pongo with rapt, yet fearful attention.

"Master, scarcely had our great Father, St. Francis, given the order when a brilliant angel appeared, way up high like the sun. He came nearer and nearer until he stood in front of our Father. Behind the great angel came the little one—so beautiful. All soft and bright like a flower. In his hands he carried a gold goblet."

"And then?" asked the patrón.

" 'Great angel, take the gold goblet and cover this gentleman with honey. Let your hands be like feathers as they pass over his body.' That was the order the great Father gave. So the heavenly angel dipped his hands into the honey and made your whole body bright, from your head to your toenails. And then you rose up tall, just you. And even against the bright sky the light from your body shone out, as if you were made of clear gold."

"Yes, that would have to be," said the patrón. Then he asked, "And you?"

"While you were shining in the sky, our great Father, St. Francis, gave another order: 'Let the angel of least worth, the commonest angel of all, come forth. Let him bring a gasoline can filled with human excrement.' "

"And then?"

"Then a worthless angel with scaly feet, not even strong enough to hold up his wings, came before our great Father. He arrived all tired out, with his wings drooping, holding a big can. 'Here, old fellow,' said our great Father to this poor angel, 'smear the little man's body with that excrement you have there in the tin can. The whole thing. Any way you like. Cover him the best you can. Quickly!' Then with his gnarled hands the old angel took the excrement out of the can and slopped it all over me. It was just as if mud were being thrown against the wall of a plain old building. And there I was up there in the bright sky, ashamed and stinking."

"That too would have to be," affirmed the patrón. "Go on. Or is that all?"

"No, my dear father, my lord. For now, though things were different, we found ourselves once again standing before our great Father, St. Francis, and now he was taking a long, long look at the two of us, you and me. His eyes were as big as the sky and he looked right into us, how far I don't know—as far as to where night becomes day, where forgetting becomes remembering. And then he said, 'The angels have done their work well. Now lick each other. Slowly. And keep on licking.' Just then the old angel became young. His wings regained their usual black color and their great strength. Then our Father charged him to watch over us, so that his will would be done."

THE QUEEN OF THE TRIBE

KWAKIUTL

When I saw Késelas, I asked him to tell it to me, for I wished to be informed regarding the word about the white man. I wanted to talk about it. I wanted to hear the story. And I said to him, "Go on, tell me, that I may listen to what is known by you." "I shall tell you." "Let me listen."

A pretty woman was wooed by many. The whole tribe wooed her against one another. But no one was good enough for her. Then, it is said, she was wooed by another tribe and there was one who was good enough for her and she desired him and he was right in her mind. Then the minds of her tribe fellows were sore, for she desired a man of another tribe.

Then her tribe fellows talked among themselves. "Let us make war on this tribe, that all of them may die." And so they made war on them. They killed them. They destroyed the whole tribe. They cut off their heads. And then they came home to their houses and took the heads of the men and put them on a scaffold on the beach. And so there were skulls on the beach.

The heart of the woman was sore. She arose and went to look at the skulls. She went down to the beach, and there in the middle of the beach was the skull of the man she had desired for her husband. The woman cried. Then she spoke to the skull: "What kind of thing are you? Are you something that might come alive? Skull, come! My vain desire, come!"

And so, it is said, the woman went straight to her house and lay down in her bed. Her heart was sore on account of the one whom she vainly desired for a husband, and night came. Then, it is said, when daylight was coming, somebody knocked on her door, saying, "Open for me."

The woman arose and opened the door. She saw at once that it was the man she desired for a husband. She rushed and embraced him.

"You are the one. I come for you," he said. "We will go and start paddling. Come, fold your bedding. We will go. We will start paddling." Then the woman gathered her bedding and clothing. "Take everything," he said. Then she folded her things and gave them to the man and they started. And so they went aboard the canoe. The man, it is said, took the bedding and spread it out in the canoe. "Lie down here in the canoe. Now we will start paddling," and the woman lay down in the canoe. He paddled. The woman was asleep. She slept in the canoe. The man was paddling. Day came. The woman raised her head and sat up in the canoe and awoke. She looked around. No land was to be seen; no mountain was to be seen, no island.

Then the man spoke: "You made fun of the way I was. I only wanted you to know I was offended by what you said.

And now I am on my way home." The man jumped out of the canoe. Then a skull was rolling over the water. He had again become a skull. And what could the woman say?

She did not know where she was headed. And so, it is said, she continued this way. A great many years she drifted. At last she saw something round on the water beside her, they say. It was foam on the water. Then with her paddle she lifted it into the canoe. Indeed, although it was in the canoe, it did not melt. Day came. What could it be? Clothing. It was calico and much thread. And still she was adrift. Still she was out on the water, but now she became glad, for now she had clothing.

There was a noise: the bow of the canoe striking land. She raised her head and looked. What should it be but a nice country! She stepped out of the canoe and pulled it after her. Then she unloaded it. She unloaded her clothing. There was much of it.

She sewed and made a house and her house was of canvas. But no people were there. Although her house was on the beach, no one came to see her.

Then there was a sound of shooting. She went out and looked to see where it was. She saw nothing. Without her seeing them, two men came around to the front of her house. And so, it is said, they came and stood at her door. "Come in!" said the woman. These were white men. Then the woman spoke to them. "Why is your clothing so bad?" she asked. Their clothing was made of deerskin, and so were their hats and shoes. "That is our clothing," said the men. "Would you like me to give you clothing?" she said. "You would be kind," said the white men.

Then she dressed them with clothing. She picked up the clothing and gave it to them. It is said the clothing was red.

And they put it on. Then the woman asked them, "Are there only two of you?" "No, we are many." "Is your village far away?" "It is not very far. It is quite near." "Go and tell your chief I am coming to talk to him, and tell him to come carry my clothing."

So they went back and told their chief. He came steering. They towed the ship and he came ashore where she lived. And so their chief came; then she gave him the clothing to be loaded in the ship, and it swelled up and became much and they filled the ship with it. Then the woman went aboard the ship. Now she was taken to their village. That woman became chief of the tribe. She was the queen of the tribe.

THE BACABAL MISSION

MUNDURUCÚ

Bacabal is on the right bank of the Tapajós River. All the people there used to work. All, that is, except for the chief, Maribashik.

Every morning at eleven o'clock they would come in from their work and take a bath. They ate at twelve. Then, in the afternoon, they would go back and work some more.

In the evening they drank banana beer and played their flutes. Whoever drank much would be drunk.

At Bacabal there were two Mundurucú blacksmiths, who did good work. They made shovels and digging tools, and they knew how to repair things.

Brazilian traders were not allowed to come there. If a trader dared to set foot in the mission, Maribashik would seize him and put him in jail, and he would have to stay there until Sunday. If the trader gave him some money, Maribashik would let him go. But he would have to leave the mission immediately.

The father had everyone learn to read and write, even the old women.

At Bacabal there were also some wild Mundurucú tribesmen who had been brought into the mission. They lived in a special house. The father found them while traveling and brought them home with him. The women joined hands and held each other tightly. But the father was good to these Indians. He gave them skirts, knives, and other things. Unfortunately, nearly all of them died of influenza. Only a few children survived.

Once some knives were stolen from one of the houses by some different Indians who lived in the Bacabal area and who were wild like the wild Mundurucú. Maribashik went after them, killed them, and brought back their children.

Bacabal was destroyed by a terrible plague. The father went away. Today the mission is abandoned.

Only the upright of its great wooden cross remains standing. The crosspiece lies on the ground.

Myths of Returning Life

"Herd of Buffalo." Drawn by
Seth Eastman, engraved by James
Smillie, published in Henry
Rowe Schoolcraft's *Indian
Tribes*, Vol. 4, 1854

Loss or deprivation may be remedied by a journey to the other world, represented in the first of the following three stories by the star realm, in the second by a garden beyond the sea, in the third by a hunting ground on the far side of an impassable mountain.

THE RING IN THE PRAIRIE

SHAWNEE

In a remote part of the forest, where birds and animals were abundant, there lived a young hunter called Waupee, or White Hawk. Tall and manly, with the fire of youth beaming from his eye, he walked unafraid through the gloomiest woods, and could follow a track made by any of the numerous kinds of birds and beasts. Every day he would return to his lodge with game, for he was one of the most skillful and celebrated hunters of his tribe.

One day, having hunted farther from home than ever before, he found himself in an open forest where he could see for great distances. Soon there was light breaking through the trees, and before long he came to the edge of a wide prairie covered with grass and flowers. Walking on, without a path, he suddenly noticed a ring worn through the sod as if by footsteps following a circle. Yet there was no path leading to it, not the least trace of footprints. Not even a crushed leaf or broken twig.

Curious to know the meaning of this strange circle, he hid himself nearby in the tall grass and waited. Presently he heard the faint sounds of music in the air. Looking up, he saw a small object coming down out of the sky. At first a mere speck, it rapidly grew in size, becoming a huge basket filled with twelve sisters of the most enchanting beauty.

As it approached, the music grew plainer and sweeter. When it had touched ground, the sisters leaped out and began to dance around the ring. Round and round they went, and as they danced they reached out with sticks to a shining ball in the center of the ring, striking it as if it were a drum.

From his hiding place Waupee gazed upon their graceful motions. He admired them all, but especially the youngest. At last, unable to restrain himself, he rushed out and attempted to seize her. But the sisters, with the quickness of birds, leaped back to the basket and were drawn up into the sky.

"They are gone," he thought, "and I shall see them no more." He returned to his lodge, but found no rest. The next day he went back to the ring. In order to deceive the sisters, he changed himself into an opossum. He had not waited long when he saw the basket descend and heard the same sweet music. Once again they began to dance, appearing even more beautiful and graceful than before.

Slowly he crept toward the ring, but the moment the sisters saw him they were startled and sprang into their basket. It had risen but a short distance when one of the elder sisters spoke. "Perhaps," she said, "he has come to show us how the game is played on earth."

"Oh no!" the youngest replied. "Quick, let us be off!" And all joining in a chant, they rose out of sight.

Waupee changed to his own form again and walked sorrowfully back to his lodge. The night seemed very long. Early the next day he returned to the ring. Not far from it, he found an old stump filled with mice. Thinking that the sisters would not be frightened by such tiny creatures, he brought the stump close to the ring and, changing his form, became one of them. Soon the sisters came down again and began to dance.

"Look!" cried the youngest sister. "That stump was not there before." Frightened, she ran toward the basket. But the others only smiled and gathered round the stump, playfully hitting at it with their sticks. As they did so, the mice, including Waupee, came running out. In a matter of moments the sisters had killed them all—all except for one, which was chased by the youngest. As she raised her stick to kill it, the form of Waupee suddenly rose up, clasping her in his arms. The other eleven sprang to their basket and were drawn up into the sky.

Waupee used all the skill he had to please his bride and win her affection. He wiped the tears from her eyes. He told her of his adventures as a hunter, and dwelt upon the charms of life on the earth. He was tireless in his attentions, picking out the way for her to walk as he led her gently toward his lodge. As she entered it, he felt his heart glow with joy, and from that moment on he was one of the happiest of men.

Winter and summer passed rapidly away, and their happiness was increased by the addition of a beautiful boy to their lodge. But Waupee's wife was a daughter of one of the stars, and as life on the earth began to lose its appeal, she longed to return to her father. She had not forgotten the charm that would carry her up, and took the opportunity, while her husband was out hunting, to construct a wicker basket, which she kept concealed when he was at home. In the meantime she collected such rarities from the earth as she thought would please her father, as well as the most dainty kinds of food.

One day, when all was ready, she went out to the ring, taking her little son with her. They stepped into the basket and she began her song. Carried by the wind, the music caught her husband's ear. It was a voice he well knew. Instantly, he ran to the prairie. But he could not reach the ring before he saw his wife and son rising up. He called out to them, but it was of no use. The basket kept on rising. He watched it till it became a small speck and finally vanished in the sky. He then bent his head down to the ground and was miserable.

Waupee bewailed his loss through a long winter and a long summer. He mourned the loss of his wife sorely, but he missed his son even more. In the meantime his wife had reached her home in the stars and had almost forgotten, in her blissful activities there, that she had left a husband on the earth. She was reminded of him only by the presence of her son, who, as he grew up, became anxious to visit the place of his birth.

One day the star said to his daughter, "Go, my child, and take your son down to his father. Ask him to come up and live with us. But tell him to bring along one of each kind of bird and animal he kills in his hunting."

Taking the boy with her, she descended once again to the earth. Waupee, who was never far from the ring, heard her voice as she came down through the sky. His heart beat with impatience as his wife and son appeared. Soon they were clasped in his arms.

When his wife had told him of the star's request, he set out with great eagerness to collect the gift. He spent whole nights, as well as days, searching for every beautiful and unusual bird or animal. He only preserved a tail, a foot, or a wing of each, and when everything was ready they went back to the ring and were carried up.

There was great joy among the stars when they arrived. The star chief invited all his people to a feast, and when they had come together, he announced that they might take whichever of the earthly gifts they liked best.

A strange confusion immediately arose. Some chose a foot, some a wing, some a tail, and some a claw. Those who selected tails or claws were changed into animals and ran off. The others were changed into birds, and flew away. Waupee chose a white hawk's feather. His wife and son did the same, and each one became a white hawk. Waupee spread his wings and, followed by his wife and son, descended with the other birds to the earth, where they are still found to this day.

THE STORY OF OKÓHI

WARRAU

There was a young man named Waiamari; he lived in the house of his uncle. One day he went down to the waterside to bathe. While he was in the water, he heard someone running along the path; he heard a splash and looked around. Recognizing his uncle's young wife, he began to swim out farther. But she swam after him. The girl wanted him very much, and as she got close to the spot where he was, she whispered, "Don't you want me?"

Instead of answering quietly, Waiamari loudly upbraided her, shouting, "Incest! Shame!" The girl drew away. Back up at the house, the uncle heard the noise and called down to his wife, "What's the matter with you? Stop bothering the boy!" For it appeared that she, not the nephew, was at fault. Then the couple got out of the water and came up to the house. The aunt went inside, but the boy kept on going until he reached the house of his other, elder, uncle, Okóhi. That night he slept in the house of Okóhi.

Now the very fact that he had not come into the house as usual with his aunt made Waiamari guilty in the eyes of her husband; and the next morning the uncle went looking for his nephew at Okóhi's place. When he found him, he reproached him for having attempted improper conduct with his wife. The charge was indignantly denied, the two began fighting, and the uncle was thrown down. They fought again and the uncle was thrown down a second time. Then Okóhi interfered and said, "Boy, that will do!" And so he stopped the fighting between his brother and his nephew.

To prevent further trouble, Okóhi thought it best to take Waiamari away with him on his journey. He told the young man to prepare the canoe, as he wished to leave the next morning. So Waiamari went down to the water's edge and painted the sign of the sun on either side of the bow of the boat. At the stern he painted a man and a moon. The next morning they set off, the nephew paddling in the bow, the uncle steering. It was a big sea they were crossing, and as the paddle blades swept along they could hear the water singing Wau-u! Wau-u! Wau-u!

At last they crossed the big sea and reached the opposite shore. They landed. Then they went up to a house nearby, where they met a pretty woman; her name was Assawako. After greeting Okóhi and telling him to be seated, she asked him to let his nephew go out to the field with her. Permission was granted and the young couple started off. When they got there, Assawako told Waiamari to rest himself while she gathered something for him to eat. She brought him plantains, pineapples, a big bundle of sugar cane, watermelons and peppers. He ate it all and spent a delightful time with her. On the way back, she asked him whether he was a good hunter. Without saying a word he stepped into the bush and reappeared with a load of armadillo meat. She was proud of him and assumed her place behind him as they walked.

Just before they got back to her house, she said, "When we get home we'll have something to drink. Can you play the kahabassa?" "Yes, I can play a little," he said. And so, when they returned, she gave him a whole jugful to drink, putting him in the mood to play music. He played beautifully; he made the kahabassa sing Waru-huru-téa. All night they reveled, but next morning Okóhi was ready to leave. Of course poor Assawako wanted Waiamari to remain with her, but he said, "Oh no, I cannot leave my uncle. He has been good to me, and he is an old man now." So she began to cry and between her sobs told him how sad she felt that he was going away. Then he too began to feel very sorry, but he consoled her, saying, "Let us weep together with the kahabassa." And there and then he sang heru-heru on the kahabassa and so comforted her before he left.

Now, when at last the uncle and his nephew got back to their own country, old Okóhi bathed his skin; he seated himself in his hammock, gathered all his family around him, and spoke to them, saying, "When I was young, I could travel day after day, as I have just done, but I am old now, and this is my last journey." He finished speaking. His head burst. And out of his head came the warmth and heat of the sun.

THE BOY AND THE OWLS

YAMANA

There once lived a widow. By her dead husband she had a son; they lived in the son's uncle's lodge.

But this uncle treated his nephew very badly and gave him only a little to eat. Day by day the nephew grew thinner. His food was not good: his uncle would give him nothing but black puddings made of guanaco gut filled with blood from people's noses. They would take a little stick and poke it around in their noses until the blood came. The uncle fed this weird pudding to his nephew. The little boy began to get very thin. Nor did any of the other people treat him kindly. No one gave him anything to eat.

At last the child could endure it no longer. Again and again he had complained to his mother, "My uncle gives me hardly anything to eat, and what he gives me is bad. I can't

stand it any more, I'm so miserable." Finally, his mother said
to him, "Go out yourself and see if you can kill a guanaco."
"But how can I go hunting," he said, "when I have no moccasins?" Immediately, the mother cut a piece of hide from
her chastity apron and used it to make her son a pair of
moccasins. He put them on and rushed off to go hunting.

He set out in the direction of a certain high ridge. His
uncle had often said, "That ridge over there is so high nobody can cross it. It's a shame, because on the other side are
plenty of guanacos." Now the little boy said to himself, "I'm
going to try to cross that ridge, and maybe I'll catch a
guanaco on the other side." So he came to where the ground
rose up and he began to climb. Then he climbed down the
other side. He saw many guanacos. He crept up to them; he
killed several big ones. Then he looked around him and saw
that the ridge had completely disappeared. He was overjoyed.
"How nice! It will be easy to get back home now." He rested
a little, then lifted one of the guanacos onto his shoulders. He
could not carry more, for he was still just a little boy and not
very strong. He left behind the other guanacos he had killed;
he would come back for them the next day. He laid them all
together in a pile.

Not until late in the evening did he get home to his mother.
When she saw him coming in with a huge guanaco, she was
delighted. He cut off a big piece and the two of them began to
eat. It wasn't long before people in nearby lodges heard them
cracking open the big bones with a rock and slurping the
marrow. They asked each other, "Who could be giving them
meat? You can hear it! That old woman is cracking bones
and getting marrow!" Finally, a few of the women went over;
they saw a huge guanaco lying there in the lodge. The mother
invited them to take some and start eating. "My little boy has

just brought in this enormous guanaco," she said. "He killed it himself!" But the women laughed and shook their heads in disbelief. "How could a little child kill such a guanaco? Then bring it home! Besides, this one must have come from the other side of the ridge. Not even a big man can get over there."

When they had eaten their fill, they went back to their own lodges. They told everybody what the old woman had said. Then the people called her in and asked her about it. She said it was all true; she gave each of them a good piece of meat from the guanaco. And still, nobody would believe her. Finally, she said, "Then go to the other side of the ridge tomorrow morning and see for yourselves all the guanacos my little boy has killed. He left them behind because he couldn't carry so many!"

The old woman went back to her lodge and said to her son, "They wouldn't believe what I said. So finally I told them to go over there in the morning and bring back all those guanacos you killed and left behind." The boy didn't like this. He had been treated badly by these people and he didn't want them to share in his kill.

Many men went with him the next day, however. And they got there easily, even though the boy's uncle had always said no one could do it. From a short distance away he showed them where the guanacos were that he had killed the day before. Now these animals were fresh indeed; the intestines had not even been pulled out. So the men could no longer doubt it: the little boy had really killed a lot of guanacos.

The boy lifted a big guanaco onto his shoulders and started for home. Then each of the men picked up a guanaco and they too started off; but it wasn't long before they found that their guanacos were very heavy. They kept having to rest.

They made very slow progress. Yet the little boy did not seem to feel his burden; he soon outdistanced all the men! It exasperated them to see this boy moving along so quickly, while they, so tired, had to stop every moment to rest. They would get up and take a few steps. Then again they would have to sit down and rest. And again they would start, and again they would tire. They worked so hard they wore themselves out: they all became owls.

After a short while the little boy came home by himself. When the other people in the camp saw him coming with a guanaco, they asked for meat. But he said to them, "I can't give you any of my guanaco. Wait a little until your relatives come back, the men who went with me this morning. You wouldn't give me anything to eat before. Now wait for your kinsmen!" They waited a long time. Not until night did the owls arrive. They brought nothing with them. They came up to the lodges where they had lived and where their relatives now were, but they did not go in. They also came close to the lodge where the little boy and his mother were sitting. They could see the two of them eating, but they themselves did not share it, nor did they go inside. They just cried kuhúruh, kuhúruh. Then they went away and stayed in the woods. Even now they come up to the lodges at night, but they don't come in, and no one gives them anything. All they do is cry kuhúruh, kuhúruh, and then they go back to the woods.

Death and Beyond

Worship of Quetzalcoatl at
Cholula. Engraved by Claude
Du Bosc after the drawing by
Bernard Picart, 1731   (*Private
collection*)

*The mystery of death-as-prelude (to revitalization) is
elaborated in six characteristic myths from North, South,
and Middle America.*

THE RED SWAN

CHIPPEWA

1

Three brothers were orphaned at an early age. The eldest,
though not yet able to provide fully for their support, did the
best he could at hunting, and by this means, and using the
stock of provisions left behind by their father, the three were
kept alive.

Yet it would seem they were protected by some power
greater than their own. For the father had been a pai-gwud-
aw-diz-zid—*a hermit*—having moved far away from the main
body of the tribe, so that when he and his wife died they left
their children without neighbors or friends, and the little

boys had no idea that there was a human being near them. They did not even know who their parents had been, for the eldest had been too young at the time of their death to remember.

Although they were alone, they did not despair. They worked hard to provide for themselves, and after a while all three learned to hunt and kill animals. The eldest soon became an expert hunter and was very successful at getting food. He was especially noted for his skill in hunting buffalo, elk, and moose. When his brothers were old enough to follow him, he taught them the ways of the forest; and as soon as they were able to take care of themselves, he announced that he would leave them and go in search of lodges, promising to return when he could bring them wives. But his brothers insisted they could not do without him. They refused to let him go. Maujeekewis—*the second eldest*—was loud in his disapproval, saying, "What will we do with those you propose to get? We have lived a long time without them, and we can still do without them." His words prevailed and the three brothers continued together for a time.

One day it was decided that each of them would kill a male of the particular kind of animal he was most skilled at hunting, and then they would use the skins for quivers. They did so, and as soon as the quivers were ready, they began making arrows to fill them, so that they would be prepared for any emergency.

Soon thereafter they bet among themselves to see who could come in first with game and prepare it as a treat for the others, with the condition that each was to shoot only those particular animals he was in the habit of killing. And so they set out in different directions. Odjibwa, the youngest, had not gone far when he saw a bear, an animal he was not allowed to kill. He followed it closely, however, and shot it and brought it down. Although contrary to the agreement, he began to skin it. Then suddenly something red tinged the air around him.

He rubbed his eyes and looked again. Still the air was red, and in the distance he heard a curious noise. At first it sounded like a human voice. He followed it. After a while he came to the edge of a lake, and there in the water he saw what he had been looking for—a beautiful red swan, its plumage glittering in the sun; and now and then it made the same noise he had heard before. He was within bow shot, and pulling the bowstring back to his ear, he aimed carefully and shot. The arrow missed; then he shot and shot again until his quiver was empty. Still the swan remained, moving round and round, stretching its long neck and dipping its bill into the water, as if unaware of the arrows.

Odjibwa ran home and got all his own and his brothers' arrows and shot them all away. He then stood and gazed at the beautiful bird. Suddenly he remembered his brother's saying that in their dead father's medicine sack were three magic arrows. Off he started. At any other time he would have thought it a sacrilege to open his father's sack, but now in his eagerness to kill the swan he seized the three arrows and ran back, leaving the other contents scattered over the lodge. The swan was still there. He shot the first arrow with great precision and came very near the mark. The second came still closer; as he took the last arrow, he felt his arm grow firmer and, drawing the arrow back with great force, saw it pass through the neck of the swan a little above the breast. At first the bird did not move; then, slowly, flapping its wings, it rose into the air and flew off toward the pungishemoo—*the sinking*—of the sun.

Odjibwa was disappointed. He knew that his brothers would be angry with him. He rushed into the water and rescued the two magic arrows; the third had been carried off by the swan. But he thought that it could not fly very far, and no matter what might happen, he was determined to follow it.

2

Off he started, on the run. He was noted for speed, for he could shoot an arrow and then out-race it. "I can run fast," he thought, "and sooner or later I will catch up with the swan."

He ran toward the west, over hills and prairies, until, just before nightfall, as he was about to take one last run and then seek a place to sleep, he heard sounds in the distance and knew there were people nearby. Men were cutting trees, and the strokes of their axes echoed through the woods. As he came out of the forest, the sun was just falling below the horizon. He felt pleased to find a place where he could rest and get something to eat, as he had left home without provisions. But though the prospect was inviting, it did not weaken his enthusiasm for the object of his quest, and he felt that if only he persevered, he would succeed.

At a distance, on a rising piece of ground, he could see the village spread out before him. As he came nearer, he heard the mudjee-kokokoho—*the watchman*—who was placed on a height where he could see all around and give notice of approaching friends or foes, calling, "We are visited!" And a loud cry indicated that all the people had heard him. The young man advanced and the watchman showed him the lodge of the chief. "It is there you must go in," he said, and left him.

"Come in, come in," said the chief. "Take a seat here," pointing to the side where his daughter sat. "It is here you must sit." He took a seat and was given food. But being a stranger, he was asked very few questions. When he spoke, he was answered; but only then was he addressed. "Daughter," said the chief, when it had grown dark, "take our son-in-law's moccasins and see if they are torn; and if so, mend them for him, and bring in his bundle." The chief's daughter was pretty. Yet Odjibwa thought it strange he should be so warmly received, and married instantly without his wishing it. He removed his moccasins. Yet it was some time before the young woman would pick them up. It displeased him to see her so reluctant, and when she did reach for them, he snatched them out of her hand and hung them up himself. He lay down and thought of the swan. Then he made up his mind to be off by dawn.

He awoke early and spoke to the young woman, but she gave no answer. He touched her. "What do you want?" she said, and turned her back toward him. "Tell me what time the swan passed. I am following it. Come out and point the way." "Do you think you can catch up to it?" she said. "Yes," he answered. "Naubesah—*foolishness!*" she said. Nevertheless, she went out and pointed in the direction he should go.

The young man went slowly until the sun rose. Then he began traveling at his usual speed. He ran all day, and when night came he was unexpectedly pleased to find himself near another village. While still at a distance, he heard the watchman crying out, "We are visited!" And soon all the men came out to see who the stranger was. He was again told to enter the lodge of the chief, and his reception was in every way the same as on the previous night, except that the young woman was more beautiful and received him very kindly.

Though he was urged to stay, his mind was fixed on the object of his journey. Before daylight he asked the young woman what time the red swan had passed and to point out the way. She did so and said that the swan had passed the day before when the sun was between midday and pungishe- moo—*its falling place.*

He again set out rather slowly, but when the sun had risen he tried his speed by shooting an arrow and running after it; it fell behind him. Nothing remarkable happened in the course of the day, and he traveled on steadily.

Sometime after dark he saw a light coming from a small low lodge. He went up to it very stealthily and, peering through the door, saw an old man alone, warming his back before the fire. His head was down on his breast, and Od- jibwa supposed that he did not yet know he had a visitor. But he was mistaken; for as soon as he looked in, the old man said, "Walk in, Nosis—*my grandchild.* Sit down across from me and remove your things and dry them. You must be tired. And I will prepare you something to eat."

Odjibwa did as he was told. Then the old magician said, "My kettle with water stands near the fire!" and immediately a small metal pot with legs appeared by the fire. Then he took one grain of corn and one blueberry and put them into the pot. Seeing this, the young man feared he would go hungry. But not a word or a look betrayed his feelings. The pot soon boiled. Then the old man spoke, commanding it to stand some distance from the fire. "Nosis," he said, "feed your- self," and he handed him a dish and ladle made of the same metal as the pot. The young man helped himself to all that there was and immediately felt ashamed at having done so. But before he could speak, the old man said, "Nosis, eat, eat," and shortly thereafter he again said, "Help yourself from the pot." Odjibwa was amazed to find it always full. He kept on emptying it; yet each time he did so, it was again filled, until at last he had completely satisfied his hunger. The magician spoke the command and the pot resumed its usual place off to one side in the lodge.

Then the young man reclined leisurely and listened to the words of his host. The old man told him that he must keep on and that he would meet with success. "To tell you more, I am not permitted. But continue as you have begun and you will not be disappointed. Tomorrow you will come to another of my fellow old men; but it will be the one after him who will tell you how to succeed. The red swan has often passed this way; those who have followed have never returned. Your mind must be strong. You must be prepared." "It will be so," answered the young man. Then they both lay down to sleep. Early in the morning the magician had his kettle prepared so his guest could eat before leaving. He gave Odjibwa his parting advice and sent him on his way.

As he set out, he found that he was in better spirits than he had been since leaving home. Again he spent the night with an old man, who treated him well and gave him directions the following morning. That day, as he traveled, his spirits were higher still, for by nightfall he expected to meet the one who would show him the way to the red swan itself.

Just as it was beginning to get dark, he reached the lodge of the third old man. And even before he got to the door, he heard him saying, "Nosis, come in," and going in immediately, he felt quite at home. The old man prepared him something to eat, just as the other magicians had done, and his kettle was exactly the same size and made of the same material. When Odjibwa had finished eating, the magician addressed him: "Young man, your errand is difficult. Many have passed with the same purpose in mind, but not one has returned. Be careful, and if your guardian spirits are powerful, you may succeed. The red swan you are following is the daughter of a magician. He is a man of great wealth, yet he values his daughter but little less than wampum. He himself once wore a cap of wampum, attached to his scalp. But powerful Indians—warriors of a distant chief—came to him and told him that their chief's daughter was near death and that she had asked for the wampum scalp so that she could be cured. If she could only see it, she would recover. And so, after repeated urging, the magician agreed to part with it, although when he took it off it left his head bare and bloody. Several years have passed, and it has not healed. The warriors deceived him; now they are making fun of his scalp, dancing it about from village to village, and with every insult it receives, the old man groans in pain. Those Indians are too powerful for the magician, and many young men have lost their lives attempting to rescue the scalp. They were enticed by the red swan, just as she has enticed you, and whoever is fortunate enough to succeed will win the red swan herself as his reward.

"In the morning you will continue on, and toward evening you will come to the magician's lodge. Before you enter, you will hear his groans. He will immediately ask you to come in; you will see no one but him. He will ask you about your dreams and about your guardian spirits. Then he will ask you to bring back the scalp. He will show you the way; and if you wish to do so, as I believe you will, go forward, my son, with a strong heart. Persevere, and I feel in my mind that you will succeed."

"I will try," said the young man, and early the next morning, after eating from the magic kettle, he started off. Toward evening he came to a lodge, as he had been told, and heard the groans of the magician; and even before he reached the door, he heard the invitation: "Come in." Upon entering, he saw that the old man's head was bloody. He was groaning terribly. "Sit down, sit down," he said, "while I prepare you something to eat." Then he made him food, just as the other magicians had done.

"You see how poor I am; I have no one to help me," he said, for he wished to conceal the fact that the red swan was there. But Odjibwa could see that the lodge was partitioned, and now and then he heard a rustling noise. He took off his leggings and his moccasins, and when he had eaten, the magician began to tell him how he had lost his scalp, about the insults it was receiving, the pain he was suffering, and the unsuccessful attempts that had already been made to get it back. He told him about those who had stolen it, how strong and how many they were. Then he appealed to the young man's pride and promised him riches. Now and then he would interrupt himself and groan, saying, "Oh, how shamefully they are treating it."

Odjibwa listened. Then the old man asked him about his dreams—enaw-baundum, *as he saw when asleep*—at the time he had fasted and blackened his face to procure guardian spirits. The young man then told him one dream; the magician groaned. "No, that is not it." The young man told him another. He groaned again. "That is not it." The young man told him two or three more. The magician groaned each time and said, rather peevishly, "No, these are not the ones." The young man thought to himself, "Who are you? You may groan as much as you like; I am inclined not to tell you any more dreams." The magician then spoke in a supplicating tone: "Have you no more dreams of another kind?" "Yes," said the young man, and told him one. "That is it, that is it," he cried. "You will cause me to live. You will go then and bring me my scalp."

"Yes," said the young man, "I will go; and the day after tomorrow, when you hear the cry of the kakak—*the hawk*—you will know by this sign that I am successful; and you must prepare yourself and lean out the door, so that the moment I arrive I can place the scalp on your head." "Yes, yes," said the magician. "As you say, it will be done."

3

Early next morning he set out, and about the time that the sun hangs toward home, he heard the shouts of a great many people. He was in a wood, and saw, as he thought, only a few men. But the farther he went, the more he saw. And then at last, as he came to an open plain, their heads appeared as numerous as the hanging leaves. In their midst he could see a post and something waving on it. It was the scalp. Now and then the air was rent with the sau-sau-quan, for they were dancing the war dance around it. Before he was noticed, he turned himself into a no-noskau-see—*a hummingbird*—and flew toward the scalp.

As he passed by the people's heads, he flew close to their ears and made the whirring sound that a hummingbird makes when it flies. They jumped to one side and asked each other what it could be. By this time he had nearly reached the scalp, but fearing he might be detected, he changed himself into a me-sau-be-wau-aun—*a tuft of down*—and floated lightly onto the scalp. He untied it and began to carry it upward. It was all he could do to keep it aloft, so heavy it was. And as it rose, they all cried out, "It is taken from us, it is taken from us." But he kept on, moving just above their heads. The rush and hum of so many people was like the dead beating surges after a storm. Soon he outdistanced them, and they gave up the pursuit. Then he became a hawk and flew away, calling out as he went.

When the old magician heard the cry of the kakak, he put his head out the door. Soon he heard the rustling of wings, and in a moment Odjibwa stood before him. Then he clapped the wampum scalp to the old man's head with such force that his limbs shot out and quivered in agony. The scalp adhered, and the young man walked in and sat down, feeling perfectly at home.

The magician was so long in recovering from the blow that he feared he had killed him. At last he began to show signs of life. He stirred, he sat up. As he rose to his full height, Odjibwa saw that he had become a handsome young man.

"Thank you, my friend," he said. "You have restored me to my former shape. It was so ordained, and now you have accomplished the victory." The young magician then urged his guest to stay, and Odjibwa remained for several days, and the two young men became fast friends. Not once, however, did the magician speak of the red swan.

At last the day arrived when Odjibwa was ready to leave. Then the magician repaid him for his bravery, giving him various kinds of wampum, robes, and many other things that would make him an influential man. But though his curiosity

was at its height, he still refrained from asking about the red
swan, feeling that it would be improper to do so, inasmuch as
his host, who had so richly rewarded him, had never once
mentioned her.

Odjibwa's traveling pack was ready and he was taking his
last smoke, when the magician addressed him at last:
"Friend, you know why you have come this far. You have
accomplished your object and conferred a lasting obligation
upon me. Your deeds shall not go unrewarded, and if you
undertake all other things in the same spirit, you will never
fail to accomplish them. My duties make it necessary for me
to remain where I am, although I would be happy to go with
you. I have given you all you will need as long as you live, and
so I see you are reluctant to speak of the red swan. Yet I
vowed that whoever returned my scalp should have her."
Then he called out and knocked on the partition. Immediately the door opened and the red swan herself appeared. She
was a most beautiful young woman, and as she stood before
Odjibwa, so great were her charms that she appeared as if she
did not belong on earth. "Take her," said the young magician. "She is my sister, treat her well. She is worthy of you,
and what you have done for me deserves even more. She is
ready to go with you to your kindred and friends, and has
been so ever since your arrival. My good wishes go with you
both." The young woman looked kindly on her husband.
Odjibwa bid farewell to his friend and, together with his wife,
began retracing his footsteps.

They traveled slowly, and after two or three days reached
the lodge of the third old magician. He welcomed them and
said, "Your heart is strong. You will succeed in all things."
And the following morning, as they were ready to start, he
pulled a bag from one side of the lodge, saying, "Nosis, I

give you this. It contains a present for you. Live happily in old age." Then they bid him farewell and proceeded on. Soon they reached the lodge of the second old man, where they were received in exactly the same manner. They went on and arrived at the first of the two villages. The watchman gave notice, and Odjibwa, as before, was shown into the chief's lodge. "Sit here, son-in-law," said the chief, pointing to a place near his daughter. "And you also," he said to the red swan.

The young woman of the lodge was busy with handwork, and she tried to show her indifference by not even raising her head to see who had come. Soon the chief said, "Let someone bring in our son-in-law's bundle." When it was brought in, the young man opened a bag he had received from one of the old men and drew out wampum, robes, and various other articles. He presented them to his father-in-law, and all were amazed at the richness of the gift. The chief's daughter glanced at the present, then at Odjibwa and his beautiful wife; she stopped working and remained silent and thoughtful the rest of the evening. They conversed about his adventures. Afterward, the chief told him that he should take his daughter along with him in the morning. The young man said, "Yes." The chief spoke again, saying, "Daughter, be ready to go with him in the morning."

But there was a Maujeekewis in the lodge, who had wanted the woman for his wife. He jumped up, saying, "Who is he, that he should take her for a few presents? I will kill him," and he raised a knife that he had in his hand. But he only waited until someone held him back, and then sat down, for he was truly a coward.

Early the next morning they went on their way and toward evening reached the other of the two villages. The watchman gave the cry, and many men, women, and children came out to see them. Again they were shown to the lodge of the chief, who greeted them, saying, "Son-in-law, you are welcome," and requested him to sit down by his daughter. The two women did the same.

When they had smoked and eaten, the chief asked the young man to relate his adventures, and those who came into the lodge to hear looked with admiration and astonishment at the red swan, for she was indeed beautiful. Odjibwa then told them everything that had happened to him; and afterward the chief said that his brothers had been to their village in search of him, but had returned home, having given up hope of ever seeing him again. He concluded by saying that since Odjibwa had been so fortunate and so manly, he should take his daughter with him. "For although your brothers were here," he said, "they were too timid to enter any of our lodges and merely asked for you and then went away. You will take my daughter; treat her well, and that will bind us more closely together."

Now it always happens in villages that someone is foolish. And so it happened here, for a Maujeekewis was in the lodge; and after the young man had given his father-in-law presents, this Maujeekewis jumped up in a rage, saying, "Who is this stranger, that he should have her? I want her myself." The chief told him to be quiet and not to quarrel with one who was enjoying their hospitality. "No, no!" he cried, and he attempted to strike the stranger. But Odjibwa was above fearing his threats and paid no attention to him. He cried all the louder: "I will have her, I will have her!" In an instant he was laid flat on the ground by the chief's war club; and when he had regained consciousness, the chief upbraided him for his foolishness and told him to go out and tell stories to the old women.

When all their arrangements were concluded, the young man invited a number of families to come along with him to visit his hunting grounds, as there was always plenty of game there. They consented, and in the morning a large party was assembled to accompany him; and the chief brought many warriors and they escorted them a long distance. When the time came for the chief to turn back, he made a speech and invoked the blessing of the Great Spirit on his son-in-law and on the entire party.

After several days' travel, Odjibwa and his followers came in sight of his former home. The party held back while he went in alone to see his brothers. As he entered the lodge, he saw that it was all dirty and covered with ashes. On one side he saw his eldest brother, sitting among the ashes with his face blackened, crying aloud. On the other side was Maujee-kewis, his other brother; his face was also blackened, but his head was covered with feathers and swan's down. Indeed he looked odd; and Odjibwa could not keep from laughing, for he made such a pretense of grief that he paid no attention to his brother's arrival. The eldest rose quickly and shook hands with him and kissed him and felt very happy to see him again.

After helping to clean up the place, Odjibwa told them that he had brought them each a wife. Hearing this, Maujeekewis jumped up and said, "Is it you? Did you just come in?" and made for the door and peeped out to see the women. Then he began jumping and laughing, saying, "Women! Women!" This was the reception he gave his brother.

Odjibwa then told them to wash and get ready, and he

would go out and bring them in. Maujeekewis began at once to wash, but every now and then he would peep out to see the women. When they came near, he said, "I will have this one; no, I will have that one." He would go and sit down for a moment, then get up and peep out again and laugh. He acted like a madman.

As soon as order was restored and all were seated, Odjibwa presented one of the women to his eldest brother, saying, "These women were given to me. I now give one to each of you. I intended so from the first." Maujeekewis spoke, and said, "I think three wives would have been *enough* for you." Then the young man led one of the women to Maujeekewis, saying, "My brother, here is one for you, and live happily." Maujeekewis hung down his head, as if he were ashamed, but now and then he would steal a glance at his wife and also at the other women. After a while, he turned toward his wife and acted as if he had been married for years. "Wife," he said, "I will go and hunt," and off he started.

4

All lived peacefully for some time. Their village prospered, the inhabitants increased, and everything was abundant among them. Yet after a while the two elder brothers began to be dissatisfied. At first they criticized Odjibwa for having taken their dead father's medicine arrows. Then they insisted that he go and find others to replace them, hoping to get him away so that one of them could take his wife. One day, after listening to them, he told them he would go. Then he and Maujeekewis went together into a sweat lodge. Even there, in that holy place, Maujeekewis kept scolding him about the arrows. Again he told him that he would go; and next day, true to his word, he set out.

After traveling a long way, he came to an opening in the earth, and descending, he entered the land of the dead. It was a beautiful country, stretching as far as the eye could see. He saw animals of various kinds in abundance. The first he came to were buffalo, and he was amazed when they spoke to him as human beings. They asked him why he had come, how he had descended, and why he dared to visit the land of the dead. He told them he had come for magic arrows to appease his brothers. "Very well," said the leader of the buffaloes, whose whole body was nothing but bone. "Yes, we know it." Then he and his followers moved back, as if they were afraid of him. "You have come to a place where a living man has never been," continued the buffalo spirit. "You will return immediately to your tribe, for your brothers are trying to dishonor your wife. Go, and you will live to a very old age. You will live and die happily. You can come no farther in this land of ours."

Odjibwa looked in the direction he thought was west and saw a bright light, as if the sun were shining, but he saw no sun. "What light is that I see?" he asked. The bone buffalo answered, "It is the place where those who were good dwell." "And that dark cloud?" Odjibwa asked. "Mudjee-izzhi-wabezewin—*wickedness*," answered the buffalo. The young man asked no more questions, and with the help of his guardian spirits he again stood on the earth and breathed the air and saw the sun giving its usual light. No one knows what else he saw in the land of the dead, or where he went or what he did when he left that place.

At last, one evening, after wandering a long time in search of knowledge to make his people happy, he returned to his village; then, passing all the other lodges, he came to his own, where he heard his brothers quarreling for possession of his wife, who had, however, remained constant, mourning the absence and probable death of her husband. The young man listened until he was certain of what he had heard, then entered the lodge and without a word placed the magic arrows in his bow, drew them to their full length, and shot his brothers dead. Thus ended the contest between the hermit's sons; and a strong and happy union was consummated between Odjibwa and the red swan.

THE MASTER OF THE RED MACAWS

KAMAIURÁ

From the forests of Brazil comes a remote variant of the Chippewa "Red Swan." The twin culture heroes, Sun and Moon, correspond to the hero Odjibwa, the ten macaws to the three brides. Vanivaní represents both the master of culture (the Chippewa magician) and the souls of the dead land (from whom Odjibwa wrests the jeweled scalp of new life).

The red macaw was always flying over the Sun's village at the Morená. In the afternoon, when the Sun was sitting in his doorway, the macaw would pass over the village. It showed up every day. It would circle the village and then head back in the direction it had come from.

"Did you see the beautiful bird that's always flying over here?" the Sun asked his brother the Moon.

The next day, when the macaw appeared, the Sun called his brother to see. The Moon immediately recognized it as Vanivaní's macaw. Wanting to see the macaw close up, the two agreed to go to Vanivaní's village the following day. The next morning they set off. When they arrived, Vanivaní asked, "What did you come here for? Do you want something?"

"We're just out for a walk," answered the Sun.

Seeing Vanivaní's macaws, the Moon commented, "Our friend here makes a lot of macaws."

Vanivaní again asked his visitors what they wanted. The Sun, under persistent questioning, answered that they had come to ask for a macaw. Vanivaní right away gave them one of his birds. And then he said, "Now I will have to scrape [bleed] you."

He performed the scarification on the Sun first, and with the blood he got from it, he made five tiny spheres. Then he called the Moon and scarified him too, making another five balls out of the blood he had drawn. After this, Vanivaní put the blood away in the same place he made macaws. He left it there for safekeeping. Then he told the Sun and the Moon to stay in his village till the next day, so they might have the macaws he was going to make. At daybreak the macaws that were being made began to scream. Vanivaní woke up the Sun and the Moon to watch. He showed them and said, "That is how I make macaws. I always do it this way."

After this remark, he gave his guests five macaws each, made with their own blood. The Sun and the Moon were delighted with Vanivaní's gift. Vanivaní had in his village two houses full of macaws. The houses were for them alone.

When the Sun and the Moon left, Ianamá arrived. Vanivaní asked him what he had come for. Ianamá replied that he was there only to visit.

The Sun went back to his village in the Morená and began to make macaws himself. He and the Moon did it together. They made them with their own blood and that of their wives. When there were enough of these manufactured macaws, they decided to build a deep ravine, to serve as dwelling place for them. They set to work, raising the riverbanks. While they were laboring, Vanivaní arrived in their village. Mavutsinim was alone there with the wives of the masters of the house. As he was leaving, Vanivaní invited the two women to come with him. They accepted the invitation and left with Vanivaní. Before leaving, Vanivaní rounded up all the macaws in the Sun's village: the ones he had given them, as well as any others he could find. And he went back to his village. When they arrived there, Mavutsinim, who had come along, asked him why he had taken the wives of the masters of the village in the Morená. Vanivaní answered, "They wanted to take my macaws. That is why I brought their women here."

There in the Morená, the village of the Sun, only the parrot was left. He belonged to the Moon. The Sun and all his people were still out building the ravine. When Vanivaní left, the parrot started calling for his masters, shouting that their wives had been stolen. This is what he shouted: "Paicã! Vanivaní Werahá né remerikó." [*My uncle, Vanivaní took your wife.*]

He shouted this over and over. The Sun heard it and said to the Moon, "Listen to what he is saying."

When the two had heard and understood what the parrot was shouting, they stopped work and went back to the village.

Only the parrot was there. When they arrived, the parrot said to them, "Your friend was here and took your wives. I don't know why they went with him."

The Sun and the Moon sat down to think and talk about what to do. One of them said, "We have to go get our wives. They belong to us, so we must go."

The following day they went off to Vanivaní's village. They crept up on it slowly, and from hiding they saw their wives sitting in Vanivaní's doorway. The Moon picked up a piece of wax, molded some motuca flies, and sent them to sit on his own wife's breast and on the leg of the Sun's wife. The motucas flew off and sat down to suck blood. As soon as they felt them, the women shooed the motucas away. They flew off and were caught by the Sun. Then the Sun and the Moon milked the blood they had sucked and deposited it in the fork of the aputereóp tree. They covered the blood carefully and spent the night there waiting. The next day the blood was already turning into people. They were laughing in the crotch of the tree.

"Listen," said the Moon, "our women are laughing up there."

Vanivaní, there in the village, said to himself, "I'm going to take these women that I have brought farther downstream." He got a canoe and went down the river with them. The Sun and the Moon were in the Morená. Vanivaní was going much farther down. He rested along the way and continued the journey the next day. He traveled without stopping, going down the river day after day. He stopped only when he came to the big river. There he settled in. Back in his village, the only person left was Mavutsinim, the old man. He stayed there, all by himself. After some time, the old man went downriver after Vanivaní. He traveled and traveled until he caught up with him, camping at the same place, on the opposite bank of the river. There he stood, shouting for a canoe, so he could come across. Vanivaní sent over a tiny canoe to get the old man. The canoe was very small and seated only one person. Mavutsinim did not want to cross in it, because he thought it wasn't safe. Vanivaní sent another one the same size as the first. Mavutsinim again refused to get into it. Again he thought it was too small. Vanivaní then sent the cayman to get the old man. The cayman leaned up against the steep bank and called to Mavutsinim to get on board. Mavutsinim said, "Now I'll go with you."

And he went across on the cayman. On the other bank he found Vanivaní's house and went inside. Vanivaní told the old man to have a seat and gave him a tiny gourd of cauim. Mavutsinim wanted to drink the whole thing, but he couldn't. The gourd kept filling up with cauim, and never ran out. Afterward, Vanivaní gave him a beiju, also very tiny. Mavutsinim tried to eat the whole thing, but there was no end to it. The beiju kept replenishing itself every time he took a bite.

If Vanivaní had not left, the red macaws would still be living up here. There are no macaws here, because he took them all downstream.

WHY THE BUZZARD IS BALD

IOWA

This neatly constructed mythlet is divided into two equal parts, the second of which is a translation of the first into a

different set of images. The hero's fall from heaven becomes
the putrefaction of his own corpse; the victory over the vul-
ture echoes his (erotic) rescue by members of the opposite
sex.

As Ishjinki was traveling, he came to a place where he saw
a buzzard flying above him. "Oh, grandfather," exclaimed
Ishjinki, "how you must enjoy yourself up there in the air.
There is nothing that can hurt you and you can see everywhere. I wish I could get up as high as that and see as far as
you do!"

"You would never get used to it, my grandson," said the
buzzard. "You belong down there and I belong up here. I'd
rather you'd stay where you are."

But Ishjinki begged and teased the buzzard until the bird
took him up a little ways and returned. Then Ishjinki pleaded
with the buzzard to take him up again and higher. This happened four times. The last time the buzzard took Ishjinki very
high, so that Ishjinki cried "Wahaha" in terror every time
the bird dipped as he soared. Finally, the buzzard went down
close over the tops of the timber until he saw a stump that was
hollow at the top. He tipped Ishjinki headfirst into it, and
Ishjinki was stuck there. It happened that there was a hunting
party of Sauk nearby, camping, and some of their women
came very close to the tree as they were gathering firewood.
Ishjinki was able to see them through a crack, so he called
out, "Big male raccoon in here!"

"Listen," said one of the women, and again Ishjinki sang
as before: "Big male raccoon in here!"

This time the women heard him plainly. They went up to the
tree and Ishjinki put his coonskin up to the crack so that they
could see it plainly. They cut a hole in the tree with their

axes, and could see it plainer. "There it is! It's big!" exclaimed Ishjinki to encourage them, so they chopped the hole still larger. At last it was large enough, and Ishjinki said, "Oh, my granddaughters, it is me, Ishjinki, let me out!"

"Oh, it's our grandfather," said the women, and Ishjinki sprang out. "Haa, now I feel good," he said. "Now you must dance, and I'll sing for you. Get your axes and hold them." So Ishjinki sang:

> *Big male raccoon here*
> *Big male raccoon here*
> *Big male raccoon here*
> *Big male raccoon here.*

Ishjinki was angry at the buzzard, so he made a trap for him. He pretended to be a dead horse and lay down until the crows pecked his buttocks. The buzzard appeared, but although Ishjinki tried three times, he could not fool him. The fourth time he became a dead elk. The birds came and ate most of his buttocks and the crows even went in and out of his body. At last the buzzard came and pecked at the edge of the opening, and then he stretched his head and reached inside. All at once Ishjinki closed the opening. "Now I've got you," he exclaimed, and walked off with the buzzard dangling from his buttocks. He kept Buzzard there for a long time, but finally he said, "I'll let you go, you've suffered enough for your trick." Then he released the poor bird. And that's why Buzzard's head is bald—and stinks.

GERIGUIGATUGO

BORORO

The legend of Geriguigatugo is the mythe de référence, *the "key myth," with which Lévi-Strauss begins* The Raw and the Cooked, *the first volume of his celebrated four-volume discourse,* Mythologiques.

The people of the ancient time were gathering leaves for the penis sheath. Korogo joined the other women and went along too. Then a boy, her son, caught sight of her and raped her—his own mother. The boy was Geriguigatugo. His father was Bokwadorireu.

When the woman returned to her lodge, the father could not help but notice that a boy's ornamental feathers were caught in his wife's girdle. To learn who had treated his wife in this manner, he ordered the people to begin the boys' soul-dance. And as they danced he looked and looked to see which boys were wearing feathers on their arms. But in vain. His son was the only one with arm feathers.

Then he called his son once more and ordered him to go tell the people there must be another dance. And as they danced again, he watched to see if any boys were wearing arm feathers. But in vain. The boys were unadorned. Only his son wore decorations, he alone wore feathers on his arms.

Now the father was enraged, and he ordered his son to go down to the nest of souls to fetch the large rattle. Then the boy ran at once to his grandmother, saying, "Grandmother, Grandmother! Father says I must get the large rattle that belongs to the souls. He wants it." And his grandmother said,

"You can't do such a difficult thing"—that's what she said. But then she said, "Go to the hummingbird! The hummingbird will help you get it." Then the boy went to the hummingbird, saying, "Hummingbird, Hummingbird, we must go to the nest of souls to get the large rattle."

Then he went with him there—went with him to the souls' nest, where the large rattle was. He went all the way down to the souls. Yet the nest is beneath the water. Thus the boy himself sat alongside the water, he stayed behind, the bird went on.

Then the hummingbird flew to the souls' nest and cut the string that held the large rattle. It dropped and went *djo-o-o!* And at that the souls cried, "Umh! umh! umh! umh!" and they tried to shoot him, but he flew swiftly away: they failed to wound him. He came a second time and cut the string. Then he returned to the boy and gave him the rattle. Then the hummingbird quickly flew off. And the boy went home to his father, saying, "Father, your rattle!"

The father had acted this way so that the souls could kill his son. But the grandmother's knowledge had been great. She had counseled her grandson.

Now the father called his son again and told him to go to the souls' nest to get the small rattle. At once the boy ran to his grandmother, saying, "Grandmother, Grandmother! Father says I must get the small rattle that belongs to the souls." Then the grandmother said, "You can't do such a difficult thing. But go to the dove! With the dove you can get it." And he went to the dove and said, "Dove, Dove, we must go to the souls' nest to get the small rattle." Then they went off together to where the souls lived, to their waterside. And the boy stayed behind and the dove went on.

Then the dove flew down to the small rattle. Then he cut

the string that held the rattle, and the rattle went *djo-o-o!* as it struck the water. At that the souls cried, "Umh! umh! umh! umh!" and they shot their arrows. But he flew so swiftly they failed to hit him. And then he returned, got the small rattle, and flew back to the boy. Then the dove disappeared. And the boy took it home to his father, saying, "Father, your rattle!"

Then the father called his son once again and told him to go to the souls' nest to get the peccary anklet. And the boy ran off to his grandmother, saying, "Grandmother, Grandmother! Father says I must get the souls' peccary anklet." Then the grandmother said, "Try the mammori. With the mammori you'll get the souls' anklet." So the boy ran to the mammori: "My father says we must get the souls' anklet." Then together they went, to get the souls' anklet. The boy stayed back, the mammori went on.

The mammori flew down to the anklet and cut the string. Then the anklet went *djo-o-o!* as it hit the water. And the souls cried, "Umh! umh! umh! umh!" and they shot at him then. And because he flew poorly, they hit him again and again in the chest. Yet they failed to kill him: he was able to bring back the peccary anklet. He gave it to the boy, then flew out of sight. And the boy went home to his father, saying, "Father, your anklet!"

Seeing that his son had returned alive, the father cried, "Hah! May you be killed by the red macaws!" Then he spoke to him again, saying, "O man! O man! We must be off now to the macaws' nest!" And the boy ran to his grandmother and said, "Grandmother, Grandmother! Father says I must go with him to the macaws' nest!" But the grandmother did not know what to do. The boy became agitated. Then at last she picked up her walking stick and gave it to him, saying, "Push this into the nest, quickly!"

Then the boy went along with his father to the base of the rock where the nest was, and there the father, finding a pole, raised it against the face of the rock so the boy could climb up. But as soon as the boy reached the cleft where the nest was, the father stopped holding the pole, thinking the boy would fall and be killed. Then quickly the boy pushed his grandmother's stick into the cleft and held on, dangling, crying for help, while the father went back to the village.

Then the boy, looking up, saw a vine hanging down within reach. He seized it and climbed to the top of the rock. Recovered somewhat from his fright and exertion, he found he was hungry. Then, using the shrubs that grew on the rock, he made a bow and many arrows and began hunting the lizards that abounded there. He killed many. Then he ate some and fastened the rest to his belt and to his arm- and ankle-bands and carried them with him.

But they started to rot and grow foul, until at last the stench overwhelmed him and he fell to the ground unconscious. Then a flock of urubus and other vultures flew down on him and greedily fed on the lizards. And when they'd finished the lizards, they attacked his buttocks. Then he frightened them off with a huge strap. But they came back and kept pecking from behind until his buttocks were eaten away.

And then with their beaks they grasped him by the belt and by the arm- and leg-bands and lifted him up. They flew far into the sky, then at last put him down at the base of the rock where the macaws' nest was.

He came to, as though waking from a long sleep. He was hungry and began eating the fruits that were plentiful there. Yet he saw that whatever he ate went immediately through him. The birds had destroyed his anus.

Then he remembered a story his grandmother had told, in which the same thing had happened and the missing parts had been molded out of soft yams. And so he did likewise, he molded new hind parts out of soft yams. Then he started to eat once again to see if they worked as they should. They did. Then he set off for home. But the village was no longer there. The people had moved.

Then for many days he wandered in search of the path that would lead him to the new village, but for a long time he looked in vain. Then at last he saw stick marks and human tracks, and he knew that the tracks had been made by his grandmother and his little brother, and the marks by his grandmother's stick. Then he felt a desire to be with her at once, and he said:

"Baigareu! Fly at once! *There!*" He changed into a baigareu, flying right to the spot he had meant. Then he changed back into himself. Then he saw that the tracks led on, and he said:

"Kugago! Fly at once! *There!*" He changed into a kugago, flew right to the spot, changed back to himself, then saw that the tracks led on, and said:

"Little Bird! Fly at once! *There!*" And he changed to a little bird, flew right to the spot, changed back to himself, then saw that the tracks led on, and said:

"Kiwareu! Fly at once! *There!*" Then he changed to a kiwareu, flew right to the spot, changed back to himself, then saw that the tracks led on. And he said:

"Butterfly! Fly at once! *There!*" Then he changed to a butterfly and flew on, and there before him he saw his grandmother, walking along with her stick, and beside her his little brother.

Then before he got there he changed back to himself and

followed along behind her. Hearing steps, the grandmother said to her little grandson, "Look back! See who's coming!" He looked, then said, "My elder brother!"

The boy was glad to see his grandmother again. Through her wisdom she had saved him from many dangers.

Then he said to her, "I will live with our people no more. They have treated me badly. And to punish my father and all the others who have made me suffer, I will send them wind, cold, and rain." Then he led his grandmother off to a distant and beautiful country and told her that she must remain there, that he would go punish the people and then return. And so in exchange for the treatment he'd received from his father, he punished the people—and turned into wind, cold, and rain.

THE GREAT CAVERN OF DARKNESS

M I C M A C

The Algonkians of the Maritime Provinces regarded Glooskap (the central figure in their mythology) as part benign father and part heroic son. As if to straddle this ambiguity, Glooskap is given a curious "family": a child, called Marten, and a mother, called Bear. In the following myth, a humdrum adventure in which Bear and Marten are kidnapped and rescued is reiterated in an impressive allegory in which the two are overcome by death and returned to life. On second reading the "humdrum" adventure appears to be an escape from

spirits of evil, or death, who have ferried their victims across
the water to the land of souls.

Now it is told in another tradition, and men tell even this differently, that pitché—*in these old times*—Glooskap's seven neighbors, who were all so many different animals, took away his family, and that he followed them, even as it has been written, unto Newfoundland. And when he came there it was night, and, finding Marten alone, he took him forth into the forest to seek food, putting his belt on the boy, which gave him such power that he hunted well and got much meat.

So it came to pass that the next morning Dame Kah-kah-gooch, the Crow, observed that Marten was drying meat on his wigwam. And this she spread abroad. But when the people learned that the child had done this, a great fear came upon them all, and they sat every man in his lodge and awaited death, for they knew that the Master had come.

And he indeed came; but when he saw them all as frightened as rabbits before the wildcat, he laughed aloud and forgave them, for he was noble and generous. And as they were hungry—for he had come in hard times—he gave them much venison, and sorrow departed from their wigwams. But as they had left him of old, he now left them. When they knew him not, they left him to die; now that they knew him, they feared lest they should perish without him. But he turned his steps towards other paths.

Now having made a canoe, the Master, with Marten and Dame Bear, went upon a mighty river. As the story says, it was broad and beautiful at first, and so they sailed away down towards its mouth. Then they came to great cliffs, which gathered round and closed over them. But the river ran on beneath these, and ever on far underground, deeper and deeper in the earth, till it dashed headlong into rapids, among rocks and ravines, and under cataracts which were so horrible that death seemed to come and go with every plunge of the canoe. And the water grew narrower and the current more dreadful, and fear came upon Marten and the woman, so that they died. But the Master sat with silent soul, though he sang the songs of magic, and so passed into the night, but came forth again into sunlight. And there was a lonely wigwam on the bank, into which he bore Marten and the grandmother, and saying, "Numchahse! *Arise!*" lo, they arose, and deemed they had only slept. And now Glooskap had gained the greatest power.

THE FLIGHT OF QUETZALCOATL

AZTEC

With Quetzalcoatl the earth itself is turned inward through a five-step progression toward death (beginning with the hero's stop at Cuauhtitlan), then outward through the stages of youth, maturity, senescence, death, and rebirth (beginning with the frolic on the mountain). The five-stage revival corresponds to the sunwise circuit of the four cardinal points— east, south, west, north, and back again to east—which in turn corresponds to the mystic cross. Note: the following is a literal translation except for added glosses and connectives, which are printed in italic.

And many another evil was done to the Toltecs that Tollan might be destroyed. And because it was so, Quetzalcoatl suffered. He grieved. Then he remembered that he was to go, that he was to leave his city of Tollan. Then he made his preparations.

It is said that he completely burned his house of gold, his house of redshell. And the other Toltec treasures, the splendid things, the precious things: all were buried, all were concealed in inaccessible places, in the interior of a mountain or in chasms.

And he also changed the cacao trees to mesquites. And all the precious birds, the quetzal, the cotinga, the roseate spoonbill—he sent them on ahead. They led him onward, they proceeded to Anahuac. So it was. And so he started out, and so he followed on.

And soon he reached the site of Cuauhtitlan—*Beneath the Tree*. The tree rose very broad and very tall. He stopped beside it. Then he asked to have his mirror, then he saw himself: he looked at his reflection, saying, "Truly I *am* old." And there he dubbed it Old-Age Cuauhtitlan—*Beneath the Old-Age Tree*.

Thereupon he stoned the tree. He pelted it. And as he pelted it, the stones grew all encrusted *and* fixed themselves upon the old-age tree. This is how it always looked—it appeared just so—beginning at the root, extending to the crown.

And as Quetzalcoatl followed on, they preceded, blowing *flutes* for him.

Again he rested—at a place where he sat himself upon a rock, leaning *forward* on his hands. Suddenly then in the distance he saw Tollan, and then he wept. Sighing, he wept. His tears rained down as hail, *and* his tears slid down his face. As they dropped, they pierced the very rock.

And as he leaned on the rock with his hands, he pressed *them* down, just as one would make impressions with one's palms in clay. His buttocks likewise were upon the rock and so were impressed *and* bemired. Indeed the indentations can be seen. So he gave *this* place the name Temacpalco—*Where the Handprints Are.*

And then he arose *and* went on to a place called Tepano-huayan—*At the Stone Bridge—where* a river lies, a river flowing, spread out wide. He laid stones to make a bridge, *and* then and there crossed over. And thereupon he called it Tepanohuayan.

And again he set forth, and arrived at a place called Coahapan—*At the Water of the Serpent.* There *were* sorcerers there who wished to turn him back, reverse him, *and* they blocked his way *and* asked him, "Where are you going? Where are you bound? Why are you leaving the city? To whom have you left *it?* Who shall do penance?"

Then Quetzalcoatl answered the sorcerers, "This cannot be permitted. I must go on."

Then the sorcerers asked Quetzalcoatl, "Where do you go?" And Quetzalcoatl answered, "Tlapallan *is* where I go *and* what I seek."

And they asked him, "What business have you *there?*" Then Quetzalcoatl said, "I have been summoned there—the sun has called me."

Then they answered, "Very well. You must relinquish all the Toltec arts."

And there he did relinquish all the Toltec arts: the art of casting gold, the art of cutting *jewels,* the art of carving wood, the art of working stone, the art of painting *books,* the art of *feather*-working.

They made him yield it all, they took it all by force—they seized it all.

So it was. Then Quetzalcoatl threw his jewels upon the water and they were swallowed up. And so he gave the place a name: Cozcahapan, *At the Water of the Jewels,* now called Coahapan, *At the Water of the Serpent.*

And then he traveled on, reaching the place called Cochtocan—*Where He Lay Sleeping.* And there a sorcerer came to meet him *and* said to him, "Where are you going?" Then he answered, "Tlapallan *is* where *I go and* what I seek."

Then the sorcerer said, "Very well. Drink this wine that I have brought here." Quetzalcoatl answered, "No, I must not drink, nor even taste but a little."

Then the sorcerer spoke to him again: "It cannot be allowed that you fail to drink, that you *even* fail to taste it. *For* I give leave to no one, I let no one pass, unless I serve him wine *and* have him drink—*and* make him drunk. Now do it! Come! *And* drink this!"

Then Quetzalcoatl drank the wine *through* a reed. And when he had drunk, he fell fast asleep in the road. He thundered as he slept: his snoring could be heard from afar. And when he woke, then he glanced from side to side. He looked at himself *and* arranged his hair; then he gave the place a name: Cochtocan, *Where He Lay Sleeping.*

Then again he set forth, climbing up between Iztactepetl and Popocatepetl. *And* all the dwarfs *and* the hunchbacks *who were* his servants went with him. It snowed on them all, they were chilled there, they died of the cold. And Quetzalcoatl was shaken by it. He wept. He sang. Weeping greatly, he sighed.

Then he saw in the distance another white mountain, called Poyauhtecatl. *And* again he set forth *and* went everywhere, touching at towns *and villages* everywhere. And they say that he left a great number of traces behind him—his signs—by which he was signified:

At a certain spot on a mountain, they say, he would frolic *and* tumble *and* fall to the bottom, and for his recovery he left in place a towline *of maguey.*

At another site he laid out a ball court all of stone. And through the middle, where the center line lay, it was entrenched. *And* the entrenchment ran deep.

And in another place he shot a ceiba, shooting it so that he himself passed through the heart of the ceiba.

And in another place he built a house underground. *And* the site is called Mictlan.

And in yet another place he erected a stone, a great stone phallus. They say that anyone might once have pushed it with his little finger.

It had indeed been set in motion, rocking back and forth. Yet, they say, when many pushed it, then it absolutely would not move. Though many together might make the effort, desiring to push it, it could not be moved.

And still many other things did he do in towns *and villages* everywhere. And they say that he named all the mountains. Here *and* throughout he bestowed all the names.

And at last he arrived at the seashore. Then he constructed a litter of serpents. *And* when it was finished, he sat himself on it: it served as his boat. And so he set off *and* was carried away by the sea.

No longer does anyone know how he reached Tlapallan.

NOTES

Introduction

page 4 / eleven brides . . . for eleven brothers: Bloomfield 1928, pp. 419–29.

page 5 / "The Roll Call of the Founders".: See Bierhorst 1974, pp. 112 ff.

page 5 / "putting the house in order": Literally, "putting their house in order" (Fenton 1957, p. 23).

page 5 / Malinowski: Malinowski 1955.

page 5 / "the germ-cell of civilization": Freud 1962, p. 61.

page 6 / Ernest Jones: Jones 1954, p. 157.

page 6 / Paul Radin: Radin 1972.

page 8 / J. N. B. Hewitt: Hewitt 1903.

page 8 / "an intuitive feeling . . .": Lévi-Strauss 1969, p. 2.

page 10 / device known as splitting: Well discussed in Ernest Jones 1954.

page 11 / myth may be described as . . . geometrical: Cf. Bierhorst 1974, pp. xiii–xvi.

page 12 / To me it seems that youth is like spring . . . : Samuel Butler, *The Way of All Flesh,* Modern Library ed., 1950, p. 38. (First published in 1903.)

page 13 / progressionism: Bierhorst 1974, p. xvi.

page 13 / a hummingbird in her belly: Cadogan 1959, p. 15.

page 13 / conceived of fluff: Sahagún 1956, Libro 3, cap. 1.

page 13 / as Lévi-Strauss has pointed out: Lévi-Strauss 1969, p. 203.

page 16 / a gradual process of becoming conscious: See Jung and Kerényi 1969, p. 86; Jung in Radin 1972, pp. 200 ff. See also Jung 1967, paragraphs 652–3. For specimens of Jungian criticism along these lines, as applied to native American subject matter, see Jung's and Radin's study of the Winnebago Trickster Cycle (Radin 1972) and Sheila Moon's analysis of the Navajo Emergence Myth (Moon 1974).

page 16 / interpretation based on the ideas of Freud: The Oedipus complex has not yet been made the theme of any noteworthy criticism devoted to American Indian literature. As Stanley Edgar Hyman has suggested, Ernest Jones's exemplary *Hamlet and Oedipus* has in a sense obviated the need for any further criticism in this particular vein. See Jones 1954; Hyman 1955, p. 160.

page 16 / by no means clear that he declined to do so: See Ernest Jones 1957, p. 332.

page 17 / Freud's myth: Freud 1938, pp. 915–16. Cf. Freud 1950, pp. 141–2.

page 17 / a second myth: Freud 1962, p. 37. The myth is defended and elucidated in Freud 1963.

page 20 / nature mythology: Still being disavowed, some fifty years after it was presumed dead (outside of Germany, that is). For a typical specimen of the genre, see D. G. Brinton's solar analysis of the Quetzalcoatl myth (Brinton 1882). German adherents, who preferred lunar themes, included Ehrenreich, Frobenius, Seler, and Lehmann. Typical naysayers are Lowie (1908), Dorson (1965), Lévi-Strauss (1969, p. 240).

page 20 / ritual theory: Has never been directly applied to American Indian literature. The theory itself is described and defended in Hyman 1965, attacked in Fontenrose 1971.

page 20 / a Menominee variant: Bloomfield 1928, pp. 419–29.

page 30 / former sporadic range of roseate spoonbill: For old sightings as far north as Wisconsin, see Allen 1942.

page 30 / "from vivid feeling within oneself . . .": Phinney 1934, p. ix.

The Dream Father

page 37 / The Beginning Life of the Hummingbird
Source: Cadogan 1959, pp. 13–15. The English translation is

mine, after the Spanish of Cadogan (who also gives the Mbyá text). Collected by Cadogan in the department of Guairá, Paraguay. Spanish text reprinted in Cadogan and Lopez Austin 1970.

page 37 / the absolute: Mbyá *pa-pa,* literally, "ultimate ultimate."

page 37 / Ñamanduí: Nyah-mahn-doo-EE, another name for the First Father.

page 38 / Hummingbird: The spirit of life, synonymous with the First Father.

page 38 / the primal time-space: Winter.

page 38 / a new space in time: Spring. The First Father is reborn with the coming of spring.

page 39 / Solitude Walker
Source: Curtis 1907–30, Vol. 14, pp. 169–70. I have given only the opening paragraphs of a slightly longer myth published by Curtis as "The Creation." Narrated by a Round Valley Yuki.

page 40 / Was It Not an Illusion?
Source: Preuss 1921–3, Vol. 1, pp. 166–7. The English translation is mine, after the lexical German of Preuss (who also gives the Uitoto text and a free German translation). Obtained by Preuss from Rïgasedyue, called Rosendo. I have given only the first half of the myth published as "The Creation." A quite different translation of the same passage appears in Astrov 1962, p. 325, reprinted by Sanders and Peek (1973, p. 60) and by Rothenberg (1968, p. 27). Yet a different version is given by

Radin (1954, p. 13), reprinted in Radin 1957 (p. 265) and in Eliade 1974 (p. 85). The passage is briefly discussed by Róheim (1952, p. 428). For Pettazoni's Italian translation, see Pettazoni 1959, p. 251.

page 40 / Who-Has-an-Illusion: Can also be translated "Who-Is-an-Illusion."

page 41 / Had he no staff?: Compare the "staff of authority" mentioned in the Mbyá myth given above (p. 37).

page 41 / gathered the void with dream-thread and pressed it together with gum: Soil particles are held together both physically and, as it were, chemically. The desert-dwelling Pima of southern Arizona also have a myth in which the Creator binds the primal soil both physically (with the erosion-inhibiting creosote bush) and quasi-chemically (with a "black gum" produced by unidentified insects). For the Pima myth, see Russell 1908, pp. 206–7.

page 41 / iseike: EE-say-ee-kay, a mysterious adhesive defined by one of Preuss's native informants as something "like tobacco smoke, like cotton flocking."

page 41 / the water flowed: To make the forest grow. The Uitoto are forest dwellers.

page 41 / when we emerged: Compare the Apache myth, p. 51.

page 41 / How Coyote Made the World
Source: de Angulo 1950, pp. 370–1. Original title: none. Narrated by Wild Bill (a professional horsebreaker) at an Indian camp near Alturas, California. Reprinted in de Angulo 1953,

p. 240. (The ellipsis " . . . " is used here to indicate a pause, not an omission.)

page 43 / Paiutes: PYE-yoots, a Nevada tribe. At the time this myth was collected, there were Paiutes living and working in the Pit River valley.

page 44 / a crazy woman, Loon: Loon Woman committed the first incest. Her story is a female variant of the kind of myth represented in the present collection by "Brother Black and Brother Red."

From the Body of Our Mother

page 49 / The Flaming Rock
Source: Fletcher and La Flesche 1911, pp. 570–1. Original title: none. Obtained from Wakídezhinga, leader of the Ínkugthi Athin [They Who Have the Translucent Pebble], an Omaha medicine society. Reprinted and discussed by Alexander (1953, p. 43); reprinted in Brown 1972, p. 15, and in Eliade 1974, p. 84.

page 50 / uprose a great rock: The imagery is phallic. Compare the "great stone phallus" of Quetzalcoatl, below, p. 312, and the rising Flint, p. 155. For an explanation, see Róheim 1952, pp. 427–8.

page 50 / Earth Goddess
Source: "Histoyre du Mechique," 1905, pp. 28–9. Original title: none. The source is a sixteenth-century French translation (by

André Thévet) of a lost Spanish original, said to have been compiled by missionaries in 1543 (see Garibay 1953–4, Vol. 1, p. 52). The English translation is mine, after the French of Thévet. Garibay (1964a, p. 1) gives a Spanish version of the same passage. Retold by Jensen (1948, p. 119), Campbell (1969, p. 224), Roy (1972, p. 15).

page 50 / Quetzalcoatl: Ket-sahl-KOH-otl, with the final syllable pronounced like the "otl" in the English word "potluck."

page 50 / Tlalteuctli: Tlahl-TAYook-tlee; literally, "earth lord"; here regarded as feminine.

page 50 / there was water already: Like the pre-existing fog in the Pit River myth, p. 42.

page 50 / two great serpents: Note that the two serpents (who represent the dual Creator) form a cross over the body of Tlalteuctli, just as the Creator in the Yuki myth (p. 39, above) constructs a world cross with his four lílkae, or stone crooks. The cross stands for the four directions, east, south, west, and north. But the Aztec myth goes on to incorporate a second idea: that the universe is half sky and half earth, sky corresponding to the upper half of the human body, earth to the lower half.

page 51 / which greatly displeased the other gods: Probably because they hoped to receive the upper, not the lower, part. The myth here reverses the expected positioning of the goddess's two halves, evidently for the sake of incorporating yet another idea: that the springs in the earth are supernatural mouths. Compare the salivating divinity in the Uitoto myth, p. 41.

page 51 / this goddess wails: The mysterious llorona ("weeping woman") may still be encountered in Mexican folklore. She is the old Aztec earth mother, crying for human blood. Cf. Sahagún, Bk. 12, ch. 1; see Horcasitas and Butterworth 1963.

page 51 / The Emergence

Source: Opler 1938, pp. 1, 16–20, 25–6. The selection presented here is a sequence of excerpts from an extensive myth cycle published by Opler as the "Origin Myth." (I use the ellipsis to indicate omissions.) Collected by Opler in 1934–5. Portions of the myth are quoted and discussed by Campbell (1969, pp. 231 ff.).

page 52 / Hactcin: Spirit powers (pronounced hosht-sheen).

page 55 / The Mother of All the People

Source: Teit et al. 1917, p. 80. I have presented only the first portion of a somewhat longer narrative published by Teit as "Old-One." Collected by Teit. Told by Kwelkweltáhen [Red Arm], a Sanpoil with Okanagon connections. Reprinted in Maria Leach 1956.

page 56 / The Origin of Nunivak Island

Source: Curtis 1907–30, Vol. 20, pp. 77–8. Collected at Nash Harbor.

page 58 / Sedna and the Fulmar

Source: Boas 1888, pp. 583–5. Boas describes it as "the particulars of the myth as I received it from the Oqomiut and the Akudnirmiut [two related Eskimo groups of southern Baffin Island]." Reprinted and discussed by Stith Thompson (1929), who gives it the title "Sedna, Mistress of the Underworld."

Reprinted in Palmer 1929; Maria Leach 1956; Feldmann 1965 (after Thompson 1929); Greenaway 1965; Appleton 1971. A German version appears in Krickeberg 1924, p. 5. Summarized and again discussed by Stith Thompson in Thompson 1946, pp. 305–6, 355.

page 59 / Inung: "Human being," especially an Eskimo; the plural is *Inuit.*

page 59 / Sedna: According to Boas, she is regarded as the Supreme Being.

page 59 / fulmar: "The gull-like Atlantic Fulmar [*Fulmarus glacialis*]—beautiful, with its intelligent dark eye set in its pure white head, its yellow bill, clear gray mantle and snowy under-parts—is one of the best known of North Atlantic sea-birds" (Forbush and May 1939, p. 13).

page 59 / Aja: Ah-yah.

page 60 / seals: The ringed seal, *Phoca hispida.* Synonym: *Pagomys foetida.*

page 60 / ground seals: The bearded seal, *Erignathus barbatus.* Synonym: *Phoca barbata.*

The Lure of the Serpent

page 65 / The Birth of Knowledge
Source: Curtis 1907–30, Vol. 15, pp. 121–2. I have given only

the opening paragraphs of a considerably longer narrative published by Curtis as "The Creation." Told by José Bastiano Lachapa, a northern Diegueño, at Los Conejos.

page 65 / The younger was blind: Because he failed to keep his eyes shut in the salty water, the salt blinded him (Gifford 1918, p. 170). Being blind, he is evil; the elder is good (Natalie Curtis 1923, p. 562).

page 66 / the mountain Wikami: The children of First Man and First Woman "lived in the east at a great mountain called Wikami. If you go there now you will hear all kinds of singing in all languages. If you put your ear to the ground, you will hear the sound of dancing. This is caused by the spirits of all the dead people . . . That is the place where everything was created first" (Waterman 1910, p. 339).

page 66 / Umai-huhlyá-wit: From *umai* ("sky"), *huhlyá* ("moon"), and *wit* (untranslated).

page 67 / How Night Appeared
Source: Magalhães 1876, pp. 162–74. The English translation is mine, after the lexical Portuguese of Magalhães (who also gives the text in lingua geral and a free Portuguese translation). Collected by Magalhães. Allain's French version is in Magalhães 1882. Carvalho-Neto (1956, p. 263) gives a Spanish version, which has been translated into English by Edmonson (1971, p. 145). Discussed in Pôrto-Carrero 1934, pp. 144–8. An English version marred by serious errors appears in Carvalho-Neto 1972, p. 189. Another Spanish version is in García de Diego 1953, p. 1460, and in Izquierdo Gallo 1956, p. 396.

page 67 / refuses to sleep with me: Because there is no privacy.

page 67 / tucuma: Too-KOO-ma, *Astrocaryum tucuma,* a palm yielding both a workable fiber and an edible fruit.

page 67 / you will be lost: If you learn to work fiber, make tools, prepare food, etc., you will lose the easy way of life you now enjoy. At the moment, as we shall see, all sorts of good things are simply lying about, waiting to be picked up.

page 67 / tan tan tan: The *n,* not pronounced, merely indicates that the (short) *a* is nasalized. In French this is written *tin tin tin.*

page 68 / The basket became a jaguar: In Indian myths of both hemispheres, the basket (or jar, or mortar, or pot, or pitcher) symbolizes culture as opposed to nature; in South American mythology the jaguar is held to be the master of culture. The imagery here suggests that man must now embark upon the dangerous and uncertain mission of obtaining cultural knowledge from the chief of beasts.

page 68 / The fisherman and his canoe were changed: Another unhappy image. The end of the fishing season means that the Amazonian Indian must now get meat from less easily caught prey—for example, waterfowl.

page 68 / cujubí: Koo-joo-BEE, a chicken-like bird that cries at dawn; one of the curassows, *Penelope cumanensis* (i.e., *Pipile pipile cujubí*), according to Magalhães. See Peters 1931–, Vol. 2, p. 22.

page 68 / urucú: A red dye used for painting the body.

page 68 / inambu: Een-ahm-BOO, one of the tinamous (*Crypturellus strigulosus*), called the "clockbird"; it screams at regular intervals during the night (Lévi-Strauss 1969, p. 204; Peters 1931–, Vol. 1, p. 22).

page 69 / monkeys: Magalhães adds: "Their black mouths and the yellow streaks on their arms, it is said, remain as a sign of the pitch that stoppered the tucuma nut and that ran over them when it melted"—thus describing the common squirrel monkey, *Siamiri sciureus.*

page 69 / The Theft of Night
Source: Wagley and Galvão 1949, p. 142. Collected along the Pindaré River in the early 1940's.

page 70 / Nephew Story
Source: Frachtenberg 1913, pp. 84–91. Original titles: "The Girl and Her Pet" (Frachtenberg's title); "Nephew Story" (narrator's title). Collected by Frachtenberg in the summer of 1909. Published in Coos and in English. Narrated by Jim Buchanan, a Coos Indian living in Acme, Lane County, Oregon, "the only member of the Coos tribe who still remembers and can relate coherently some of the myths and traditions of the bygone generations."

page 71 / the two tips: Literally, "the two heads."

page 72 / So they *let it rest:* I.e., out of fear they stayed away from it?

page 72 / nephew: Evidently a term of endearment. Note that the serpent of this myth represents not only culture but salvation. Cf. the raft of serpents, p. 312.

page 73 / The Boy and the Deer
Source: Tedlock 1972b, pp. 1–30. Narrated by Andrew Peynetsa (in the Zuni language) on the evening of January 20, 1965. Recorded on tape, and later translated into English, by Tedlock, with the assistance of Joseph Peynetsa. Published in English only. Reprinted in Rothenberg 1972. Discussed in Tedlock 1972a.

page 73 / the boy's father, a serpent in other, related myths: E.g., "Deer Boy" (Benedict 1935, Vol. 2, p. 12).

page 74 / Son'ahchi . . . Sonti long ago: Strictly untranslatable, but analogous to "Once upon a time . . . Once long ago" (Tedlock 1972b, 1973; cf. Sanchez and Tedlock 1975). The "apostrophe" is a glottal stop, pronounced as a catch in the throat, like the catch between the *tt* and the *o* in the usual pronunciation of the English word "button."

page 74 / eeso: Eh-so (the doubled vowel is pronounced like a single vowel, but held a little longer). Untranslatable, but roughly equivalent to "So it was" (Sanchez and Tedlock 1975).

page 74 / There were villagers at He'shokta: Zuni tales customarily begin by setting the locale. He'shokta is a pueblo ruin about three miles northwest of Zuni.

page 75 / Kachina Village: "This lies beneath the surface of a lake and comes to life only at night; it is the home of all the kachinas, the ancestral gods of the Zunis. Kachinas are impersonated by the Zunis in masked dances" (Tedlock's note).

page 76 / Kyaklo . . . Long Horn . . . Huututu . . . Pawtiwa: Names of kachina priests; Pawtiwa is the chief priest.

page 77 /daylight person: "Living human beings are 'daylight people'; all other beings, including animals, some plants, various natural phenomena, and deceased humans (kachinas), are called 'raw people,' because they do not depend on cooked food" (Tedlock's note).

page 77 / the young man: I.e., the little boy's uncle.

page 78 / Bow Priest: "In charge of hunting, warfare, and public announcements; he shouts announcements from the top of the highest house" (Tedlock's note).

page 83 / Tisshomahhá: A common interjection, roughly equivalent to "Oh no!" (Sanchez and Tedlock 1975).

page 84 / When they reached the roof: "In the 'long ago,' houses were entered through a trap-door in the roof; the boy and his grandfather go up an outside ladder to reach the roof and then down a second ladder into the house. Just before they enter the grandfather makes a 'corn-meal road' by sprinkling a handful of corn-meal in front of them, thus treating the boy as an important ritual personage" (Tedlock's note).

page 84 / a grandfather to anyone: A priest is everyone's "grandfather."

page 86 / put strands of turquoise beads on them: Joseph Peynetsa commented: "When deer die, they go to Kachina Village. And from there they go to their re-make, transform into another being, maybe a deer. That's in the prayers the Zunis say for deer, and that's why you have to give them corn-meal and put necklaces on them, so that they'll come back to your house once again."

page 87 / Lee semkonikya: A standard closing, for which Tedlock has proposed the translation "The word is just so——short." See Sanchez and Tedlock 1975.

A Gift of Honey

page 91 / Brother Black and Brother Red
Source: Parker 1923, pp. 290–2. Original title: "A Youth's Double Abuses His Sister."

page 94 / The Price of a Wife
Source: Curtis 1907–30, Vol. 20, pp. 92–3.

page 95 / umiak: OO-mee-ack, an Eskimo boat.

page 95 / Unugchoaóchin: Uh-nug-cho-ah-OH-ching.

page 97 / The Red Parrot
Source: Preuss 1921–3, Vol. 1, pp. 207–11. The English translation is mine, after the German of Preuss, who also gives the Uitoto text—which I have carefully compared. Obtained by Preuss from Rïgasedyue, called Rosendo. Original title: "The Flood Due to the Mutilation of a Brilliant Parrot."

page 97 / Dyaere: DYAH-eh-reh.

page 97 / Seigerani: SAY-ee-gay-rah-nee.

page 98 / cacao: Translation uncertain.

page 98 / calabash: The calabash tree (*Crescentia cujete*), with gourdlike fruits used as vessels—and sometimes compared to skulls.

page 98 / Nadyerekudu: NAH-dyeh-reh-koo-doo, the chief of the calabash people. The context suggests that these "people" represent the dead or the stars or both. Preuss thinks *Nadyerekudu* is derived from a root meaning "star" (Preuss 1921–3, Vol. 1, p. 62).

page 99 / ran back and forth: "Face to face against one another as they went by, as was demonstrated for me" (Preuss's note). The paragraph is a concatenation of images in which we may dimly perceive the "fallen woman" and her equally guilty partner, appearing as the incestuous Brother Sun and Sister Moon, running along in their diurnal courses, yet joined in flagrante delicto (as in fact we often find them in Indian myths of both continents).

page 100 / grating trough: Used for grating cassava.

page 101 / A Gift of Honey
Source: Ixtlilxochitl 1891–2, Vol. 1, pp. 15, 16, 23–55, 67–70. Original title: none. Recorded in the Nahuatl language by Ixtlilxochitl and translated into Spanish by "Ramirez, an interpreter of Otumba" (Garibay 1953–4, Vol. 1, p. 55; but see Ixtlilxochitl 1891–2, Vol. 2, p. 4, and Garibay 1964a, p. 89).

The Nahuatl text has not survived. My English version, based on the Spanish, is a condensation of Ixtlilxochitl's much fuller account of the fall of Tollan. Another, briefer condensation is in Garibay 1964a. The story is discussed by Diaz Infante (1963, pp. 39–41). Retold in verse by Roa Bárcena (1862, pp. 13–64).

page 101 / another . . . version of the same "history": See Bierhorst 1974, pp. 44 ff.

page 101 / 1 Flint: The number and name of a sacred-almanac day. (Years were named after the almanac day on which the first day of the calendar year happened to fall.)

page 101 / Tlapallan: Tlah-PAHL-lahn.

page 101 / Huematzin: Way-MOTT-seen.

page 102 / rainstorms: The text has "lizards," suggesting that the ultimate source is a pictographic book; in the ancient picture writing, lizards were used to symbolize water (cf. *Il Manoscritto Messicano Vaticano 3738,* p. 25).

page 103 / maguey: MAH-gay, name given to various species of the genus *Agave,* commonly called "century plants." The sap may be collected in a cavity hollowed out at the base of the plant when it starts blooming; Mexicans call this "honey water" (Pesman 1962, p. 247).

page 106 / jadestone, redshell, whiteshell, and turquoise—and with it a ball of redstone: Ixtlilxochitl has "emerald, ruby, diamond, and hyacinth—and with a carbuncle for a ball." But with the exception of the emerald, these jewels were not known in ancient Mexico. I have therefore substituted more probable materials, borrowing from a description given by Sahagún (Bk.

10, ch. 29, section 1). See Anderson and Dibble 1950–, Bk. 10, p. 166.

page 106 / score a goal: A goal is scored by sending the ball through a fixed stone ring.

Tales of War

page 111 / The Legend of Korobona
Source: Brett 1880, pp. 64–74. The prose version is mine, after the metrical (English) text given by Brett. A different prose version, also after Brett, is given in Lambert 1931. A German version appears in Koch-Grünberg 1921.

page 114 / Carib warrior: The Caribs were an aggressive, expansionist tribe, occupying areas of Brazil, Venezuela, Guyana, and the Antilles.

page 114 / had come down to earth from the sky: Alludes to an origin legend (Brett 1880, p. 55) in which the Warrau are shown to have descended from a paradisal sky world.

page 114 / Home Boy
Source: Curtis 1907–30, Vol. 4, pp. 165–71.

page 115 / coupsticks: Sticks or switches carried into battle, used for "counting coup" (pronounced KOO); that is, for touching the body of an enemy—considered an act of honor.

page 116 / Dahpiké: Hidatsa name for the Sun Dance.

page 119 / coulee: KOO-lay, ravine.

page 124 / The Rival Chiefs
Source: Hunt 1906, pp. 108–36. The source gives the text in Kwakiutl and lexical English only. My version is adapted from the lexical translation, preserving the Kwakiutl phraseology to the fullest extent possible. Text collected by Hunt.

page 124 / There were Kwakiutl . . . : I have shortened the full designation, galasa kwakiutl ("First of the Kwakiutl"), to "Kwakiutl." The term evidently refers to the Kwakiutl proper (one of twenty Kwakiutl-speaking groups native to Vancouver Island and the inlets along the north shore of Queen Charlotte Strait). For a description of Kwakiutl social organization, see Boas 1966.

page 124 / Sun tribe . . . Hair-Turned-Up-in-Front tribe: The word "tribe," as used here, is synonymous with "clan," called by Boas "numayma." Several "clans" living in close proximity comprise a village. See the following note.

page 124 / Our tribe will be happy: Here the term "tribe" is synonymous with "village." See the preceding note.

page 125 / grease: Oil of the eulachon (YOO-la-kahn), or candle-fish—a delicacy.

page 126 / as if you had much: As if you were a man of great wealth. What follows is a form of the famous potlatch ceremony, in which rivals attempted to outdo each other in boastful displays of wealth.

page 126 / copper: A sheet of placer copper, usually two and a half feet high and about one and a half feet wide, tooled with an anthropomorphic design—a very valuable piece of property.

page 128 / now he was dancing his fool-dance: Flaunting his membership in the prestigious society of fool-dancers.

page 129 / son and daughter disappeared: The main feature of the winter ceremonial is the initiation of young people into the mysteries of Kwakiutl religion. The ceremonial takes the form of a drama in which the initiate is supposedly kidnapped by a spirit who gives him sacred knowledge, then returns him (or her) safely home. Masks, costumes, and ingenious stage effects are employed. In the rites described here, the female initiates wear sea-monster masks and are called "war dancers"; the males are "grizzly bears." As we shall see, the initiation is regarded as a symbolic death and resurrection.

page 129 / had her head cut off: A stage trick.

page 130 / arose and stood up: Was "resurrected"—but with little pomp. Fast-Runner's daughters, in the description that follows, will be "resurrected" in style.

page 132 / Fast-Runner killed his slave: A tremendous demonstration of privilege. Remember that in the parallel passage above, Throw-Away was only able to have a canoe destroyed (by his "grizzly bear" son).

page 133 / "O shamans . . .": Refers to the whole company—in keeping with the calculated fakery of the winter ceremonial (much as modern physicians address their students as "doctor" in the presence of unsuspecting patients).

page 134 / go make war on the Nootka: Throw-Away proceeds from Kwakiutl territory, on the eastern shore of Vancouver Island, across the mountainous interior to the western shore (inhabited by the Nootka).

Winter and Spring

page 139 / Sapling and Flint
Source: Hewitt 1903, pp. 309–12. Original title: none. The story is part of an episodic origin myth obtained by Hewitt from Seth Newhouse at the Six Nations Reserve near Brantford, Ontario, in 1896–7. My version is adapted from the lexical English of Hewitt (who also gives both the Mohawk text and a free English translation).

page 139 / a bridge out of stone: Suggests an ice sheet.

page 140 / bluebird: "The bluebird is here mentioned as it is among the first of the migratory birds to return in the spring, which is a token that spring of the year has come, and that the power of the Winter power is broken" (Hewitt's note).

page 140 / "Kwa!" etc.: The Iroquois death cry.

page 140 / as fast as he fled, the bridge he had made disappeared: "That is, so fast as winter recedes, so rapidly the ice on rivers and lakes disappears" (Hewitt's note).

page 141 / Raw Gums and White Owl Woman
Source: Dorsey and Kroeber 1903, pp. 231–6. Collected by

Dorsey among the Southern Arapaho of Oklahoma. Told by River-Woman.

page 142 / the good classes of people: Refers to chiefs, or "rulers," of the tribe.

page 146 / bluestem: Grass.

page 147 / pemmican: Dried shreds of meat mixed with fat.

page 147 / I shall ask some more questions . . . : The following test of wit recalls the ancient Maya custom of interrogating chiefs at regular intervals. If unable to answer certain riddles, a chief could be deposed or perhaps even executed. For typical questions, see Roys 1933, pp. 88–98.

page 149 / The Man Who Loved the Frog Songs
Source: Skinner and Satterlee 1915, p. 470. I have made a few minor changes in the wording of the myth as given by Skinner and Satterlee. The story is retold and discussed by Lévi-Strauss (1968, p. 63), who calls it "The Song of the Frogs."

page 150 / Ibis Story
Source: Gusinde 1937, pp. 1232–3. Original titles: "Ibis Story" (native title) ; "The Touchy Ibis-Woman" (Gusinde's title). The English translation is mine, after the German of Gusinde. Collected by Gusinde between 1919 and 1923. Retold and discussed by Guyot (1968, p. 105).

page 150 / Ibis: Theristicus melanopis.

The Birth of the Hero

page 155 / Up from the Earth
Source: Hoffman 1896, pp. 87, 113–14. Original title: none. Version A recited in 1890 by Shúnien, Version B in 1891 by Niópet. Both informants were leaders in the Mitawit, the grand medicine society of the Menominee. Collected by Hoffman at Keshena, Wisconsin. (In each case I have given only the opening portion of a somewhat longer myth.) Version A and, in part, Version B are reprinted and discussed in Alexander 1916, pp. 39–40; both versions appear in Krickeberg 1924, p. 43; Version B is reprinted in Appleton 1971, p. 36.

page 155 / Manabush: MAH-nah-bush (from *mashá,* "great," and *wabús,* "rabbit"), better known to English speakers as Manabozho. Manabozho is both culture hero and deliverer. Possibly he is identified with the rabbit because this animal was an important source of food.

page 156 / Out of the Wind
Source: Skinner and Satterlee 1915, pp. 239–41. I have given only the opening portion of a slightly longer narrative, published by Skinner and Satterlee as "Birth of Mánabus." The same passage is reprinted by Stith Thompson (1966), who gives it the title "Manabozho's Birth."

page 158 / Múhwase: MUH-wah-seh.

page 159 / Born for the Sun
Source: O'Bryan 1956, pp. 75–7. Narrated in the Navajo language by Hastin Tlótsi hee [Old Man Buffalo Grass], called

Sandoval, in the autumn of 1928 at Mesa Verde National Park, with Sandoval's nephew, Sam Ahkeah, acting as interpreter. Recorded in English by O'Bryan. Original title: "The White Bead Maiden's Marriage with the Sun." The passage given here is excerpted from a much longer origin myth.

page 160 / pollen from a pair of blue birds: Pollen that has been sprinkled over a pair of blue birds (probably should be "bluebirds").

The Hero as Provider

page 167 / The Mice's Sun Dance
Source: Dorsey and Kroeber 1903, pp. 107–8. Original title: "Nihansan and the Mice's Sun Dance." Collected by Kroeber. I have made a few minor changes in the wording of the myth as given by Kroeber.

page 167 / Nihansan: The Arapaho trickster.

page 168 / Raven
Source: Boas 1916, pp. 58–60. Original title: "Origin of Txäm-sem." Recorded in Tsimshian by Henry W. Tate, himself a Tsimshian, sometime during the period 1904–14 (Tate died in 1914). Published in English only (translated by Boas). Discussed by Boas (1916, pp. 634–41). I here give merely the first portion of a considerably longer Raven cycle. The same passage is reprinted by Stith Thompson (1929), who, borrowing a phrase from Boas, calls it "Raven Becomes Voracious."

page 168 / Queen Charlotte Islands: Haida territory. The Tsim-shian lived to the east, on the mainland side of the broad Hecate Strait.

page 168 / Kúngalas: Probably the name of a Haida town (per Boas).

page 169 / animal people: The events described herein are sup-posed to have occurred during a remote mythic time "when animals appeared in the form of human beings" (Boas 1916, p. 565).

page 170 / Mouth-at-Each-End: Evidently a manifestation of the serpent that imparts cultural knowledge (see above, pp. 65 ff.) Boas himself regards it as a "faint echo" of the double-headed serpent prominent in Kwakiutl lore. See Boas 1966, p. 307.

page 171 / away inland to the other side of the ocean: Meaning "to the mainland" (Boas's note).

page 172 / His father named him Giant: Having made the transi-tion from nature to culture, the hero is no longer the "shining youth" described earlier. Henceforth he is regarded as larger than ordinary men, "a great man," "a giant," having a "large rough face" and "a long beard," with "rough skin," very ugly, frightful. When he wishes to fly, he puts on his "raven garment." See Boas 1916, pp. 74, 76, 77, 79, 100, 101, 104.

page 172 / all kinds of fish . . . full of fruits: Henry Tate com-ments: "All these works he did in order to support the people. [. . .] The first thing he did was to leave his father; the second was to fly over the sea to the mainland; the third, to scatter all kinds of fishes in the rivers and streams; the fourth, to scatter all kinds of berries over the dry land" (Boas 1916, p. 67).

page 173 / The Hungry Old Woman
Source: Magalhães 1876, pp. 270–80. Original title: "Legend of the Old Gluttoness." Collected by Magalhães in 1865 near the Itaboca rapids of the Tocantins River. The English version is mine, after the lexical Portuguese of Magalhães (who also gives the text in lingua geral). A free Portuguese version is in Magalhães 1913; Allain's French translation is in Magalhães 1882. Retold and discussed by Lévi-Strauss (1966a, p. 233).

page 173 / the hungry old woman came by: "Hungry old woman" (literally, "old gluttoness") is another name for Ceiuci, the Pleiades, portrayed as a desirable young maiden in other Amazonian myths.

page 173 / I'll send wasps . . . I'll send stinging ants: Thus the "old woman" makes a sexual overture. The wasps and the stinging ants (tucanderas) symbolize sexual arousal—as suggested in Stradelli 1890, p. 674.

page 174 / smearing it [the mortar] with resin: Compare the hollow, pitch-stoppered tucuma nut in the story called "How Night Appeared," above; the symbolism is almost certainly the same. In each case a receptacle is made apparent by the melting of what in the native texts is called iráiti, usually translated "wax," but also, according to Magalhães, "resin" or "pitch." See Mauro 1950, p. 208.

page 174 / buccan: BUCK-un, a wooden frame for roasting meat.

page 174 / marajá: Mah-rah-ZHAH, a spiny palm, *Bactris minor;* the fruit is used to make a highly nutritious drink (Lévi-Strauss 1950, p. 470).

page 174 / kaw-kaw: Kaw-KAW, pronounced with a nasal vowel. Lévi-Strauss (1966a, p. 233) suggests that the bird in question may be one of the caracaras (viz., *Ibycter americanus*). These are vulturelike falcons.

page 175 / bushmaster: A large viper (*Lachesis muta*), called surucucu in Brazil.

page 175 / makauan: Ma-ka-WAW, pronounced with the final syllable nasalized; it is the Laughing Falcon, *Herpetotheres cachinnans* (García 1929).

page 175 / How many burrows do they have?: The question has been interpreted to mean "How many entrances does their burrow have?" (Magalhães 1882). It should be pointed out that in South American mythology the snake's burrow is often equated with the human vagina. That the hero intends to enter this "burrow" (in order to be reborn) is suggested by the appearance of a stork in the following passage. As in Old World lore, the stork here delivers the "child" to its mother.

page 175 / stork: The tuyuyú, which may be the enormous jabiru stork, *Jabiru mycteria*, though the name tuyuyú has usually been applied to the not-quite-so-large wood stork, or "wood ibis," *Mycteria americana*. See Lévi-Strauss 1969, p. 278; García 1929, *tuyuyú* entry.

page 175 / agouti: Dasyprocta agouti, a long-legged rabbit-size rodent—a proverbial garden pest and a final reminder of the hero's former pursuer. In a myth of upper Amazonia, the agouti "represents that fearful old woman who, expecting the sky to fall on the earth at every moment, plants not a single seed, living on that which others have planted; and because of this, the nocturnal monkey (*Aotus trivirgatus*) transformed her into an agouti" (Stradelli 1890, p. 803). Francis Huxley writes: "The agouti is a notoriously randy animal [. . .] that rodent famous for its sexual powers" (Huxley 1957, pp. 159, 207).

page 175 / manioc: Cassava, a large herb cultivated for its starchy rootstock, used in making a kind of bread.

page 176 / Coniraya and Cahuillaca
Source: Trimborn and Kelm 1967, pp. 21–9. The English version is mine, after the German translation of Trimborn (who also gives the Quechua text). Recorded in Quechua by Francisco de Avila between 1597 and 1608 in the province of Huarochiri (department of Lima), Peru. Avila's Quechua manuscript and his Spanish paraphrase of 1608 are both preserved in the Biblioteca Nacional, Madrid. For an English translation of the Spanish paraphrase, see Markham 1873. The first translation from the Quechua is Trimborn 1939 (German), followed by Avila 1942 (Latin and Spanish), Lara 1960 (Spanish, partial), Arguedas 1966 (Spanish), Trimborn and Kelm 1967 (German), Lara 1973 (Spanish, partial). The story of Coniraya and Cahuillaca is discussed by Ehrenreich (1905, pp. 94–5), more fully by Bierhorst, *(Black Rainbow,* in press); retold by Brundage (1963, pp. 64–5), and by Lara (1969, pp. 109–11); it also appears in Alexander 1920, Krickeberg 1928, Eells 1938, Pettazoni 1959, Osborne 1968.

page 177 / Viracocha: Weer-ah-COACH-ah.

page 177 / Cahuillaca: Kah-weel-YAH-kah.

page 177 / eggfruit tree: Lucuma bifera. The fruit was an important element in the diet of the ancient Peruvians (Towle 1961).

page 178 / Anchicocha: "A very cold inhospitable spot between the villages of Chorrillo and Huarochiri" (Markham 1873, p. 125). Maps reproduced in Trimborn and Kelm 1967 show this "spot" to be in the mountains about seventy miles east of Lima.

The Hero as Deliverer

page 185 / The Cannibal Dwarfs
Source: Dorsey and Kroeber 1903, pp. 122–3. Original title: "How the Cannibal Dwarfs Were Killed." Collected by Dorsey among the Southern Arapaho of Oklahoma. Told by Adopted. I have made a few minor changes in Dorsey's wording.

page 185 / a small man: Literally, a "dwarf person."

page 187 / doing mischief: Killing and eating human beings.

page 187 / Two Friends
Source: Rink 1875, pp. 119–23. Original title: "The Friends." Rink writes: "This is a very famous Greenland story, and is, in its present form, compiled from three copies." I have made a few minor revisions in Rink's text.

page 189 / angakok: A person gifted with the ability to communicate with supernatural powers.

page 189 / guardian spirit: The Eskimo word is *tornak.*

page 190 / as if compelled to do so: Rink uses italics for emphasis.

page 192 / How the Fog Came
Source: Rasmussen 1921, pp. 84–5. Collected by Rasmussen at Smith Sound. English version by W. Worster. A different translation of the same text appears in Rasmussen 1908, p. 183, entitled "The Origin of the Fog." Told by Agpalerssuarssuk, a young man.

page 194 / Hiawatha
Source: Parker 1923, pp. 403–6. Original title: "The Origin of the Long House." Related by Delos B. Kittle, known as Chief Big Kittle, January 1905, at Newtown, Cattaraugus reservation.

page 194 / the cannibal motif: See Wallace 1946.

page 195 / among the Mohawks: The idea of uniting the five Iroquois nations is supposed to have originated among the Mohawks. (The four remaining nations are the Oneida, the Onondaga, the Cayuga, and the Seneca.)

page 195 / Deganawidah: Deh-gah-nah-WEE-dah. Parker spells it "Dekanawida."

page 195 / Kwa: A greeting.

page 196 / Hiawatha: High-ah-WAH-thah. I have changed Parker's spelling to the more familiar form. Parker gives Haiówent'ha (high-OH-wuht-hah).

page 196 / Hadiondas: Hod-YON-duz, "white men" (Chafe 1963, p. 56). But the league as it is known today was probably founded in the fifteenth or sixteenth century, long before the Iroquois could have felt the pressure of encroaching whites.

page 196 / Atotarho: Ah-do-DAHR-ho, the leader of the Onondaga nation; this is the familiar spelling. Parker gives it in the Seneca dialect: "Tatodaho."

page 196 / onward to Onondaga: The capital of the Onondaga nation is called Onondaga.

page 197 / Long House: A figurative expression meaning "the five united nations of the Iroquois."

Comedy of Horrors

page 201 / The Fox
Source: Grinnell 1903, pp. 169–70.

page 201 / Old Man: The Blackfoot trickster.

page 203 / Juan Tul
Source: Rosado Vega 1957, pp. 192–9. Original title: "Concerning the Wicked Pranks of Juan Tul." The English version is mine, adapted from the Spanish of Rosado Vega. A study of the origin of this tale might begin with a reading of the strikingly similar story included in Paredes 1970 (pp. 54–8). See also

Thompson 1919, pp. 419–26; Aarne and Thompson 1961, type 1530.

page 203 / Tul: The Maya word for "rabbit," pronounced tuh-HOOL.

page 206 / balche: Ball-CHAY, a tree (*Lonchocarpus longistylus*) ; the bark is used in making an alcoholic beverage of the same name.

page 207 / How He Got Tongue
Source: Grinnell 1926, pp. 299–301.

page 207 / Wihio: The Cheyenne trickster.

page 209 / The Buffalo Wife
Source: Teit et al. 1917, pp. 76–9. Original title: "Coyote and Buffalo." Collected by Teit. Told by Kwelkweltáhen [Red Arm], a Sanpoil with Okanagon connections.

page 210 / snahauq: SNAH-owk, a person who steals and then lives with another man's wife.

Jaguar and Fox

page 217 / "A man is careful . . .": Opler 1946, p. 57.

page 217 / Old Man-Coyote and the Strawberry
Source: Simms 1903, p. 284. Related to Simms during the

summer of 1902 through an interpreter, "the second-oldest man of the tribe, known as Bull-that-goes-hunting." I have made a few minor revisions in Simms's text.

page 218 / Old-Man-Coyote and the Mouse
Source: Lowie 1918, p. 43. I have made a number of minor revisions in Lowie's text.

page 219 / It's First-Worker's: With reference to Coyote as Creator.

page 220 / Jaguar and Fox
Source: Kruse 1946–9, pp. 631–2. Original title: "The Story of the Fox." The English translation is mine, after the German of Kruse. The appearance in this tale of the stock episode catalogued by Aarne and Thompson (1961) as 66A ("Hello, House!") suggests the possibility of Old World influence.

page 220 / fox: The forest fox, *Dusicyon thous* (Gilmore 1950, p. 377).

page 222 / Turtle and Fox
Source: Magalhães 1876, pp. 199–203. The English translation is mine, after the Portuguese of Magalhães (who also gives the text in lingua geral). Collected by Magalhães. Allain's French version is in Magalhães 1882.

page 222 / narrator sings: See Magalhães 1882, p. 25.

page 223 / Coyote and Wren
Source: Jacobs 1934, pp. 243–4. Original title: none. I here give

only one episode from a much longer Coyote cycle. Dictated to Jacobs in Upper Cowlitz by Lewy Costima (a man in his sixties) at Costima's farm in Bremer, near Morton, Washington, in August 1927. Later translated into English by Jacobs and Sam N. Eyley, Jr. For the Upper Cowlitz text, see Jacobs 1937, pp. 208–9.

page 224 / But after an hour she became tired: "Costima takes pleasure in introducing white terms, phraseology, ideas, and humor into purely Indian narration; he is known to tell in myth recitals that this or that happened one hour later or that Coyote had tea at five o'clock in the afternoon. [. . .] Costima exhibits a constant, malicious, and somewhat crude urge to violate tradition" (Jacobs 1934, p. 238).

Ghosts

page 229 / The Two Jeebi-Ug
Source: Schoolcraft 1839, Vol. 2, pp. 61–6. (A much embellished version was published by Schoolcraft in 1825; see Schoolcraft 1825, pp. 412–20.) Original title: "The Two Jeebi-Ug, or A Trial of Feeling." Reprinted by Schoolcraft (1856), Williams (1956). Adapted by Longfellow (*The Song of Hiawatha*, XIX: "The Ghosts"). Retold by Jones (1829), Matthews (1869), Bache (1871), Emerson (1884, p. 193).

page 229 / jeebi-ug: Ghosts.

page 233 / The Ghost Country
Source: Boas 1935–43, Pt. 1, pp. 111–12. Collected by Boas at

Fort Rupert during the winter of 1930–1. Told by Yákolas.
Published in English only. (I have made a few minor changes
in Boas's text.)

page 233 / crying under the grave: Indicating a tree burial.

page 234 / Do not eat what is offered: Alluding to the belief
that one may not return from the land of the dead if one has
eaten there.

page 234 / they took the board into the winter-dance house:
Compare the resurrection scene in "The Rival Chiefs," above,
pp. 133–4.

pages 234–5 / Koskimo . . . Newettee . . . Nákwado: Names
of Kwakiutl tribal groups.

page 235 / The Dead Wife
Source: Swanton 1929, pp. 144–5. Obtained by Swanton be-
tween 1908 and 1914 "from the Alabama Indians living in Polk
County, Tex."

page 235 / They passed through her body: A husband is similarly
killed in an Eskimo myth given above (p. 57).

page 235 / she went to a dance: Dancing is widely regarded as
the typical activity of the dead.

page 236 / The Vampire Skeleton
Source: Beauchamp 1888, pp. 47–8. Original title: "The Terrible
Skeleton." ("The Vampire Skeleton" is the title given to a
variant of the same story in Hewitt 1918.) I have made a few

changes in Beauchamp's wording. The story was obtained by Beauchamp from Sa-go-na-qua-de, called Albert Cusick. Reprinted with minor changes (some of which have been incorporated here) in Beauchamp 1922.

page 236 / a fox, which the Onondaga recognize . . . as a symbol of sexual love: This symbolism is perhaps more transparent in an Onondaga version of the great Iroquois cosmological myth (Hewitt 1928, p. 479), in which the doomed heroine, Awenhai, the fallen woman, is tempted by a fox-man as part of the prelude to her expulsion from paradise.

page 238 / Forty Dead Men
Source: Curtis 1907–30, Vol. 11, pp. 108–10. Original title: "The Whaler Who Killed His Brother."

page 238 / Ozette: A Makah settlement (now a reservation) on the Washington coast, about fifteen miles south of Cape Flattery.

page 239 / The way he obtained his power: "The use of corpses in ceremonial preparation for whaling is accurately described in this Makah tradition" (Curtis's note).

Tales of the White Man

page 245 / The Land Sale
Source: Andrade 1931, pp. 207–11. Original title: "The Advent of the Whites." Recorded by Leo J. Frachtenberg in 1915 or 1916. Published in Quileute and in English. Told by Hallie George, "a half-blood Quileute."

page 246 / knew how to speak Chinook: A trade language.

page 246 / Stevens: Isaac Ingalls Stevens, appointed in 1853 as first governor of the Washington Territory.

page 248 / The Pongo's Dream
Source: Arguedas 1965. Obtained by Arguedas, in Lima, from a native of the district of Ccatca (about thirty miles east-south-east of the old Inca capital of Cuzco). Published in Quechua and in Spanish. Reprinted in Arguedas and Carrillo 1967. Reprinted with minor revisions in Arguedas 1969. The English version is mine, after the Spanish of Arguedas.

page 249 / pongo: An Indian menial of the lowest order, charged with kitchen and stable work, traditionally a kind of doorman whose more or less permanent station was the vestibule. Hence the name "pongo," from the Quechua *punku,* "door" (Luna 1957).

page 250 / viscacha: A rodent (*Lagostomus maximus*) resembling the chinchilla, but larger. Viscachas live in colonies, like prairie dogs.

page 254 / The Queen of the Tribe
Source: Boas 1935–43, Pt. 1, pp. 227–9; Pt. 2, pp. 218–20. Original title: "The Woman Carried Away by a Skull." Collected by Boas at Fort Rupert during the winter of 1930–1. Told by Guyósdedzas. Published in Kwakiutl and in English. (I have made numerous revisions in Boas's English text.)

page 257 / The Bacabal Mission
Source: Kruse 1946–9, p. 615. The English version is mine, after the German of Kruse.

page 257 / Tapajós: Tah-pah-ZHOHS.

page 257 / their work: Collecting rubber and other forest products (Murphy 1958, p. 7).

page 258 / traders were not allowed: The Indians were permitted to trade only with the priests, who sold directly to agents in Belém (ibid.).

page 258 / The crosspiece lies on the ground: The story refers to a Capuchin mission, founded in 1872, abandoned in 1876 (see Murphy, pp. 6–7). The narrator adds: "Many years later [i.e., in 1912] other fathers came to the Mundurucú and built the 'Mission of Saint Francis on the Cururú [River].'" (Father Kruse, who published this text, was a Franciscan.)

Myths of Returning Life

page 263 / The Ring in the Prairie
Source: Schoolcraft 1839, Vol. 1, pp. 67–73. Original title: "The Celestial Sisters." A metrical version appears in Whiting 1831, where the collector of the myth is named as C. C. Trowbridge. Reprinted by Schoolcraft (1856, p. 116), Williams (1956), Macfarlan (1968). Versified by Schoolcraft (1856, p. 335). Retold by Schoolcraft (1851–7, Vol. 1, p. 327) with the title "The Magic Circle in the Prairie" and with the hero's name

changed to the ersatz "Algon." Retold by Domenech (1860, Vol. 1, p. 303), Matthews (1869), Emerson (1884, p. 59), Choate and Curtis (1916), Spence (1916, p. 152), Potter and Robinson (1963, p. 295), Bierhorst (1970), Zolla (1973, p. 150). The version presented here (in which virtually every sentence of the original Schoolcraft text has been reworded) is reprinted from Bierhorst 1970; a passage that had been omitted from the 1970 edition is here restored.

page 264 / a ring worn through the sod: "You may also remark in the Great Prairies small circular places entirely denuded of vegetation, which travelers have called the 'Circles of the Prairies.' The inhabitants or the frequenters of the desert [i.e., wilderness] have not failed to attribute to them origins which are more or less contestable; our simple belief is, that some of these circles were formed by the buffaloes during their sojourn in the same spot, and that the others are the traces of ancient cabins which formerly belonged to the savages" (Domenech 1860, Vol. 1, p. 303). From this it would appear that the "ring" of Schoolcraft's 1839 version ought properly to have been "circle," as indeed he has it in the otherwise inferior text of 1851–7.

page 267 / The Story of Okóhi
Source: Roth 1915, pp. 255–6. I have made numerous revisions in Roth's text. Retold and discussed by Lévi-Strauss (1968, p. 111), who calls it "Story of the Beautiful Assawako." Reprinted by Wilbert (1970).

page 268 / Okóhi: "This word *okóhi* among the Warraus means the hottest part of the day; it refers to the warmth and heat of the sun as distinguished from its power of producing light" (Roth's note).

page 269 / Wau-u! Wau-u! Wau-u!: "This sound would correspond with the English 'Swish! Swish! Swish!'" (Roth's note).

page 269 / Assawako: "This is the Warrau term for any smart, sensible female" (Roth's note).

page 269 / assumed her place behind him: "On the march the Indians always walk in file, the men leading" (Roth's note).

page 269 / kahabassa: Probably a gourd flute.

page 269 / Waru-huru téa: "This sound would correspond with our hootiti-tootiti, etc." (Roth's note)—meaningless syllables, presumably, intended to convey the idea of gourd-flute music.

page 270 / The Boy and the Owls
Source: Gusinde 1937, pp. 1190–3. Original title: "Owl Story." The English translation is mine, after the German of Gusinde. Collected by Gusinde between 1919 and 1923. Retold and discussed by Guyot (1968, p. 78).

page 270 / guanaco: Lama guanicoe, a mammal similar to the llama, but slimmer (weighing up to 220 lbs.). (Gilmore 1950, pp. 447–51).

page 270 / this weird pudding: The Yamana did in fact relish a kind of black pudding or blood sausage, called keti. But the hypothetical keti described here refers to a ceremony (associated with puberty rites) in which the adult men sought to validate their masculinity. The blood they drew from their noses was part of an attempt to frighten the women. See Gusinde 1937, p. 1191; Métraux 1943, p. 117. (I take this to mean that the young hero is being treated like a woman, being told, in effect, that he is not a man. It will be part of his mission to overcome this discrimination.)

page 271 / cut a piece . . . from her chastity apron: The chastity apron, or vaginal shield, is a small triangular covering made of hide. Note that the boy's "foot" is to be inserted in the "piece" cut from this covering. The passage can have only one meaning.

page 273 / they wore themselves out: I.e., to death.

page 273 / they all became owls: Owls are associated with death and evil in various Indian mythologies; the species referred to here is *Bubo magellanicus.*

Death and Beyond

page 277 / The Red Swan
Source: Schoolcraft 1839, Vol. 2, pp. 9–33. (I have made numerous changes in Schoolcraft's wording.) Reprinted by Schoolcraft (1856), Williams (1956), Macfarlan (1968). Retold by Matthews (1869), Bache (1871), Choate and Curtis (1916), Krickeberg (1924), Lyback (1925–38), Bierhorst (1969). Discussed by Lévi-Strauss (1968, p. 284).

page 278 / Maujeekewis: "A term indicative of the heir or successor to the first place in power" (Schoolcraft 1839, Vol. 1, p. 130). The word may be used either as a descriptive term or as a proper name. See p. 289.

page 278 / those you propose to get: Italicized by Schoolcraft, probably to indicate that this is the literal translation of a Chippewa term (which he does not give).

page 278 / Odjibwa: Oh-JIB-way.

page 280 / rescued the two magic arrows: An ill-considered, perhaps merely wishful, detail. (I believe that this is the myth's only significant flaw.) All three arrows must be regarded as gone for good. Compare the fourth from last paragraph of the story (where it is made clear that the arrows are gone) and see the discussion above, pp. 25–6.

page 280 / the strokes of their axes: Metal axes are implied, suggesting a superior level of material culture. Compare the metal pot, mentioned below.

page 282 / a small metal pot: The reference to metal is the only definitely non-aboriginal intrusion in this myth. But the allusion is not to European material culture per se, rather to an exalted form of Chippewa culture, for which the pot serves as a precious emblem.

page 282 / blueberry: Schoolcraft has "whortleberry."

page 284 / she had asked for the wampum scalp so that she could be cured: I.e., she had asked for the *precious penis* so that she could be cured *of a sexual itch that was "killing"* her. The penis is synonymous with youth; its removal is the cause of the old magician's senescence. For the genital symbolism of the scalp, see Edmund Leach 1957; Lévi-Strauss 1968, p. 329. See also p. 358, below. For the penis as a youth symbol, see Bierhorst 1975. For an Aztec version of the sick maiden "cured" by a penis, see Bierhorst 1974, pp. 44–6. Note that there need be no conflict between the solar symbolism of the scalp as (white) wampum (strands of) hair (see p. 20, above) and the genital symbolism of the wampum (i.e., precious) scalp as quasi-pubic hair. The piecing together of odd bits of lore, such as we see in this case, has been aptly termed bricolage ("tinkering") by Lévi-Strauss. For bricolage, see Lévi-Strauss 1966b, pp. 16–33.

page 285 / The magician groaned each time . . . : This whole passage is a satire on the role of the mentor in puberty ritual.

page 286 / the time that the sun hangs toward home: Afternoon.

page 286 / sau-sau-quan: A war cry (Schoolcraft 1839, Vol. 1, p. 101)—probably pronounced saw-saw-KWAH, with the last syllable nasalized.

page 289 / there was a Maujeekewis: See note above, p. 354.

page 291 / the blessing of the Great Spirit: Possibly, but not definitely, an idea borrowed from missionaries.

page 293 / the place where those who were good dwell: Another idea possibly derived from missionaries.

page 294 / The Master of the Red Macaws
Source: Villas Boas and Villas Boas 1972, pp. 163–6. Original title: "Vanivaní / The Master of the Red Macaws"; I presume that the native title is "Vanivaní." The English translation given here (after the Portuguese of the Villas Boas brothers) is by Susana Hertelendy Rudge (reprinted from Villas Boas and Villas Boas 1973).

page 294 / Morená: The junction of the headwaters of the Xingu River—a holy place.

page 294 / It showed up . . . *:* Rudge erroneously translates the pronoun as "he" and thereby throws several ensuing verbs to the wrong gender. I have corrected this slip.

page 296 / Ianamá: Name of a Kamaiurá hero who appears to be an ordinary mortal, unlike the supernatural heroes, Sun and Moon. I take this to mean that the adventure of Sun and Moon could have happened to Ianamá. In other words, it is applicable to humanity.

page 296 / Mavutsinim: The first man, the grandfather of the twin culture heroes, Sun and Moon—pronounced mah-voot-see-NEE, with the final syllable nasalized.

page 298 / cauim: "A drink prepared from fermented manioc" (Villas Boas and Villas Boas 1973)—pronounced kah-WEE, with the second syllable nasalized.

page 298 / beiju: "A thin white bread or pancake made from manioc flour" (ibid.)—pronounced bay-ZHOO.

page 298 / Why the Buzzard Is Bald
Source: Skinner 1925, pp. 486–7. I have made a number of changes in Skinner's wording. Original title: "Ishjinki Is Tricked by the Buzzard." Reprinted by Coffin (1961), who calls it "Why Buzzard Is Bald."

page 299 / Ishjinki: The Iowa trickster.

page 299 / Sauk: A neighboring tribe.

page 299 / put his coonskin up to the crack: A euphemism. (In

a Kickapoo variant the hero is said to be showing his pubic hair.
See Jones and Michelson 1915, pp. 9–13.)

page 301 / Geriguigatugo
Source: Colbacchini 1925, pp. 223–36; appendix, pp. 92–9.
Original title: "Legend of Geriguigatugo." The English version
is mine, after Colbacchini, who gives the first portion of the
text (down through the second sentence of the thirteenth paragraph) in the original Bororo and in lexical Italian, and the
whole text in a free Italian version. A Portuguese translation
with a somewhat different ending and with the bird transformation passage woefully truncated is given by Colbacchini and
Albisetti (1942, pp. 225–8), who append a related fragment
entitled "Geriguiguiatugo's Vengeance." Lévi-Strauss's retelling
in French—a mélange of Colbacchini 1925 and Colbacchini and
Albisetti 1942, including "Geriguiguiatugo's Vengeance"—appears in Lévi-Strauss 1964, translated into English in Lévi-
Strauss 1969 (pp. 35–7). Reprinted, after Colbacchini 1925, in
Petazzoni 1959, p. 419. Retold and discussed by Kirk, 1970,
pp. 63–73; and by Greimas, 1971. Reprinted, together with
other excerpts from *The Raw and the Cooked* (Lévi-Strauss
1969), in Maranda 1972. Repeatedly discussed by Lévi-Strauss
(1964, 1966a, 1968, 1971).

page 301 / the penis sheath: A palm-leaf wrapper, customarily
worn by men and presented to boys on the occasion of their
initiation. Thus the stage is set for a boys' puberty rite. The
soul-dance, mentioned later, is part of the ceremony.

page 301 / Korogo . . . Geriguigatugo . . . Bokwadorireu:
Bororo polysyllables are stressed on the penult. Hence: ko-RO-go,
jay-ree-ghee-ga-TOO-go, bo-kwa-doh-ree-RAY-oo.

page 301 / nest of souls: Beneath the water, where the dead reside.

page 303 / peccary anklet: A jingle string made of peccary hooves, used in the boys' soul-dance. Note the decreasing power of the three musical instruments—the large rattle, the small rattle, the anklet jingles—as the hero draws closer and closer to death.

page 303 / mammori: A giant grasshopper, *Acridium cristatum.*

page 305 / Baigareu: An unidentified bird, the first in a series of five bird-like creatures, evidently decreasing in size.

page 306 / The Great Cavern of Darkness
Source: Leland 1884, pp. 60–1. Original title: "How Glooskap Sailed through the Great Cavern of Darkness." Versified by Leland in Leland and Prince 1902.

page 307 / pitché: "Long ago" in the Passamaquoddy dialect.

page 307 / as it has been written: Phrase inserted by Leland, refers to a similar myth given earlier in the same collection (Leland 1884, p. 31).

page 307 / Dame Kah-kah-gooch, the Crow: "The Crow is represented in several stories as always peeping, spying, begging, pilfering, and tale-bearing about a town" (Leland's note).

page 308 / The Flight of Quetzalcoatl
Source: Anderson and Dibble 1950–, Bk, 3, ch. 12–14; also Seler 1927, pp. 286–92. Original title: none. The English trans-

lation is mine (reprinted from Bierhorst 1974, pp. 57–63), after the Nahuatl as paleographed by Seler and by Anderson and Dibble. The Nahuatl text, recorded in the sixteenth century by Fray Bernardino de Sahagún, is preserved in manuscripts in Florence and in Madrid. Other published translations: Sahagún 1956 (Spanish), Bandelier 1932 (English, after the Spanish of Sahagún), Seler 1927 (German), Cornyn 1930 (English), Anderson and Dibble 1950– (English). Excerpts from "The Flight of Quetzalcoatl" have been adapted in prose by Garibay (1964a); in verse by Garibay (1964b), by Rothenberg (1968, 1972) after Garibay 1964a, and by Kissam (1971). The passage is discussed by Spence (1930, pp. 269–71) and more fully by Bierhorst (1974, pp. 11, 89–94); see also Bierhorst 1975. Portions of one or another of the translations listed above have been reprinted by authors too numerous to list here.

page 309/ that Tollan might be destroyed: For the story of Tollan's destruction, see above, pp. 101–6. The unfortunate figure of Huemac in that account is here represented by his spiritual counterpart, the god-hero Quetzalcoatl.

page 309 / Anahuac: Ah-NAH-wahk, the seacoast.

page 311 / Tlapallan: Tlah-PAHL-lahn, "Red Land"; in the present context, it refers to the eastern horizon—where the sun comes up.

page 312 / maguey: See note on p. 330.

page 312 / ceiba: SAY-buh, the silk-cotton tree (*Ceiba pentandra*).

page 312 / Mictlan: MEEK-tlahn, "Dead Land."

REFERENCES

Aarne, Antti, and Thompson, Stith. 1961. *The Types of the Folktale: A Classification and Bibliography*. Helsinki.

Albisetti, C., and Venturelli, A. J. 1962. *Enciclopédia Bororo*, Vol. 1. Campo Grande.

Alexander, Hartley Burr. 1916. *The Mythology of All Races*, Vol. 10: *North American* (Louis Herbert Gray, ed.). Boston.

———. 1920. *The Mythology of All Races*, Vol. 11: *Latin-American* (Louis Herbert Gray, ed.). Boston.

———. 1953. *The World's Rim: Great Mysteries of the North American Indians*. Lincoln, Neb.

Allen, Robert P. 1942. *The Roseate Spoonbill*. Research Report No. 2. National Audubon Society. New York.

Anderson, Arthur J. O., and Dibble, Charles E. 1950–. *Florentine Codex*. 12 "books" in 13 vols. Santa Fe.

Andrade, Manuel J. 1931. *Quileute Texts*. Columbia University Contributions to Anthropology, Vol. 12. New York.

Appleton, Le Roy H. 1971. *American Indian Design and Decoration*. New York. (Originally published as *Indian Art of the Americas*, 1950.)

Arguedas, José María. 1965. *El Sueño del Pongo: Cuento Quechua*. Lima.

——. 1966. *Dioses y Hombres de Huarochiri*. Lima.

——. 1969. *El Sueño del Pongo: Cuento Quechua / Canciones Quechuas Tradicionales*. Santiago de Chile.

Arguedas, José María, and Carrillo, Francisco. 1967. *Poesía y Prosa Quechua*. Lima.

Astrov, Margot. 1962. *American Indian Prose and Poetry*. New York. (Originally published as *The Winged Serpent*, 1946.)

Avila, Francisco de. 1942. *De Priscorum Huaruchiriensium Origine et Institutis*. Madrid.

Bache, Richard Meade. 1871. *American Wonderland*. Philadelphia.

Bandelier, Fanny R. 1932. *A History of Ancient Mexico*. Nashville.

Beauchamp, William M. 1888. "Onondaga Tales." *Journal of American Folklore*, Vol. 1, pp. 44–8.

——. 1922. *Iroquois Folk Lore*. Empire State Historical Publication 31. Albany.

Benedict, Ruth. 1935. *Zuni Mythology*. 2 vols. Columbia University Contributions to Anthropology, Vol. 21. New York.

Bierhorst, John, ed. 1969. *The Fire Plume: Legends of the American Indians* (collected by Henry Rowe Schoolcraft). New York.

——. 1970. *The Ring in the Prairie: A Shawnee Legend* (collected by Henry Rowe Schoolcraft, illustrated by Leo and Diane Dillon). New York.

——. 1974. *Four Masterworks of American Indian Literature: Quetzalcoatl, The Ritual of Condolence, Cuceb, The Night Chant.* New York.

——. 1975. "American Indian Verbal Art and the Role of the Literary Critic." *Journal of American Folklore,* Vol. 88, no. 350, pp. 401–8.

——. In press. *Black Rainbow: Legends of the Incas and Myths of Ancient Peru.* New York.

Bloomfield, Leonard. 1928. *Menominee Texts.* Publications of the American Ethnological Society, Vol. 12. New York.

Boas, Franz. 1888. "The Central Eskimo." *Sixth Annual Report of the Bureau of [American] Ethnology, 1884–1885,* pp. 399–669.

——. 1916. "Tsimshian Mythology." *Thirty-first Annual Report of the Bureau of American Ethnology, 1909–1910,* pp. 29–1037.

——. 1935–43. *Kwakiutl Tales: New Series.* 2 vols. Columbia University Contributions to Anthropology, Vol. 26, pts. 1 and 2. New York.

——. 1966. *Kwakiutl Ethnography* (Helen Codere, ed.). Chicago.

Brett, William Henry. [1880.] *Legends and Myths of the Aboriginal Indians of British Guiana*. London.

Brinton, D. G. 1882. *American Hero-Myths*. Philadelphia.

Brown, Joseph Epes, comp. 1972. *The North American Indians: A Selection of Photographs by Edward S. Curtis*. New York.

Brundage, Burr Cartwright. 1963. *Empire of the Inca*. Norman, Okla.

Cadogan, León. 1959. *Ayvu Rapyta* [The Origin of Human Speech]: *Textos míticos de los Mbyá-Guaraní del Guairá*. Universidade de São Paulo, Faculdade de Filosofia, Ciências e Letras, Boletim 227, Antropologia 5. São Paulo.

Cadogan, León, and López Austin, Alfredo. 1970. *La Literatura de los Guaranies*. 2nd ed. Mexico City.

Campbell, Joseph. 1969. *The Masks of God: Primitive Mythology*. 2nd ed. New York.

Carvalho-Neto, Paulo de. 1956. *Folklore y psicoanalisis*. Buenos Aires.

———. 1972. *Folklore and Psychoanalysis* (an English translation by Jacques M. P. Wilson of Carvalho-Neto's *Folklore y psico-análisis*, 2nd ed., 1968, Mexico City). Coral Gables.

Chafe, Wallace L. 1963. *Handbook of the Seneca Language*. New York State Museum and Science Service, Bulletin 388. Albany.

Choate, Florence, and Curtis, Elizabeth. 1916. *The Indian Fairy Book*. New York.

Coffin, Tristram P., ed. 1961. *Indian Tales of North America.* Philadelphia.

Colbacchini, Antonio. [1925.] *I Bororos Orientali, "Orarimugudoge," del Matto Grosso.* Contributi Scientifici delle Missioni Salesiane del Venerabile Don Bosco, 1. Turin.

Colbacchini, Antonio, and Albisetti, Cesar. 1942. *Os Boróros Orientais, Orarimogodogue do Planalto Oriental de Mato Grosso.* São Paulo.

Couto de Magalhães, [J. Vieira]. See Magalhães, [J. Vieira] Couto de.

Curtis, Edward S. 1907–30. *The North American Indian.* 20 vols. Vols. 1–5: Cambridge, Mass. Vols. 6–20: Norwood, Mass.

Curtis, Natalie. 1923. *The Indians' Book: Songs and Legends of the American Indians.* 2nd ed. New York.

de Angulo, Jaime. 1950. "Indians in Overalls." *The Hudson Review,* Vol. 3, no. 3, pp. 327–79.

———. 1953. *Indian Tales.* New York.

Diaz Infante, Fernando. 1963. *Quetzalcoatl: Ensayo psicoanalítico del mito nahua.* Xalapa, Mexico.

Domenech, Em[manuel Henri Dieudonné]. 1860. *Seven Years' Residence in the Great Deserts of North America.* 2 vols. London.

Dorsey, George A. 1904. *Traditions of the Osage.* Field Columbian Museum Publication 88; Anthropological Series, Vol. 7, no. 1. Chicago.

Dorsey, George A., and Kroeber, Alfred L. 1903. *Traditions of the Arapaho*. Field Columbian Museum Publication 81; Anthropological Series, Vol. 5. Chicago.

Dorson, Richard M. 1965. "The Eclipse of Solar Mythology." In *Myth: A Symposium* (Thomas A. Sebeok, ed.). Bloomington, Ind.

——. 1968. "Theories of Myth and the Folklorist." In *Myth and Mythmaking* (Henry A. Murray, ed.). Boston.

Edmonson, Munro S. 1971. *Lore: An Introduction to the Science of Folklore and Literature*. New York.

Eels, Elsie Spicer. 1938. *Tales from the Amazon*. New York.

Ehrenreich, Paul. 1905. *Die Mythen und Legenden der Südamerikanischen Urvölker und ihre Beziehungen zu denen Nordamerikas und der alten Welt* [The myths and legends of the South American aborigines and their connections with those of North America and the Old World]. Berlin.

Eliade, Mircea. 1974. *Gods, Goddesses, and Myths of Creation*. New York. (A paperback edition of chapters 1 and 2 of Eliade's *From Primitives to Zen*.)

Emerson, Ellen Russell. 1884. *Indian Myths*. Boston.

Feldmann, Susan, ed. 1965. *The Storytelling Stone: Myths and Tales of the American Indians*. New York.

Fenton, William. 1957. *American Indian and White Relations to 1830*. Chapel Hill.

Fletcher, Alice C., and La Flesche, Francis. 1911. "The Omaha

Tribe." *Twenty-seventh Annual Report of the Bureau of American Ethnology, 1905–1906*, pp. 16–672.

Fontenrose, Joseph. 1971. *The Ritual Theory of Myth.* Berkeley.

Forbush, Edward Howe, and May, John Bichard. 1939. *A Natural History of American Birds of Eastern and Central North America.* Boston.

Freud, Sigmund. 1938. "Totem and Taboo." In *The Basic Writings of Sigmund Freud* (A. A. Brill, trans.), pp. 807–930. New York.

———. 1950. *Totem and Taboo* (James Strachey, trans.). New York.

———. 1962. *Civilization and Its Discontents* (James Strachey, trans.). New York.

———. 1963. "The Acquisition of Power over Fire" (Joan Riviere, trans.). In *Character and Culture* (Philip Rieff, ed.), pp. 294–300. New York.

García, Rodolpho. 1929. "Nomes de Aves em lingua Tupi." *Boletim do Museu Nacional,* Vol. 5, no. 3, pp. 1–54. Rio de Janeiro.

García de Diego, V. 1953. *Antología de leyendas,* Vol. 2. Madrid.

Garibay K., Ángel María. 1953–4. *Historia de la Literatura Náhuatl.* 2 vols. Mexico City.

———. 1964a. *Épica náhuatl.* 2nd ed. Mexico City.

———. 1964b. *La Literatura de los Aztecas*. Mexico City.

Gifford, Edward Winslow. 1918. "Clans and Moieties in Southern California." University of California Publications in American Archaeology and Ethnology, Vol. 14, pp. 155–219. Berkeley.

Gilmore, Raymond M. 1950. "Fauna and Ethnozoology of South America." In *Handbook of South American Indians* (Julian H. Steward, ed.), Vol. 6, pp. 345–464. Bureau of American Ethnology, Bulletin 143, Vol. 6.

Greenaway, John, ed. 1965. *The Primitive Reader*. Hatboro, Penn.

Greimas, A. Julien. 1971. "The Interpretation of Myth: Theory and Practice." In Pierre Maranda and E. K. Maranda, eds., *Structural Analysis of Oral Tradition*. Philadelphia.

Grinnell, George Bird. 1903. *Blackfoot Lodge Tales*. New York.

———. 1926. *By Cheyenne Campfires*. New Haven.

Gusinde, Martin. 1937. *Die Yamana (Die Feuerland Indianer*, Vol. 2). Mödling bei Wien.

Guyot, Mireille. 1968. *Les mythes chez les Selk'nam et les Yamana de la Terre de Feu*. Université de Paris, travaux et mémoires de l'Institut d'Ethnologie, 65. Paris.

Hewitt, J. N. B. 1903. "Iroquoian Cosmology," first part. *Twenty-first Annual Report of the Bureau of American Ethnology, 1899–1900*, pp. 127–339.

———. 1928. "Iroquoian Cosmology," second part. *Forty-third*

Annual Report of the Bureau of American Ethnology, 1925–1926, pp. 449–819.

Hewitt, J. N. B., ed. 1918. "Seneca Fiction, Legends, and Myths." *Thirty-second Annual Report of the Bureau of American Ethnology, 1910–1911,* pp. 37–813.

" 'Histoyre du Mechique': Manuscrit français inédit du XVIᵉ siècle." 1905. Edited by Édouard de Jonghe. *Journal de la Société des Americanistes de Paris,* n.s. Vol. 2, pp. 1–41.

Hoffman, Walter James. 1896. "The Menominee Indians." *Fourteenth Annual Report of the Bureau of [American] Ethnology, 1892–1893,* pp. 3–328.

Horcasitas, Fernando, and Butterworth, Douglas. 1963. "La Llorona." *Tlalocan,* Vol. 4, no. 3. Mexico City.

Hunt, George. 1906. "The Rival Chiefs: A Kwakiutl Story." In *Boas Anniversary Volume.* New York.

Huxley, Francis. 1957. *Affable Savages: An Anthropologist among the Urubu Indians of Brazil.* New York.

Hyman, Stanley Edgar. 1955. *The Armed Vision.* Rev. ed. New York.

——. 1965. "The Ritual View of Myth and the Mythic." In *Myth: A Symposium* (Thomas A Sebeok, ed.). Bloomington, Ind.

Il Manoscritto Messicano 3738, detto il Codice Rios, riprodotto . . . a spese di Sua Eccellenza il Duca di Loubat, per cura della Biblioteca Vaticano. 1900. Rome.

Ixtlilxochitl, Fernando de Alva. 1891–2. *Obras históricas.* 2 vols. Mexico City.

Izquierdo Gallo, R. P. Mariano. 1956? *Mitología americana.* Madrid.

Jacobs, Melville. 1934. *Northwest Sahaptin Texts.* Columbia University Contributions to Anthropology, Vol. 19, pt. 1. New York.

——. 1937. *Northwest Sahaptin Texts.* Columbia University Contributions to Anthropology, Vol. 19, pt. 2. New York.

Jensen, Adolf E. 1948. *Das religiöse Weltbild einer frühen Kultur.* Stuttgart.

Jones, Ernest. 1954. *Hamlet and Oedipus.* Garden City, N.Y.

——. 1957. *The Life and Work of Sigmund Freud,* Vol. 3: *The Last Phase, 1919–1939.* New York.

Jones, James A. 1829. *Tales of an Indian Camp.* 3 vols. London. (Reissued in 1830 as *Traditions of the North- American Indians.*)

Jones, William, and Michelson, Truman. 1915. *Kickapoo Tales.* Publications of the American Ethnological Society, Vol. 9. New York.

Jung, C. G. 1967. *Symbols of Transformation* (R. F. C. Hull, trans.). 2nd ed. Princeton.

Jung, C. G., and Kerényi, C. 1969. *Essays on a Science of Mythology* (R. F. C. Hull, trans.). Princeton.

Kirk, G. S. 1970. *Myth: Its Meaning and Functions in Ancient and Other Cultures.* London and Berkeley.

Kissam, Edward. 1971. "Aztec Poems." *Antaeus,* 4. New York.

Koch-Grünberg, Theodor. 1921. *Indianermärchen aus Südamerika.* Jena.

Krickeberg, Walter. 1924. *Indianermärchen aus Nordamerika.* Jena.

——. 1928. *Märchen der Azteken und Inkaperuaner.* Jena.

Kruse, Albert. 1946–9. "Erzählungen der Tapajoz-Munduruků." *Anthropos,* Vols. 41–4, pp. 314–30, 614–56.

Lambert, Leonard, ed. 1931. *Guiana Legends Collected by the Late William Henry Brett.* London.

Lara, Jesús. 1960. *Leyendas Quechuas.* [La Paz.]

——. 1969. *La Literatura de los Quechuas: Ensayo y Antología.* 2nd ed. La Paz.

——. 1973. *Mitos, Leyendas y Cuentos de los Quechuas.* La Paz.

Leach, Edmund. 1957. "Magical Hair." *Journal of the Royal Anthropological Institute,* Vol. 87, pp. 147–64.

Leach, Maria. 1956. *The Beginning: Creation Myths around the World.* New York.

Leland, Charles G[odfrey]. 1884. *The Algonquin Legends of New England.* Boston.

Leland, Charles Godfrey, and Prince, John Dyneley. 1902. *Kulóskap the Master, and Other Algonkin Poems.* New York.

Lévi-Strauss, Claude. 1950. "The Use of Wild Plants in Tropical South America." In *Handbook of South American Indians* (Julian H. Steward, ed.), Vol. 6, pp. 465–86. Bureau of American Ethnology, Bulletin 143, Vol. 6.

———. 1964. *Le Cru et le cuit (Mythologiques,* Vol. 1). Paris.

———. 1966a. *Du Miel aux cendres (Mythologiques,* Vol. 2). Paris.

———. 1966b. *The Savage Mind.* Chicago.

———. 1968. *L'Origine des manières de table (Mythologiques,* Vol. 3). Paris.

———. 1969. *The Raw and the Cooked (Mythologiques,* Vol. 1) (John and Doreen Weightman, trans.). New York.

———. 1971. *L'Homme nu (Mythologiques,* Vol. 4). Paris.

Lowie, Robert H. 1908. "The Test-Theme in North American Mythology." *Journal of American Folklore,* Vol. 21, pp. 97–148.

———. 1918. *Myths and Traditions of the Crow Indians.* Anthropological Papers of the American Museum of Natural History, Vol. 25, pt. 1. New York.

Luna, Lizandro. 1957. "El Pongo." *Tradición: Revista Peruana de Cultura,* Nos. 19–20, pp. 19–24.

Lyback, Johanna R. M. 1925–38. *Indian Legends*. [Chicago.]

Macfarlan, Allan A. 1968. *American Indian Legends*. New York.

Magalhães, [J. Vieira] Couto de. 1876. *O Selvagem*. Rio de Janeiro.

———. 1882. *Contes Indien du Brésil* (Émile Allain, trans.). Rio de Janeiro.

———. [1913?] *O Selvagem* (edição prefaciada e revista pelo sobrinho do auctor). São Paulo and Rio de Janeiro.

Malinowski, Bronislaw. 1954. "Myth in Primitive Psychology." In *Magic, Science and Religion*, pp. 93–148. Garden City, N.Y.

———. 1955. *Sex and Repression in Savage Society*. Cleveland and New York.

Maranda, Pierre, ed. 1972. *Mythology: Selected Readings*. Harmondsworth, England.

Markham, Clements R. 1873. *Narratives of the Rites and Laws of the Yncas*. Works Issued by the Hakluyt Society, No. 48. London.

Matthews, Cornelius. 1869. *The Indian Fairy Book*. New York.

Matthews, Washington. 1897. *Navaho Legends*. Memoirs of the American Folk-Lore Society, Vol. 5. Boston.

Mauro, Humberto. 1950. "Vocabulário dos têrmos Tupis de 'O Selvagem' de Couto de Magalhães." *Revista do Instituto*

Histórico e Geográfico Brasileiro, Vol. 208, julho-setembro, pp. 197–242.

Métraux, Alfred. 1943. "A Myth of the Chamacoco Indians and Its Social Significance." *Journal of American Folklore,* Vol. 56, pp. 113–19.

Moon, Sheila. 1974. *A Magic Dwells: A Poetic and Psychological Study of the Navaho Emergence Myth.* Middletown, Conn.

Murphy, Robert F. 1958. *Mundurucú Religion.* University of California Publications in American Archaeology and Ethnology, Vol. 49, no. 1. Berkeley.

Nimuendaju, Curt. 1952. *The Tukuna.* University of California Publications in American Archaeology and Ethnology, Vol. 45. Berkeley.

O'Bryan, Aileen. 1956. *The Dîné: Origin Myths of the Navaho Indians.* Bureau of American Ethnology, Bulletin 163.

Opler, Morris Edward. 1938. *Myths and Tales of the Jicarilla Apache.* Memoirs of the American Folklore Society, Vol. 31. New York.

———. 1946. *Childhood and Youth in Jicarilla Apache Society.* Publications of the Frederick Webb Hodge Anniversary Publication Fund, Vol. 5. Los Angeles.

Osborne, Harold. 1968. *South American Mythology.* London.

Owen, Roger C.; Deetz, James J. F.; and Fisher, Anthony D., eds. 1967. *The North American Indians: A Sourcebook.* New York.

Palmer, Rose A. 1929. *The North American Indians.* Smithsonian Scientific Series, Vol. 4.

Paredes, Américo. 1970. *Folktales of Mexico.* Chicago.

Parker, Arthur C. 1923. *Seneca Myths and Folk Tales.* Buffalo.

Pesman, M. Walter. 1962. *Meet Flora Mexicana.* Globe, Ariz.

Peters, James Lee. 1931–. *Check-List of Birds of the World.* Cambridge, Mass.

Pettazoni, Raffaele. 1959. *Miti e Leggende,* Vol. 4: *America Centrale e Meridionale.* Turin.

Phinney, Archie. 1934. *Nez Percé Texts.* Columbia University Contributions to Anthropology, Vol. 25. New York.

Pôrto-Carrero, J. P. 1934. *A psicologia profunda ou psicanálise.* 3rd rev. ed. Rio de Janeiro.

Potter, Robert R., and Robinson, H. Alan. 1963. *Myths and Folk Tales around the World.* New York.

Preuss, Konrad Theodor. 1921–3. *Religion und Mythologie der Uitoto.* 2 vols. Göttingen.

Radin, Paul. 1954. *Monotheism among Primitive Peoples.* Basel.

———. 1957. *Primitive Religion: Its Nature and Origin.* 2nd ed. New York.

———. 1972. *The Trickster: A Study in American Indian Mythology* (with commentaries by Karl Kerényi and C. G. Jung). New York.

Rasmussen, Knud. 1908. *The People of the Polar North: A Record* (compiled from the Danish originals and edited by G. Herring). London.

———. 1921. *Eskimo Folk-Tales* (W. Worster, ed. and trans.). London.

Rink, Henry. 1875. *Tales and Traditions of the Eskimo*. Edinburgh and London.

Roa Bárcena, José María. 1862. *Leyendas mexicanas*. Mexico City.

Róheim, Géza. 1952. *The Gates of the Dream*. New York.

Rosado Vega, Luis. 1957. *El Alma Misteriosa del Mayab: Tradiciones, Leyendas y Consejas*. Mexico City.

Roth, Walter E. 1915. "An Inquiry into the Animism and Folklore of the Guiana Indians." *Thirtieth Annual Report of the Bureau of American Ethnology, 1908–1909*, pp. 103–386.

Rothenberg, Jerome, ed. 1968. *Technicians of the Sacred*. New York.

———. 1972. *Shaking the Pumpkin: Traditional Poetry of the Indian North Americas*. New York.

Roy, Cal. 1972. *The Serpent and the Sun: Myths of the Mexican World*. New York.

Roys, Ralph. 1933. *The Book of Chilam Balam of Chumayel*. Washington, D.C.

Russell, Frank. 1908. "The Pima Indians." *Twenty-sixth Annual Report of the Bureau of American Ethnology, 1904–1905,* pp. 3–389.

Sahagún, Bernardino de. 1956. *Historia general de las cosas de Nueva España* (Ángel M. Garibay, ed.). 12 "books" in 4 vols. Mexico City.

Sanchez, Walter, and Tedlock, Dennis. 1975. "The Girl and the Protector: A Zuni Story." *Alcheringa,* n.s. Vol. 1, no. 1, pp. 110–50. Boston.

Sanders, Thomas E., and Peek, Walter W. 1973. *Literature of the American Indian.* Beverly Hills.

Schoolcraft, Henry Rowe. 1825. *Travels in the Central Portion of the Mississippi Valley.* New York.

———. 1839. *Algic Researches.* 2 vols. New York.

———. 1851–7. *Information Respecting the History, Condition and Prospects of the Indian Tribes of the United States.* (Also issued as *Historical and Statistical Information Respecting the Indian Tribes of the United States.*) 6 vols. Philadelphia.

———. 1856. *The Myth of Hiawatha and Other Oral Legends.* Philadelphia.

Seler, Eduard. 1927. *Einige Kapitel aus dem Geschichtswerk des Fray Bernardino de Sahagun.* Stuttgart.

Simms, S. C. 1903. *Traditions of the Crows.* Field Columbian Museum Publication 85; Anthropological Series, Vol. 2, no. 6. Chicago.

Skinner, Alanson. 1925. "Traditions of the Iowa Indians." *Journal of American Folklore,* Vol. 38, pp. 425–506.

Skinner, Alanson, and Satterlee, John V. 1915. *Folklore of the Menomini Indians.* Anthropological Papers of the American Museum of Natural History, Vol. 13, pt. 3. New York.

Spence, Lewis. [1916.] *The Myths of the North American Indians.* New York.

———. 1930. *The Magic and Mysteries of Mexico.* London.

Stradelli, Ermanno. 1890. "Leggenda dell'Jurupary." *Bollettino della Società Geografica Italiana,* Serie III, vol. III, pp. 659–89, 798–835. Rome.

Swanton, John R. 1929. *Myths and Tales of the Southeastern Indians.* Bureau of American Ethnology, Bulletin 88.

Tedlock, Dennis. 1972a. "On the Translation of Style in Oral Narrative." In *Toward New Perspectives in Folklore* (Américo Paredes and Richard Bauman, eds.). Austin.

———. 1972b. *Finding the Center: Narrative Poetry of the Zuni Indians.* New York.

———. 1973. "The Story of How a Story Was Made." *Alcheringa,* No. 5, pp. 120–5.

Teit, James A.; Gould, Marian K.; Farrand, Livingston; and Spinden, Herbert J. 1917. *Folk-Tales of Salishan and Sahaptin Tribes* (Franz Boas, ed.). Memoirs of the American Folklore Society, Vol. 11. Lancaster, Penn.

Thompson, Stith. 1919. *European Tales among the North American Indians.* Colorado Springs.

——. 1929. *Tales of the North American Indians.* Cambridge, Mass.

——. 1946. *The Folktale.* New York.

Towle, Margaret A. 1961. *The Ethnobotany of Pre-Columbian Peru.* Chicago.

Trimborn, Hermann. 1939. *Dämonen und Zauber im Inkareich.* Leipzig.

Trimborn, Hermann, and Kelm, Antje. 1967. *Francisco de Avila.* Quellenwerke zur alten Geschichte amerikas aufgezeichnet in den Sprachen der Eingeborenen, Vol. 8. Berlin.

Velázquez, Primo Feliciano. 1945. *Códice Chimalpopoca.* Mexico City.

Villas Boas, Orlando, and Villas Boas, Claudio. 1972. *Xingu: os índios, seus mitos.* 2nd, rev. ed. Rio de Janeiro.

——. 1973. *Xingu: The Indians, Their Myths* (Susana Hertelendy Rudge, trans.). New York.

Wagley, Charles, and Galvão, Eduardo. 1949. *The Tenetehara Indians of Brazil.* Columbia University Contributions to Anthropology, Vol. 35. New York.

Wallace, Paul A. W. 1946. *The White Roots of Peace.* Garden City, N.Y.

Waterman, T. T. 1910. "The Religious Practices of the Diegueño Indians." University of California Publications in American Archaeology and Ethnology, Vol. 8, pp. 271–357. Berkeley.

Whiting, Henry. 1831. *Sannilac*. Boston.

Wilbert, Johannes. 1970. *Folk Literature of the Warao Indians: Narrative Material and Motif Content*. Los Angeles.

Williams, Mentor L., ed. 1956. *Schoolcraft's Indian Legends*. East Lansing, Mich.

Zolla, Elémire. 1973. *The Writer and the Shaman: A Morphology of the American Indian* (Raymond Rosenthal, trans.). New York.

GLOSSARY OF TRIBES, CULTURES, AND LANGUAGES

ALABAMA. A Muskhogean tribe, formerly of southern or central Alabama. Member of the Creek confederacy.

ALGONKIAN. A large family of tribes, related by language, formerly occupying much of the northeastern and north central United States and adjacent Canada. Includes the Chippewa, the Micmac, the Shawnee, the Menominee, the Secotan, the Arapaho, and many others.

ANAMBÉ (ah-nahm-BAY). A Tupian tribe of southeastern Amazonia. Now completely extinct.

ARAPAHO. An Algonkian-speaking Plains tribe, consisting of two divisions: the Southern Arapaho, who have settled in Oklahoma, and the Northern Arapaho, now on reservation lands in central Wyoming.

ASSINIBOIN. A Siouan tribe of the northern Plains.

AZTEC. A people of the central Mexican highlands, conquered by Cortés in 1519. Also a language, more properly called Nahuatl, spoken by the Aztecs and some of their neighbors. (Nahuatl is spoken today by over a million persons.)

BLACKFOOT. An Algonkian tribe of the northern Plains, now on reservation lands in northwestern Montana.

BORORO. A people of southern Brazil near the Bolivian border.

CENTRAL ESKIMO. General name for the Eskimo of Canada.

CHEYENNE. An Algonkian tribe of the western Plains, with reservation lands in southern Montana.

CHINOOK. An extinct tribe (and language) of southwestern Washington. Also a widely spoken trade language based on Chinook.

CHIPPEWA (CHIP-a-wah). Also called Ojibwa (o-JIB-way). An Algonkian people of the western Great Lakes region. Now mostly on reservations in Michigan, Wisconsin, Minnesota, and North Dakota.

COOS (rhymes with "moose"). A people formerly inhabiting the shores of Coos Bay, Oregon.

CROW. A Siouan tribe of southern Montana.

DIEGUEÑO (dyeh-GAY-nyoh). A native people of San Diego County, California.

HIDATSA. A Siouan tribe of North Dakota.

IOWA. A Siouan people of the eastern Plains, assigned to reservations in Kansas and Oklahoma.

IROQUOIS. A native people of eastern North America, comprising the "five nations" of New York and adjacent Canada (the Mohawk, the Oneida, the Onondaga, the Cayuga, and the Seneca) and a sixth nation, the Tuscarora, formerly of North Carolina, now of western New York and southern Ontario.

JICARILLA APACHE (hee-kah-REE-yah a-PATCH-ee). An Apache

band of northeastern New Mexico. (In language and mythology the Apache are closely related to the Navajo.)

KAMAIURÁ (kah-my-yoo-RAH). A small Tupian tribe of the Upper Xingu region of Brazil.

KIOWA APACHE. An Apache band of the southern Plains.

KWAKIUTL (kwah-kyootl, with the "ootl" as in "bootleg"). A group of twenty closely related tribes native to Vancouver Island and the mainland shore of Queen Charlotte Strait, British Columbia.

LINGUA GERAL (ling-gwa zheh-RAHL). A trade language based on Tupi, widely spoken in the Amazon basin.

MAKAH. A small tribe native to the Olympic Peninsula of Washington.

MAYA. The native people of Yucatan, whose language is still spoken by more than 300,000 persons.

MBYÁ (embuh-YAH). A native people of Paraguay.

MENOMINEE. An Algonkian tribe of Michigan and Wisconsin.

MICMAC. An Algonkian people of the Maritime Provinces of Canada.

MOHAWK. One of the five nations of the Iroquois, q.v.

MUNDURUCÚ. A Tupian tribe of the upper Tapajós River valley of Brazil.

MUSKHOGEAN. A group of linguistically related tribes native to the southeastern United States. Includes the Alabama, the Choctaw, the Seminole, the Natchez, and others.

NAVAJO. The largest Indian tribe in the United States today, numbering over 100,000 persons, mostly in northeastern Arizona and adjacent New Mexico.

NUNIVAK ESKIMO. An Eskimo people of southwestern Alaska, native to Nunivak Island in the Bering Sea.

OKANAGON. A Salishan people of Washington and British Columbia.

OMAHA. A Siouan Plains tribe now on reservation lands in eastern Nebraska.

ONONDAGA. One of the five nations of the Iroquois, q.v.

PIT RIVER. A native people of the Pit River valley of California, more properly called Achomawi.

QUECHUA (KETCH-wuh). An Andean people (and language) of Ecuador, Peru, and parts of Bolivia, Chile, and Argentina. Formerly the language of the Incas. Spoken today by approximately five million people.

QUILEUTE (kwil-ee-OOT). A native people of the Olympic Peninsula of Washington.

SALISHAN. A linguistic family ranging from Oregon to southern British Columbia and westward to Montana. Includes the Shuswap, the Okanagon, and the Thompson, among others.

SECOTAN. A vanished Algonkian tribe of coastal North Carolina. Known from sixteenth-century reports.

SENECA. One of the five nations of the Iroquois, q.v.

SHAWNEE. An Algonkian people formerly wide-ranging through the east central United States, now assigned to reservation lands in Oklahoma.

SIOUAN. A linguistic family ranging mostly through the upper Plains. Includes the Omaha, the Hidatsa, the Sioux proper, and many others.

SMITH SOUND ESKIMO. An Eskimo people of northwestern Greenland, near Smith Sound.

TENETEHARA. A Tupian people of northeastern Brazil.

TSIMSHIAN. A people of coastal British Columbia, related culturally to the Kwakiutl.

TUPI (TOO-pee). A linguistic family of South America, especially of the Amazon basin.

UITOTO (wee-TOH-toh). A forest-dwelling people of southeastern Colombia.

UPPER COWLITZ. A small Salishan band of the upper Cowlitz River of southwestern Washington.

WARRAU (WAHR-ow). A native people of northeastern Venezuela and adjacent Guyana.

YAMANA (YAH-mah-nah). Also called Yahgan. A native people of Tierra del Fuego. Now virtually extinct.

YUKI (YOO-kee). A native people of northern California. Now virtually extinct.

ZUNI (ZOO-nee). A Pueblo tribe of western New Mexico. The spelling "Zuñi" and especially its corresponding pronunciation (ZOON-yee) are falling into disuse.